CW01654936

The Open University

MST125

Essential mathematics 2

Unit 7

Topics in calculus

Introduction

This unit introduces you to various important concepts and techniques in calculus. In particular, you'll be led through a number of integration methods, so that by the end of the unit you should feel comfortable in integrating a wide range of functions.

In Section 1 you'll revise some of the integration methods that you should have met already, such as integration by substitution and integration by parts. Make sure you fully understand this revision section before you continue.

Sections 2 and 3 are about an extremely useful method for writing rational expressions such as

$$\frac{x-5}{(x-2)(3x^2-2x+1)} \quad \text{or} \quad \frac{x^2}{(2x+1)(x+1)}$$

in terms of simpler expressions called *partial fractions*. You'll also learn a handy technique known as *polynomial long division*, which is similar to long division of integers, but uses polynomial expressions rather than integers. Some of the procedures in these sections are quite involved, but working through them will improve your algebra skills, and the methods you learn will enable you to integrate a large collection of rational functions.

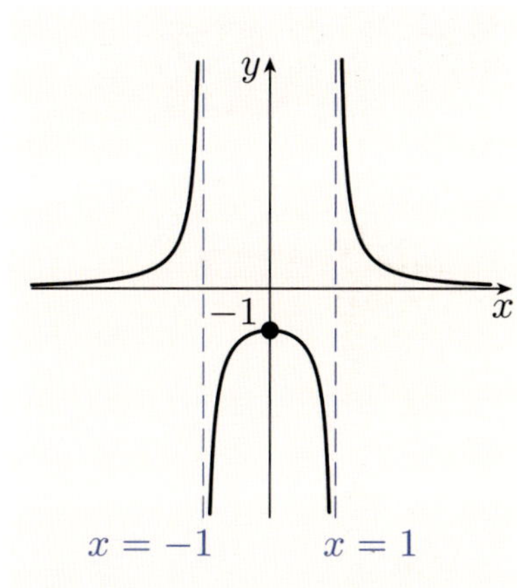

Figure 1 The graph of $y = \dfrac{1}{x^2-1}$

In Section 4 we take a break from integration to look at graph sketching. We focus on the graphs of rational functions, such as the graph of

$$y = \frac{1}{x^2-1},$$

shown in Figure 1. Such graphs are often made up of a number of 'pieces' separated by vertical lines known as *vertical asymptotes* (shown as dashed lines in the figure). You'll see a detailed strategy of how to sketch the graphs of rational functions.

Section 5 is about the role of the trigonometric functions in integration. You'll learn how to find integrals involving trigonometric expressions, such as

$$\int \cos^5 x \, dx,$$

and you'll also learn how to find integrals such as

$$\int \frac{\sqrt{x^2-16}}{x} \, dx$$

by substituting x with a trigonometric expression.

In Section 6 you'll meet a class of functions called the *hyperbolic functions*, which you may have encountered before in MST124 Unit 11. These functions share many properties with the trigonometric functions, but there are also significant differences between the two classes of functions; for example, unlike trigonometric functions, hyperbolic functions are not periodic. You'll see how hyperbolic functions can be used to add yet more strategies to your toolbox of integration techniques.

Finally, in Section 7 there is a guide to choosing a suitable method of integration. Remember that there are often many ways to integrate a function, which is one of the reasons that integration is such a rich, but challenging, subject.

This is a long unit that covers a number of key calculus topics needed for later modules, so the study planner allows extra time for it. Don't be discouraged if you struggle with some of the examples and activities at first; you'll master them with plenty of practice, and working through them will help give you the mathematical skills that you need to advance with your studies.

1 Revision of integration methods

In this section you'll revise some methods of integration that you should have met before, and which will prove to be essential later on. All the material in this section is covered in detail in MST124 Unit 8.

1.1 Standard indefinite integrals

Let's begin by reminding ourselves of some definitions. Given a function f, an **antiderivative** of f is any function F whose derivative is f. There are many antiderivatives of f because, if F is an antiderivative of f, then any function given by an expression $F(x) + c$, where c is a constant, is also an antiderivative of f. The collection of all such functions, for all values of c, is called the **indefinite integral** of f, and we write

$$\int f(x)\,dx = F(x) + c.$$

The expression $f(x)$ being integrated is called the **integrand**.

Informally, you should think 'integration reverses differentiation' because you differentiate $F(x)$ to obtain $f(x)$, and integrate $f(x)$ to obtain $F(x) + c$. Don't forget the constant (usually denoted by c), which can take any value and so is often referred to as an **arbitrary constant**.

Using this fundamental observation about antiderivatives, you can construct the following table of standard indefinite integrals, which is copied here from MST124 for convenience. You can confirm that each row in the table is correct by differentiating the expression in the right-hand column, and checking that you obtain the expression in the left-hand column.

Standard indefinite integrals

Function	Indefinite integral
a (constant)	$ax + c$
$x^n \ (n \neq -1)$	$\dfrac{1}{n+1}x^{n+1} + c$
e^x	$e^x + c$
$\dfrac{1}{x}$	$\ln\lvert x\rvert + c$
	or $\ln x + c$, for $x > 0$
$\sin x$	$-\cos x + c$
$\cos x$	$\sin x + c$
$\sec^2 x$	$\tan x + c$
$\operatorname{cosec}^2 x$	$-\cot x + c$
$\sec x \tan x$	$\sec x + c$
$\operatorname{cosec} x \cot x$	$-\operatorname{cosec} x + c$
$\dfrac{1}{\sqrt{1-x^2}}$	$\sin^{-1} x + c$
	or $-\cos^{-1} x + c$
$\dfrac{1}{1+x^2}$	$\tan^{-1} x + c$

In order to become proficient at integration, you'll need to be familiar with a number of standard integrals such as those listed above. By the time you've finished this unit, you'll have met all of the standard integrals in the longer list given in the *Handbook*.

You should also remember the following rules for finding integrals of sums and constant multiples of functions. These rules allow you to integrate many more functions than those listed in the table above.

Constant multiple rule and sum rule for indefinite integrals

$$\int k\,f(x)\,\mathrm{d}x = k\int f(x)\,\mathrm{d}x, \quad \text{where } k \text{ is a constant}$$

$$\int (f(x) + g(x))\,\mathrm{d}x = \int f(x)\,\mathrm{d}x + \int g(x)\,\mathrm{d}x$$

There is another useful rule, which we'll call the linear expression rule, that allows you to integrate a still wider variety of functions.

Linear expression rule for indefinite integrals

If f is a function with antiderivative F, and a and b are constants with $a \neq 0$, then

$$\int f(ax+b)\,\mathrm{d}x = \frac{1}{a}F(ax+b) + c.$$

For example, you know from the table of standard indefinite integrals that

$$\int \cos x\,\mathrm{d}x = \sin x + c.$$

Here $\sin x$ is an antiderivative of $\cos x$. The linear expression rule tells you that, for instance,

$$\int \cos(7x+5)\,\mathrm{d}x = \tfrac{1}{7}\sin(7x+5) + c.$$

You can confirm this by differentiating $\frac{1}{7}\sin(7x+5) + c$ using the chain rule, and checking that you obtain $\cos(7x+5)$.

Here are some more examples of applying these rules.

Example 1 *Integrating by modifying and combining standard integrals*

Find the following integrals.

(a) $\displaystyle\int (\sec x)(2\sec x + \tan x)\,\mathrm{d}x$ (b) $\displaystyle\int \frac{1}{\sqrt{1-25x^2}}\,\mathrm{d}x$

Solution

(a) Expand the brackets, and then use the constant multiple rule and the sum rule to write the integral as a combination of simpler integrals.

$$\begin{aligned}\int (\sec x)(2\sec x + \tan x)\,\mathrm{d}x &= \int (2\sec^2 x + \sec x\tan x)\,\mathrm{d}x \\ &= 2\int \sec^2 x\,\mathrm{d}x + \int \sec x \tan x\,\mathrm{d}x\end{aligned}$$

The integrals of $\sec^2 x$ and $\sec x \tan x$ both appear in the table of standard indefinite integrals.

$$= 2\tan x + \sec x + c$$

Only one constant is needed, even though there are two integrals. This is because the sum of two arbitrary constants is again an arbitrary constant, so we may as well use the single letter c to refer to the sum.

(b) Try to write the integrand as f(linear expression), where f is a function from the table of standard indefinite integrals.

$$\int \frac{1}{\sqrt{1-25x^2}}\,dx = \int \frac{1}{\sqrt{1-(5x)^2}}\,dx$$

The expression $\dfrac{1}{\sqrt{1-(5x)^2}}$ has the form f(linear expression), where $f(x) = \dfrac{1}{\sqrt{1-x^2}}$ and the linear expression is $5x$. Refer to the table of standard indefinite integrals to find the integral of $\dfrac{1}{\sqrt{1-x^2}}$, and then use the linear expression rule.

$$= \tfrac{1}{5}\sin^{-1}(5x) + c$$

Remember that, when you've found an indefinite integral, you can always check your answer by differentiating it. For instance, in part (b) of the above example, you can differentiate the answer $\frac{1}{5}\sin^{-1}(5x) + c$ using the chain rule, and check that you obtain the integrand $\dfrac{1}{\sqrt{1-25x^2}}$.

From now on in this unit, we'll use the constant multiple rule, the sum rule and the linear expression rule without comment, and we won't usually refer explicitly to the table of standard indefinite integrals.

Here are some integrals for you to find using the methods we've described so far.

Activity 1 *Integrating by modifying and combining standard integrals*

Find the following integrals.

(a) $\displaystyle\int (3-x)x^2\,dx$ (b) $\displaystyle\int e^{-8x+2}\,dx$

(c) $\displaystyle\int (\operatorname{cosec} x)(\cot x - 3\operatorname{cosec} x)\,dx$ (d) $\displaystyle\int \frac{1}{\sqrt{1-9x^2}}\,dx$

(e) $\displaystyle\int \left(\sqrt{x} + \frac{1}{\sqrt{x}}\right)^2 dx$

1.2 Integration by substitution

In this subsection you'll revise an integration technique that was covered in MST124, namely *integration by substitution.* You should use this method when you have an integrand of the form

$$f(\text{something}) \times \text{the derivative of the something},$$

where f is a function that you know how to integrate. For example, the expression $e^{\sin x}\cos x$ is of this form, because you can write it as

$$e^{\text{something}} \times \text{the derivative of the something},$$

where the 'something' is $\sin x$.

Here's a summary of how to carry out integration by substitution.

Integration by substitution

1. Recognise that the integrand is of the form

   $$f(\text{something}) \times \text{the derivative of the something},$$

   where f is a function that you can integrate.
2. Set the something equal to u, and find $\mathrm{d}u/\mathrm{d}x$.
3. Hence write the integral in the form

   $$\int f(u)\,\mathrm{d}u,$$

   by using the fact that $\displaystyle\int f(u)\,\frac{\mathrm{d}u}{\mathrm{d}x}\,\mathrm{d}x = \int f(u)\,\mathrm{d}u.$
4. Do the integration.
5. Substitute back for u in terms of x.

The effect of substituting the variable u in place of the 'something' in the integral is to reduce the integral to a simpler integral in terms of u. This principle is illustrated in the next example.

Example 2 *Integrating by substitution*

Find the integral

$$\int \left(\frac{1}{2x^4+1}\right)(8x^3)\,\mathrm{d}x.$$

Solution

Since the derivative of $2x^4+1$ is $8x^3$, the integrand is of the form

$$\frac{1}{\text{something}} \times \text{the derivative of the something}.$$

So set the something equal to u.

Let $u = 2x^4 + 1$; then $\dfrac{du}{dx} = 8x^3$.

Imagine 'cross-multiplying' in the second equation to obtain $du = (8x^3)\,dx$.

So

$$\int \left(\frac{1}{2x^4+1}\right)(8x^3)\,dx = \int \frac{1}{u}\,du$$

Do the integration.

$$= \ln|u| + c$$

Substitute back for u in terms of x.

$$= \ln|2x^4 + 1| + c$$

Simplify the answer if possible. Here, notice that $2x^4 + 1$ is always positive.

$$= \ln(2x^4 + 1) + c.$$

There's usually more than one choice for the 'something' when integrating by substitution, and some choices are better than others. For instance, you can choose $u = 2x^4$ (rather than $u = 2x^4 + 1$) in the above example because this still gives

$$\frac{du}{dx} = 8x^3.$$

However, after making this substitution the integrand becomes $1/(u+1)$, which is slightly harder to integrate than $1/u$.

Here are some examples of integration by substitution for you to try.

Activity 2 *Integrating by substitution*

Find the following integrals.

(a) $\displaystyle\int e^{\sin x}\cos x\,dx$ (b) $\displaystyle\int (x^2 + x + 2)^{1/3}(2x+1)\,dx$

(c) $\displaystyle\int \left(\frac{1}{\sqrt{1-\tan^2 x}}\right)\sec^2 x\,dx$

The integrands in the preceding example and activity were given in the form

$$f(\text{something}) \times \text{the derivative of the something}$$

to help you integrate by substitution. Often you'll need to integrate expressions that must be rearranged before they take this form. Here's an example of this type.

Example 3 *Rearranging an integral before using substitution*

Find the integral

$$\int \frac{\sin(x^{1/2})}{x^{1/2}}\, dx.$$

Solution

The derivative of $x^{1/2}$ is $\frac{1}{2}x^{-1/2}$, which is 'nearly' equal to $x^{-1/2} = \dfrac{1}{x^{1/2}}$ (it just has the wrong coefficient). So if you separate the numerator and denominator of the fraction in the integrand, then it will nearly be in the required form.

Let $u = x^{1/2}$; then $\dfrac{du}{dx} = \frac{1}{2}x^{-1/2}$.

Imagine 'cross-multiplying' in the second equation to obtain $du = (\frac{1}{2}x^{-1/2})\, dx$. Separate the numerator and denominator of the fraction in the integrand.

So

$$\int \frac{\sin(x^{1/2})}{x^{1/2}}\, dx = \int \left(\sin(x^{1/2})\right) x^{-1/2}\, dx$$

The only problem is that you need $\frac{1}{2}x^{-1/2}$ in place of $x^{-1/2}$. To achieve this, multiply by $1/2$ inside the integral, and multiply by 2 outside to compensate.

$$= 2\int \left(\sin(x^{1/2})\right)\left(\tfrac{1}{2}x^{-1/2}\right) dx$$

Now do the substitution.

$$\begin{aligned} &= 2\int \sin u\, du \\ &= -2\cos u + c \\ &= -2\cos(x^{1/2}) + c. \end{aligned}$$

Activity 3 *Rearranging integrals before using substitution*

Find the following integrals.

(a) $\int x^3 e^{x^4}\,dx$ (b) $\int \frac{\sin x}{2+\cos x}\,dx$ (c) $\int \frac{x}{1+x^4}\,dx$

Hint for part (c): choose $u = x^2$.

Sometimes a substitution can help you to deal with an integrand that isn't of the form

f(something) × the derivative of the something.

This is illustrated in the following example.

Example 4 *Finding a more complicated integral by substitution*

Find the integral

$$\int x\sqrt{x-1}\,dx.$$

Solution

To simplify the expression $\sqrt{x-1}$, try the substitution $u = x - 1$. You must also express the other factor in the integrand, namely x, in terms of u.

Let $u = x - 1$; then $\frac{du}{dx} = 1$.

Also, rearranging the equation $u = x - 1$ gives $x = u + 1$. So

$$\begin{aligned}\int x\sqrt{x-1}\,dx &= \int (u+1)\sqrt{u}\,du\\ &= \int \left(u^{3/2} + u^{1/2}\right)du\\ &= \tfrac{2}{5}u^{5/2} + \tfrac{2}{3}u^{3/2} + c\\ &= \tfrac{2}{5}(x-1)^{5/2} + \tfrac{2}{3}(x-1)^{3/2} + c.\end{aligned}$$

For more complicated integrals, such as the one in the previous example, you may be wondering how you 'spot' a suitable substitution. This is a skill that develops with practice and experience. In this unit, we'll always suggest a suitable substitution for more complicated integrals.

Activity 4 *Finding more complicated integrals by substitution*

Find the following integrals.

(a) $\displaystyle\int x(x+1)^{3/2}\,\mathrm{d}x$ (b) $\displaystyle\int \frac{x+1}{(x-2)^2}\,\mathrm{d}x$

Hints: in part (a) use the substitution $u = x + 1$, and in part (b) use the substitution $u = x - 2$.

You'll remember from MST124 Unit 8 that, if f is a continuous function and a and b are numbers in its domain, then the **definite integral**

$$\int_a^b f(x)\,\mathrm{d}x$$

is defined to be the signed area between the graph of f and the x-axis from $x = a$ to $x = b$. This signed area is illustrated in Figure 2 for the simple case where $a < b$ and the graph of f lies above the x-axis between $x = a$ and $x = b$. The numbers a and b are the **lower** and **upper limits of integration**, respectively. We can find the signed area using the **fundamental theorem of calculus**, which says that

$$\int_a^b f(x)\,\mathrm{d}x = F(b) - F(a),$$

where F is an antiderivative of f.

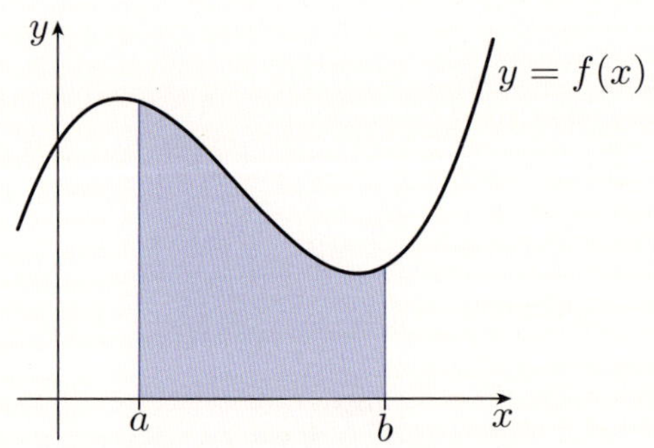

Figure 2 The signed area between the graph of f and the x-axis from $x = a$ to $x = b$

In this unit you'll have to find a number of definite integrals by substitution. There are two ways to do this. The first way is to find the *indefinite* integral

$$\int f(x)\,\mathrm{d}x$$

first, and then apply the limits of integration $x = a$ and $x = b$ only at the end of the calculation. An alternative way is to work with the definite integral from the start and, when you change the variable from x to u, also change the limits of integration to the corresponding values of u. The second method is demonstrated in the next example.

Example 5 *Evaluating a definite integral by substitution*

Evaluate the definite integral

$$\int_0^1 \frac{x}{(4-x^2)^2}\,dx.$$

(It represents the area of the shaded region in Figure 3.)

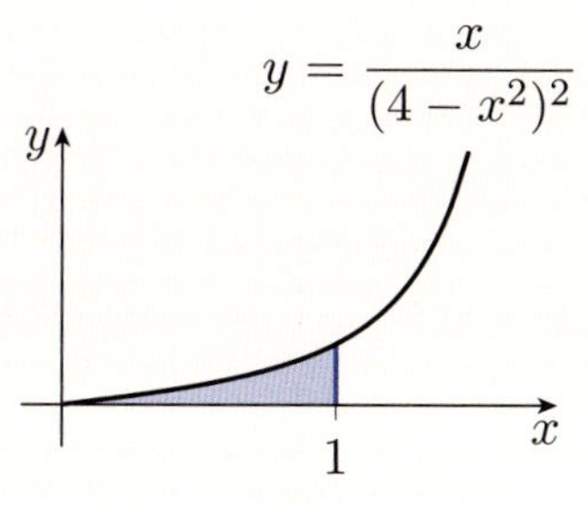

Figure 3 The definite integral in Example 5

Solution

Use integration by substitution.

Let $u = 4 - x^2$; then $\dfrac{du}{dx} = -2x$.

Find the values of u that correspond to the values of x that are the limits of integration.

Putting $x = 0$ into $u = 4 - x^2$ gives $u = 4$.

Putting $x = 1$ into $u = 4 - x^2$ gives $u = 3$.

Change the variable from x to u, remembering that you also have to change the limits of integration.

So

$$\begin{aligned}\int_0^1 \frac{x}{(4-x^2)^2}\,dx &= -\tfrac{1}{2}\int_0^1 \left(\frac{1}{(4-x^2)^2}\right)(-2x)\,dx \\ &= -\tfrac{1}{2}\int_4^3 \frac{1}{u^2}\,du\end{aligned}$$

The upper limit is smaller than the lower limit. This doesn't matter – you can continue to evaluate the definite integral in the usual way. However, you can switch the upper and lower limits if you wish, but if you do so then you must change the sign of the integrand (in this case, remove the minus sign).

$$\begin{aligned} &= \tfrac{1}{2}\int_3^4 \frac{1}{u^2}\,du \\ &= \tfrac{1}{2}\int_3^4 u^{-2}\,du \\ &= \tfrac{1}{2}\left[-u^{-1}\right]_3^4 \\ &= \tfrac{1}{2}\left(\left(-\tfrac{1}{4}\right) - \left(-\tfrac{1}{3}\right)\right) \\ &= \tfrac{1}{24}.\end{aligned}$$

When finding definite integrals, you must be sure that it's possible to evaluate the integrand at all values of x between the limits of integration.

For example, consider the same integral as in the preceding example, but this time with limits $x = 0$ and $x = 3$:

$$\int_0^3 \frac{x}{(4-x^2)^2}\,dx.$$

Even though you could repeat the working of the example with these new limits, the answer you obtain would not be valid. This is because the integrand is not defined at $x = 2$, since the denominator $(4-x^2)^2$ equals 0 when $x = 2$.

The graph of $y = \dfrac{x}{(4-x^2)^2}$ is shown in Figure 4; there is an asymptote through the value $x = 2$ at which the integrand is not defined.

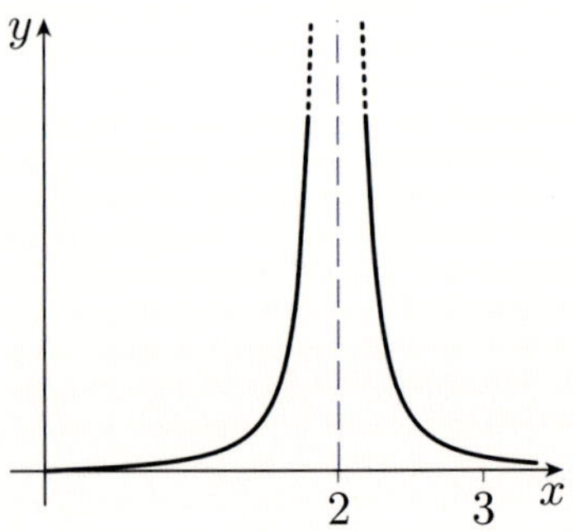

Figure 4 The graph of $y = \dfrac{x}{(4-x^2)^2}$ between $x = 0$ and $x = 3$

Although you should be aware of this pitfall, it needn't concern you in the examples and activities in this unit, as you'll always be given definite integrals with valid limits.

Activity 5 *Evaluating definite integrals by substitution*

Evaluate the following definite integrals.

(a) $\displaystyle\int_0^1 x^2\sqrt{x^3+1}\,dx$ (b) $\displaystyle\int_{\pi/16}^{\pi/8} \operatorname{cosec}^2(4x)\,dx$ (c) $\displaystyle\int_0^{\ln 3} \frac{e^x}{1+e^x}\,dx$

The solutions to the examples and activities in this subsection have set out all of the steps used to integrate by substitution. With practice, you should find that you can carry out some of the steps 'in your head' without writing them down in full, in which case your solutions can be shorter.

1.3 Integration by parts

Another technique that you should already be familiar with is *integration by parts*, which is useful for integrating some products of the form $f(x)g(x)$, where f and g are functions. Integration by parts is not used much in the rest of this unit, but you should revise it carefully now because it will be needed for MST125 Unit 8.

This technique is based on the following formula.

Integration by parts formula

$$\int f(x)g(x)\,dx = f(x)G(x) - \int f'(x)G(x)\,dx.$$

Here G is an antiderivative of g.

This formula is useful when

- you know how to integrate the expression $g(x)$, giving you $G(x)$, and
- the product $f'(x)G(x)$ is easier to integrate than $f(x)g(x)$.

You may find the following informal version of the integration by parts formula more convenient and easier to remember.

Integration by parts formula (informal)

$$\begin{aligned}\text{integral of product} &= (\text{first}) \times \begin{pmatrix}\text{antiderivative}\\ \text{of second}\end{pmatrix}\\ &\quad - \text{integral of}\left(\begin{pmatrix}\text{derivative}\\ \text{of first}\end{pmatrix} \times \begin{pmatrix}\text{antiderivative}\\ \text{of second}\end{pmatrix}\right)\end{aligned}$$

Here's an example of how to apply the integration by parts formula.

Example 6 *Integrating by parts*

Find the integral $\displaystyle\int x\cos x\,\mathrm{d}x$.

Solution

The integrand is a product of two expressions, x and $\cos x$. You can integrate the second expression, $\cos x$, and differentiating the first expression, x, makes it simpler. So try integration by parts.

Integrating by parts gives

$$\begin{aligned}\int x\cos x\,\mathrm{d}x &= x\sin x - \int 1\times\sin x\,\mathrm{d}x\\ &= x\sin x - \int \sin x\,\mathrm{d}x\\ &= x\sin x - (-\cos x) + c\\ &= x\sin x + \cos x + c.\end{aligned}$$

Try the following activity. If you find that integration by parts gives you an integral that is more complicated than the original integral, then try swapping the 'first' and 'second' expressions in the integrand, and apply integration by parts again.

Activity 6 *Integrating by parts*

Find the following integrals.

(a) $\int xe^{-3x}\,\mathrm{d}x$ (b) $\int x^4 \ln x\,\mathrm{d}x$ (c) $\int x(x+1)^{1/2}\,\mathrm{d}x$

Bernhard Riemann (1826–1866)

Henri Lebesgue (1875–1941)

Riemann and Lebesgue integration

The first part of this unit is about methods and applications of integration. In more advanced modules on calculus, you'll learn about the formal theory of integration, and study different ways of thinking about integrals. One of the first people to give the subject of integration a rigorous framework was the German mathematician Bernhard Riemann. Using his theory, which today is called **Riemann integration**, he was able to explain in a formal mathematical way what it means to integrate a variety of functions, including continuous functions such as those that you'll meet in this module. However, his methods were unable to cope with some obscure functions that aren't continuous. For example, his theory doesn't tell you how to integrate the function q given by

$$q(x) = \begin{cases} 1 & \text{if } x \text{ is a rational number} \\ 0 & \text{if } x \text{ is an irrational number.} \end{cases}$$

In order to deal with peculiar functions such as this one, the French mathematician Henri Lebesgue developed a richer theory of integration, which today is called **Lebesgue integration**. Using Lebesgue integration, it can be shown that

$$\int_0^1 q(x)\,\mathrm{d}x = 0.$$

This is because, informally speaking, there are 'far more irrational numbers than rational numbers', so the values of q at the rational numbers don't affect the value of the integral.

2 Partial fractions of proper rational expressions

In this section and the next, you'll learn a useful technique for simplifying certain expressions (known as *rational expressions*) by writing them as sums of simpler expressions, called *partial fractions*. You'll see that this technique enables you to integrate a large class of rational expressions by first writing them in this way.

2.1 Rational expressions

One of the most important classes of functions in mathematics is the class of *rational functions*, such as the functions whose rules are

$$f(x) = \frac{2x^3 + 7}{x^2 - 9}, \quad g(x) = \frac{\frac{4}{7}x^3 + x^2}{1} \quad \text{and} \quad h(x) = \frac{x^9}{8x(x^2 - x + 5)}.$$

The expressions on the right-hand sides of these rules are examples of *rational expressions*.

In general, a **rational expression** in x is an expression formed by dividing one polynomial expression in x by another. A **rational function** is a function whose rule is given by a rational expression.

You'll recall that the **degree** of a polynomial expression or function is the highest power of x in that expression or function. For example, the highest power of x in the polynomial expression $\frac{4}{7}x^3 + x^2$ is x^3, so the degree of this polynomial expression is 3. Polynomial expressions of degrees 2 and 3 are called **quadratic** and **cubic** expressions, respectively.

A polynomial expression of the form $ax + b$, where a and b are constants, is called a **linear expression**. You use these when you apply the linear expression rule for indefinite integrals, which you revised in the previous section. The linear expression $ax + b$ has degree 1 provided $a \neq 0$. If $a = 0$, so that the expression is equal to the constant b, then it has degree 0 unless $b = 0$, in which case it has no degree at all.

Since a constant is a form of polynomial expression, it follows that either the numerator or the denominator (or both) of a rational expression can be a constant. However, the polynomial expression in the denominator cannot be equal to the constant 0, since division by zero is not defined.

When you add or subtract two or more rational expressions you obtain another rational expression. Here are some examples of this.

Example 7 *Adding and subtracting rational expressions*

Express each of the following as a single rational expression.

(a) $\dfrac{1}{x+2}+\dfrac{2}{x-3}$ (b) $\dfrac{2}{x+3}-\dfrac{1}{x-1}+\dfrac{3}{(x-1)^2}$

Solution

(a) Write both fractions with a common denominator, found by multiplying the two given denominators together to give $(x+2)(x-3)$. So multiply the top and bottom of the left-hand expression by $x-3$, and multiply the top and bottom of the right-hand expression by $x+2$.

$$\frac{1}{x+2}+\frac{2}{x-3}=\frac{x-3}{(x+2)(x-3)}+\frac{2(x+2)}{(x+2)(x-3)}$$

Combine the two rational expressions.

$$=\frac{(x-3)+2(x+2)}{(x+2)(x-3)}$$
$$=\frac{(x-3)+(2x+4)}{(x+2)(x-3)}$$
$$=\frac{3x+1}{(x+2)(x-3)}$$

You could now expand the brackets in the denominator, but there is no need, as the rational expression is already in a simple form.

(b) Write the fractions with a common denominator. To find a common denominator, you could multiply all the given denominators together to give

$$(x+3)\times(x-1)\times(x-1)^2=(x+3)(x-1)^3.$$

However, the denominators $x-1$ and $(x-1)^2$ already share a factor of $x-1$, so a simpler common denominator is

$$(x+3)\times(x-1)^2=(x+3)(x-1)^2,$$

found by multiplying just the first and last of the given denominators.

$$\frac{2}{x+3}-\frac{1}{x-1}+\frac{3}{(x-1)^2}$$
$$=\frac{2(x-1)^2}{(x+3)(x-1)^2}-\frac{(x+3)(x-1)}{(x+3)(x-1)^2}+\frac{3(x+3)}{(x+3)(x-1)^2}$$

Combine the three rational expressions.

$$= \frac{2(x-1)^2 - (x+3)(x-1) + 3(x+3)}{(x+3)(x-1)^2}$$

$$= \frac{2(x^2-2x+1) - (x^2+2x-3) + (3x+9)}{(x+3)(x-1)^2}$$

$$= \frac{x^2-3x+14}{(x+3)(x-1)^2}$$

Activity 7 *Adding and subtracting rational expressions*

Express each of the following as a single rational expression.

(a) $\dfrac{2}{x+2} + \dfrac{1}{x-1}$ (b) $\dfrac{9}{x+1} + \dfrac{x+4}{x^2+1}$ (c) $\dfrac{3}{x} - \dfrac{1}{x+4} - \dfrac{1}{(x+4)^2}$

You've just seen how to add or subtract two or more rational expressions to give another rational expression. The focus of much of the rest of this section and the next is the reverse process of how to split up a rational expression into a sum of simpler rational expressions called *partial fractions.*

In this section, we'll restrict our attention to **proper** rational expressions, which are those for which the degree of the polynomial expression in the numerator is smaller than the degree of the polynomial expression in the denominator. Rational expressions that are not proper are said to be **improper**. We'll return to these in the next section.

The next box gives the definition of partial fractions and the general form of the partial fraction expansion of a proper rational expression. Don't worry if this doesn't mean much to you at first: you'll come to understand its significance as you work through the section.

Partial fractions of proper rational expressions

Any proper rational expression $f(x)$ can be written as a sum of expressions of the form

$$\frac{A}{(ax+b)^n} \quad \text{and} \quad \frac{Ax+B}{(ax^2+bx+c)^n},$$

where n is a positive integer and a, b, c, A and B are constants. Such a sum is called the **partial fraction expansion** of $f(x)$, and the terms of the sum are called the **partial fractions** of $f(x)$.

For example, the right-hand side of the equation

$$\frac{-4x^2+3x+11}{(2x+1)(x^2+2x+5)} = \frac{2}{2x+1} - \frac{3x-1}{x^2+2x+5}$$

is the partial fraction expansion of the proper rational expression on the left-hand side. The partial fractions are the two terms on the right-hand side.

Much of the remainder of this section is about methods for finding the partial fractions of proper rational expressions. Before you learn these methods, however, you should try the next activity, which asks you to use the computer algebra system to calculate some partial fraction expansions.

Activity 8 *Using the computer algebra system to calculate partial fraction expansions*

Work through Section 6.1 of the *Computer algebra guide*, where you'll learn how to use the computer algebra system to find partial fraction expansions.

2.2 Distinct linear factors

In this subsection, you'll learn how to find the partial fraction expansions of proper rational expressions whose denominators are products of *distinct linear factors*. Partial fraction expansions of proper rational expressions whose denominators include *repeated linear factors* or *quadratic factors* are covered in Subsections 2.3 and 2.4 respectively.

As examples of these types, consider the rational expressions

$$\frac{x+8}{(x-2)(x+3)}, \quad \frac{x^2-11x+3}{(2x-1)(x+7)^2} \quad \text{and} \quad \frac{13}{(x+5)(x^2+1)}.$$

The first expression has distinct linear factors $x-2$ and $x+3$ in its denominator, so its partial fraction expansion can be found using the methods in this subsection.

However, in the second expression the linear factor $x+7$ is repeated in the denominator (that is, the factor is raised to a power greater than 1), while the third expression has the quadratic factor x^2+1 in its denominator. To find the partial fraction expansions of these expressions, you'll need the methods of the next two subsections.

The following rule tells you the form of the partial fraction expansion of a proper rational expression whose denominator is a product of distinct linear factors.

Partial fractions of proper rational expressions with distinct linear factors

Each linear factor $ax + b$ gives rise to a partial fraction of the form $\dfrac{A}{ax+b}$, where A is a constant. In general, this constant will be different for different linear factors.

For example, the partial fraction expansion of the rational expression

$$\frac{x+8}{(x-2)(x+3)}$$

is of the form

$$\frac{x+8}{(x-2)(x+3)} = \frac{A}{x-2} + \frac{B}{x+3},$$

where A and B are constants. Note that we have used different letters for the constants, since they may have different values.

Once you've written down the form of a partial fraction expansion of a rational expression, you must determine the values of the constants. There are several methods of doing this, which are demonstrated in the examples that follow.

Example 8 *Finding partial fractions by equating coefficients*

Find the partial fraction expansion of the rational expression $\dfrac{x+8}{(x-2)(x+3)}$.

Solution

Write down the form of the partial fraction expansion of $\dfrac{x+8}{(x-2)(x+3)}$.

We have

$$\frac{x+8}{(x-2)(x+3)} = \frac{A}{x-2} + \frac{B}{x+3},$$

where A and B are constants.

Multiply both sides by $(x-2)(x+3)$ to give polynomial expressions on each side.

Multiplying both sides by $(x-2)(x+3)$ gives

$$x + 8 = A(x+3) + B(x-2)$$

Expand the brackets, then collect the terms in x and the constant terms.

$$= (Ax + 3A) + (Bx - 2B)$$
$$= (A + B)x + (3A - 2B).$$

You can find A and B by 'equating coefficients' in the equation $x + 8 = (A + B)x + (3A - 2B)$. The coefficients of x on each side of the equation must be equal. Similarly the constant terms on each side must be equal.

Comparing the coefficients of x in the equation

$$x + 8 = (A + B)x + (3A - 2B)$$

gives $1 = A + B$. Comparing constant terms gives $8 = 3A - 2B$. So

$$A + B = 1$$
$$3A - 2B = 8.$$

These are simultaneous equations, which you can solve in the usual way.

Multiplying the first equation by 2 gives

$$2A + 2B = 2.$$

Adding this equation to the second equation gives

$$5A = 10, \quad \text{so} \quad A = 2.$$

Substituting $A = 2$ into the first equation $A + B = 1$ gives

$$B = 1 - A = 1 - 2 = -1.$$

So

$$\frac{x+8}{(x-2)(x+3)} = \frac{2}{x-2} + \frac{-1}{x+3}$$

It's neater to write $-\frac{1}{x+3}$ rather than $\frac{-1}{x+3}$.

$$= \frac{2}{x-2} - \frac{1}{x+3}.$$

It's easy to make a mistake when calculating partial fractions, so you should check your answer at the end. One way to do this is to add together the partial fractions you've found, and check that you obtain the original rational expression. This can be a long process, so to save time you can instead test your answer for a particular value of x. This quick check is useful for picking up mistakes, but you should remember that you can't be sure that an equation is correct for all values of x just by checking one value of x.

For example, suppose you wish to check the partial fraction expansion

$$\frac{x+8}{(x-2)(x+3)} = \frac{2}{x-2} - \frac{1}{x+3}.$$

Let's check whether the left-hand side (LHS) and right-hand side (RHS) are equal for a particular value of x, say $x = 0$. You should work out the value of the LHS and RHS at $x = 0$ *separately*, one after the other, as follows:

$$\text{LHS} = \frac{0+8}{(0-2)(0+3)} = \frac{8}{-6} = -\frac{4}{3}$$

and

$$\text{RHS} = \frac{2}{0-2} - \frac{1}{0+3} = -1 - \frac{1}{3} = -\frac{4}{3}.$$

The two sides of the equation agree at $x = 0$, which indicates that the partial fraction expansion is likely to be correct.

It's usually simplest to choose $x = 0$ for the check, unless one of the factors in the denominator is x itself, in which case you must choose another value of x (because choosing $x = 0$ in that case would lead to division by 0).

You can also check your answers using the computer algebra system.

The procedure demonstrated in Example 8 for finding the constants in a partial fraction expansion is called the **method of equating coefficients**. This method relies on the fact that, if you have two polynomial expressions such as

$$ax^2 + bx + c \quad \text{and} \quad Ax^2 + Bx + C$$

that are equal for all values of x, then $a = A$, $b = B$ and $c = C$. The method works in a similar way for polynomial expressions of higher degree.

Try out the method of equating coefficients by finding the partial fraction expansions of the rational expressions in the next activity. Remember to check your answers!

Activity 9 *Finding partial fractions by equating coefficients*

Find the partial fraction expansions of the following rational expressions using the method of equating coefficients.

(a) $\dfrac{x-3}{(x-1)(x+1)}$ (b) $\dfrac{5}{x(2x+1)}$

You can *always* find the constants in the partial fraction expansion of a rational expression by using the method of equating coefficients – even rational expressions whose denominators are *not* a product of distinct linear factors. However, this method can be time-consuming, especially if there are three or more factors. There are often quicker methods of finding at least some of the constants. One such method is demonstrated in the example below. The rational expression in part (a) of this example is the same as in Example 8.

Example 9 *Finding partial fractions by substituting values*

Find the partial fraction expansions of the following rational expressions.

(a) $\dfrac{x+8}{(x-2)(x+3)}$ (b) $\dfrac{x-3}{2(x-1)(x+2)(2x-1)}$

Solution

(a) Write down the form of the partial fraction expansion of $\dfrac{x+8}{(x-2)(x+3)}$.

We have

$$\frac{x+8}{(x-2)(x+3)} = \frac{A}{x-2} + \frac{B}{x+3},$$

where A and B are constants.

Multiply both sides by $(x-2)(x+3)$ to give polynomial expressions on each side.

Multiplying both sides by $(x-2)(x+3)$ gives

$$x+8 = A(x+3) + B(x-2).$$

This equation is valid for all values of x, so to find A and B you can substitute into the equation *any* convenient values of x. A good choice is $x=2$, because then $x-2=0$, so the term $B(x-2)$ disappears, leaving an equation in A. Use a similar method to find B.

Choosing $x=2$ gives

$$\begin{aligned} 2+8 &= A \times (2+3) \\ 10 &= 5A, \end{aligned}$$

so $A = \dfrac{10}{5} = 2$.

Choosing $x=-3$ gives

$$\begin{aligned} -3+8 &= B \times (-3-2) \\ 5 &= -5B, \end{aligned}$$

so $B = \dfrac{5}{-5} = -1$.

Hence

$$\begin{aligned} \frac{x+8}{(x-2)(x+3)} &= \frac{2}{x-2} + \frac{-1}{x+3} \\ &= \frac{2}{x-2} - \frac{1}{x+3}. \end{aligned}$$

(Check: when $x=0$, LHS $= \frac{8}{-6} = -\frac{4}{3}$ and RHS $= -1 - \frac{1}{3} = -\frac{4}{3}$.)

(b) Write down the form of the partial fraction expansion of $\dfrac{x-3}{2(x-1)(x+2)(2x-1)}$. Notice that the constant factor 2 in the denominator makes no difference to the form of the partial fraction expansion.

We have

$$\frac{x-3}{2(x-1)(x+2)(2x-1)} = \frac{A}{x-1} + \frac{B}{x+2} + \frac{C}{2x-1},$$

where A, B and C are constants.

Multiply both sides by $2(x-1)(x+2)(2x-1)$ to give polynomial expressions on each side.

Multiplying both sides by $2(x-1)(x+2)(2x-1)$ gives
$x-3 = 2A(x+2)(2x-1) + 2B(x-1)(2x-1) + 2C(x-1)(x+2)$.

To find A, B and C, substitute into the equation values of x that make the linear factors $x-1$, $x+2$ and $2x-1$ equal to 0. For example, choose $x=1$, because then $x-1=0$, so the terms $2B(x-1)(2x-1)$ and $2C(x-1)(x+2)$ disappear, leaving an equation in A. Use a similar method to find B and C.

Choosing $x=1$ gives

$$\begin{aligned} 1-3 &= 2\times A\times(1+2)(2\times 1-1)\\ -2 &= 2\times A\times 3\times 1\\ -1 &= 3A, \end{aligned}$$

so $A = -\frac{1}{3}$.

Choosing $x=-2$ gives

$$\begin{aligned} -2-3 &= 2\times B\times(-2-1)(2\times(-2)-1)\\ -5 &= 2\times B\times(-3)\times(-5)\\ 1 &= -6B, \end{aligned}$$

so $B = -\frac{1}{6}$.

Choosing $x=\frac{1}{2}$ gives

$$\begin{aligned} \tfrac{1}{2}-3 &= 2\times C\times\left(\tfrac{1}{2}-1\right)\left(\tfrac{1}{2}+2\right)\\ -\tfrac{5}{2} &= 2\times C\times\left(-\tfrac{1}{2}\right)\times\tfrac{5}{2}\\ -1 &= -1\times C, \end{aligned}$$

so $C = 1$.

Hence

$$\begin{aligned} \frac{x-3}{2(x-1)(x+2)(2x-1)} &= \frac{-\frac{1}{3}}{x-1} + \frac{-\frac{1}{6}}{x+2} + \frac{1}{2x-1}\\ &= -\frac{1}{3(x-1)} - \frac{1}{6(x+2)} + \frac{1}{2x-1}. \end{aligned}$$

(Check: when $x = 0$,

$$\text{LHS} = \frac{-3}{2\times(-1)\times2\times(-1)} = -\frac{3}{4} \quad \text{and} \quad \text{RHS} = -\frac{1}{-3} - \frac{1}{12} + \frac{1}{-1} = -\frac{3}{4}.)$$

The procedure for finding the constants in a partial fraction expansion demonstrated in Example 9 is called the **method of substituting values**.

Activity 10 *Finding partial fractions by substituting values*

Using the method of substituting values, find the partial fraction expansions of the following rational expressions.

(a) $\dfrac{x-2}{(x-1)(x-3)}$ (b) $\dfrac{-7x-11}{(x+2)(x+1)(x-1)}$

There is yet another method of finding the partial fraction expansion of a proper rational expression with distinct linear factors. It is essentially a streamlined version of the method of substituting values, which can be used when the values you are substituting are those that make the linear factors in the denominator of the rational expression equal 0. To describe this method, let's return to the rational expression

$$\frac{x+8}{(x-2)(x+3)}$$

considered in the last two examples. Its partial fraction expansion has the form

$$\frac{x+8}{(x-2)(x+3)} = \frac{A}{x-2} + \frac{B}{x+3},$$

where A and B are constants. In Example 9(a), we found A by multiplying both sides of this equation by $(x-2)(x+3)$ to give

$$x + 8 = A(x+3) + B(x-2),$$

and then substituting $x = 2$. With this substitution, the term involving B vanishes and we are left with

$$A = \frac{2+8}{2+3} = \frac{10}{5} = 2.$$

A quicker way to obtain this value is to 'cover up' the linear factor $x - 2$ in the original rational expression to leave

$$\frac{x+8}{\boxed{(x-2)}(x+3)},$$

and substitute $x = 2$ into the uncovered part. This leaves us with exactly the same calculation for A as before, and we can perform a similar manipulation to find B.

This technique is called the **cover-up method**. It is demonstrated again in the next example, which uses the same rational expression as in Example 9(b).

Example 10 *Finding partial fractions using the cover-up method*

Use the cover-up method to find the partial fraction expansion of the rational expression

$$\frac{x-3}{2(x-1)(x+2)(2x-1)}.$$

Solution

Write down the form of the partial fraction expansion of $\dfrac{x-3}{2(x-1)(x+2)(2x-1)}$. Note that this is not affected by the presence of the constant factor 2 in the denominator.

We have

$$\frac{x-3}{2(x-1)(x+2)(2x-1)} = \frac{A}{x-1} + \frac{B}{x+2} + \frac{C}{2x-1},$$

where A, B and C are constants.

Use the cover-up method to find A. To do this, cover up the linear factor $(x-1)$ in the original rational expression to leave

$$\frac{x-3}{2(x-1)(x+2)(2x-1)},$$

and substitute $x = 1$ into the uncovered part. You choose $x = 1$ because it is this value of x that gives $x - 1 = 0$.

Using the cover-up method with $x = 1$ gives

$$A = \frac{1-3}{2(1+2)(2\times 1-1)} = \frac{-2}{2\times 3\times 1} = -\frac{2}{6} = -\frac{1}{3}.$$

Use the cover-up method to find B. To do this, cover up the linear factor $(x+2)$ in the original rational expression to leave

$$\frac{x-3}{2(x-1)(x+2)(2x-1)},$$

and substitute $x = -2$ into the uncovered part. You choose $x = -2$ because it is this value of x that gives $x + 2 = 0$.

Using the cover-up method with $x = -2$ gives

$$B = \frac{-2-3}{2(-2-1)(2\times(-2)-1)} = \frac{-5}{2\times(-3)\times(-5)} = \frac{-5}{30} = -\frac{1}{6}.$$

Use the cover-up method to find C. To do this, cover up the linear factor $(2x-1)$ in the original rational expression to leave

$$\frac{x-3}{2(x-1)(x+2)\boxed{(2x-1)}},$$

and substitute $x=\frac{1}{2}$ into the uncovered part. You choose $x=\frac{1}{2}$ because it is this value of x that gives $2x-1=0$.

Using the cover-up method with $x=\frac{1}{2}$ gives

$$C=\frac{\frac{1}{2}-3}{2\left(\frac{1}{2}-1\right)\left(\frac{1}{2}+2\right)}=\frac{-\frac{5}{2}}{2\times\left(-\frac{1}{2}\right)\times\frac{5}{2}}=\frac{-\frac{5}{2}}{-\frac{5}{2}}=1.$$

So

$$\frac{x-3}{2(x-1)(x+2)(2x-1)}=-\frac{1}{3(x-1)}-\frac{1}{6(x+2)}+\frac{1}{2x-1}.$$

(Check: when $x=0$,

$$\text{LHS}=\frac{-3}{2\times(-1)\times 2\times(-1)}=-\frac{3}{4}\quad\text{and}\quad\text{RHS}=-\frac{1}{-3}-\frac{1}{12}+\frac{1}{-1}=-\frac{3}{4}.)$$

Activity 11 *Finding partial fractions using the cover-up method*

Using the cover-up method, find the partial fraction expansions of the following rational expressions.

(a) $\dfrac{x}{(x+1)(3x+2)}$ (b) $\dfrac{1}{2x(x+3)}$ (c) $\dfrac{3x-1}{(x-2)(x+3)(2x+1)}$

Oliver Heaviside (1850–1925)

Heaviside cover-up method

The cover-up method is also sometimes called the **Heaviside cover-up method**, named after the British mathematician and scientist Oliver Heaviside who popularised the technique. ('Heaviside' is pronounced as 'heavy side'.) Heaviside is remembered in physics for his great advances in electricity and magnetism, developing the work of the eminent Scottish mathematical physicist James Clerk Maxwell (1831–1879). Heaviside also made substantial contributions to mathematics, particularly in the subject known as vector calculus.

2.3 Repeated linear factors

In this subsection you'll learn how to find the partial fraction expansions of proper rational expressions whose denominators are products of linear factors, some of which may be repeated. For example, in the denominator of the rational expression

$$\frac{x+7}{(x-2)^2},$$

the linear factor $x-2$ is repeated: it appears twice, to give $(x-2)^2$. You can obtain the partial fraction expansion for this particular expression by rearranging the numerator, as follows:

$$\frac{x+7}{(x-2)^2} = \frac{(x-2)+2+7}{(x-2)^2} = \frac{(x-2)+9}{(x-2)^2} = \frac{1}{x-2} + \frac{9}{(x-2)^2}.$$

Notice that there is a partial fraction with denominator $x-2$ *and* a partial fraction with denominator $(x-2)^2$. More generally, the following rule tells you the form of partial fractions for proper rational expressions that have repeated linear factors in their denominator.

Partial fractions of proper rational expressions with repeated linear factors

Each repeated linear factor $(ax+b)^2$ gives rise to *two* partial fractions of the form $\dfrac{A}{ax+b} + \dfrac{B}{(ax+b)^2}$, where A and B are constants.

Each repeated linear factor $(ax+b)^3$ gives rise to *three* partial fractions of the form $\dfrac{A}{ax+b} + \dfrac{B}{(ax+b)^2} + \dfrac{C}{(ax+b)^3}$, where A, B and C are constants, and so on.

In general, the constants will be different for different linear factors.

Any linear factors $ax+b$ that aren't repeated just give rise to a single partial fraction of the form $\dfrac{A}{ax+b}$, as before.

For example,

$$\frac{x^3+8x-7}{(x+5)(x-2)^3} = \frac{A}{x+5} + \frac{B}{x-2} + \frac{C}{(x-2)^2} + \frac{D}{(x-2)^3},$$

where A, B, C and D are constants.

Unfortunately, when there are repeated linear factors, the cover-up method can be used to find only *some* of the constants. Specifically, for each repeated factor $(ax+b)^n$ in the denominator of a rational expression, the cover-up method can only be used to find the value of the constant for the partial fraction with $(ax+b)^n$ in its denominator – it won't tell you the values of the constants for the partial fractions with other powers of $(ax+b)$ in their denominators. So in the above example, you could use the cover-up method to find A and D, but not B or C.

To find the remaining constants, you should take the following approach.

If only one unknown constant remains, then find it by using the method of substituting values. Usually you should choose $x = 0$.

If more than one unknown constant remains, then find them by using the method of equating coefficients.

If only one unknown constant remains, then you should substitute $x = 0$ unless x itself is a factor of the denominator of the rational expression. In that exceptional case, you can substitute another simple value of x, such as $x = 1$.

Example 11 *Finding partial fractions when there are repeated linear factors*

Find the partial fraction expansions of the following rational expressions.

(a) $\dfrac{x^2 + 10x + 7}{(x-1)(x+2)^2}$ (b) $\dfrac{-x^2 + 8x - 11}{(x-3)^3}$

Solution

(a) Write down the form of the partial fraction expansion of $\dfrac{x^2 + 10x + 7}{(x-1)(x+2)^2}$.

We have

$$\frac{x^2 + 10x + 7}{(x-1)(x+2)^2} = \frac{A}{x-1} + \frac{B}{x+2} + \frac{C}{(x+2)^2},$$

where A, B and C are constants.

Use the cover-up method to find A. To do this, cover up the linear factor $(x - 1)$ in the original rational expression to leave

$$\frac{x^2 + 10x + 7}{(x-1)(x+2)^2},$$

and substitute $x = 1$ into the uncovered part.

Using the cover-up method with $x = 1$ gives

$$A = \frac{1^2 + 10 \times 1 + 7}{(1+2)^2} = \frac{1 + 10 + 7}{3^2} = \frac{18}{9} = 2.$$

You cannot use the cover-up method to find B, so ignore B for now and use the cover-up method to find C. To do this, cover up the repeated linear factor $(x+2)^2$ in the original rational expression to leave

$$\frac{x^2+10x+7}{(x-1)(x+2)^2},$$

and substitute $x=-2$ into the uncovered part.

Using the cover-up method with $x=-2$ gives

$$C=\frac{(-2)^2+10\times(-2)+7}{-2-1}=\frac{4-20+7}{-3}=\frac{-9}{-3}=3.$$

So

$$\frac{x^2+10x+7}{(x-1)(x+2)^2}=\frac{2}{x-1}+\frac{B}{x+2}+\frac{3}{(x+2)^2}.$$

To find the single remaining constant B, substitute into the equation a convenient value of x, such as $x=0$. Before doing so, it helps to multiply both sides of the equation by $(x-1)(x+2)^2$ to give polynomial expressions on each side.

Multiplying both sides by $(x-1)(x+2)^2$ gives

$$x^2+10x+7=2(x+2)^2+B(x+2)(x-1)+3(x-1).$$

Substituting $x=0$ gives

$$7=2\times2^2+B\times2\times(-1)+3\times(-1)$$
$$7=8-2B-3$$
$$2=-2B.$$

So $B=\dfrac{2}{-2}=-1$. Hence

$$\frac{x^2+10x+7}{(x-1)(x+2)^2}=\frac{2}{x-1}-\frac{1}{x+2}+\frac{3}{(x+2)^2}.$$

You should now check your answer. Since you used $x=0$ to find B, you cannot also use $x=0$ to check your answer. Instead, choose another simple value of x. You cannot use $x=1$ because $x-1$ is a factor of the denominator of the rational expression, so use $x=-1$ or $x=2$.

(Check: when $x=-1$, LHS $=\frac{-2}{-2}=1$ and RHS $=\frac{2}{-2}-\frac{1}{1}+\frac{3}{1}=1$.)

(b) Write down the form of the partial fraction expansion of $\dfrac{-x^2+8x-11}{(x-3)^3}$.

We have

$$\frac{-x^2+8x-11}{(x-3)^3} = \frac{A}{x-3} + \frac{B}{(x-3)^2} + \frac{C}{(x-3)^3},$$

where A, B and C are constants.

You cannot use the cover-up method to find A or B, so ignore A and B for now and use the cover-up method to find C. To do this, cover up the repeated linear factor $(x-3)^3$ in the original rational expression to leave

$$\frac{-x^2+8x-11}{(x-3)^3},$$

and substitute $x = 3$ into the uncovered part. As the whole denominator is covered, replace it by 1 when you use the cover-up method.

Using the cover-up method with $x = 3$ gives

$$C = \frac{-3^2+8\times 3-11}{1} = -9+24-11 = 4.$$

So

$$\frac{-x^2+8x-11}{(x-3)^3} = \frac{A}{x-3} + \frac{B}{(x-3)^2} + \frac{4}{(x-3)^3}.$$

You could substitute simple values of x to find A and B. However, as there are two unknowns, you'll need two substitutions and then you'll have to solve a pair of simultaneous equations. A quicker way to find A and B is to multiply both sides of the equation by $(x-3)^3$, and then equate coefficients.

Multiplying both sides by $(x-3)^3$ gives

$$-x^2+8x-11 = A(x-3)^2 + B(x-3) + 4$$

Expand the brackets, then collect terms in x^2, terms in x and constant terms.

$$\begin{aligned} &= A(x^2-6x+9) + B(x-3) + 4 \\ &= (Ax^2-6Ax+9A) + (Bx-3B) + 4 \\ &= Ax^2 + (-6A+B)x + (9A-3B+4). \end{aligned}$$

The coefficients of x^2 on each side of the equation $-x^2 + 8x - 11 = Ax^2 + (-6A + B)x + (9A - 3B + 4)$ must be equal. Similarly the coefficients of x on each side must be equal. With this information you can find A and B. The constant terms of the equation must also be equal, but you don't need to use this, as you can find A and B by equating the coefficients of the terms in x and x^2 only. However, you could equate the constant terms as a check on your values of A and B.

Comparing coefficients of x^2 gives $A = -1$. Comparing coefficients of x gives

$$8 = -6A + B, \quad \text{so} \quad B = 8 + 6A = 8 + 6 \times (-1) = 2.$$

So

$$\frac{-x^2 + 8x - 11}{(x-3)^3} = -\frac{1}{x-3} + \frac{2}{(x-3)^2} + \frac{4}{(x-3)^3}.$$

(Check: when $x = 0$,

$$\text{LHS} = \tfrac{-11}{-27} = \tfrac{11}{27} \quad \text{and} \quad \text{RHS} = -\tfrac{1}{-3} + \tfrac{2}{9} + \tfrac{4}{-27} = \tfrac{11}{27}.)$$

Activity 12 *Finding partial fractions when there are repeated linear factors*

Find the partial fraction expansions of the following rational expressions.

(a) $\dfrac{x+7}{(x+1)^2}$ (b) $\dfrac{x}{(3x-1)(x-1)^2}$ (c) $\dfrac{x^2}{(2x-1)^3}$

2.4 Quadratic factors

In each of the examples about finding partial fraction expansions that you've seen so far, the denominator of the given rational expression has been written as a product of linear factors. However, a rational expression needn't be presented in such a form. Consider, for example, the expression

$$\frac{x+8}{x^2+x-6}.$$

To find the partial fraction expansion of this expression, you must first factorise the denominator. You can do this to obtain

$$\frac{x+8}{(x-2)(x+3)},$$

and then proceed as before. In this case the denominator factorised neatly into a product of two linear factors with integer coefficients. Other rational expressions do not behave so well; for example, if you factorise the denominator of the rational expression

$$\frac{2x+3}{x^2-2x-1},$$

then you obtain

$$\frac{2x+3}{(x-(1+\sqrt{2}))(x-(1-\sqrt{2}))}.$$

This is a more complicated expression because the coefficients of the linear factors in the denominator are not all integers. Nonetheless, you can still find the partial fraction expansion of this rational expression using the same methods that you've learned already.

In each of these examples, the denominator of the rational expression is a quadratic expression of the form $ax^2 + bx + c$ for which the discriminant $b^2 - 4ac$ is positive. As you know, you can factorise quadratic expressions whose discriminant is positive or zero, but you can't factorise quadratic expressions whose discriminant is negative.

In this subsection, we look at how to find the partial fraction expansions of rational expressions whose denominators contain quadratic factors with a negative discriminant. Consider, for example, the expression

$$\frac{x-7}{2x^2-x+3}.$$

You cannot factorise the quadratic $2x^2 - x + 3$ because the discriminant $b^2 - 4ac$ is negative:

$$(-1)^2 - 4 \times 2 \times 3 = 1 - 24 = -23.$$

So you cannot hope to simplify this rational expression further.

The following box tells you the form of the partial fractions of a proper rational expression that correspond to such quadratic factors (that aren't repeated).

Partial fractions of proper rational expressions for distinct quadratic factors with negative discriminant

Each quadratic factor $ax^2 + bx + c$ whose discriminant $b^2 - 4ac$ is negative gives rise to a partial fraction of the form

$$\frac{Ax+B}{ax^2+bx+c},$$

where A and B are constants. In general, the constants will be different for different quadratic factors.

Any linear factors in the denominator of such a rational expression contribute partial fractions in the same way that you've seen already.

For example,

$$\frac{x-2}{(x+1)(3x^2-x+2)} = \frac{A}{x+1} + \frac{Bx+C}{3x^2-x+2},$$

where A, B and C are constants. You can find the constant A using the cover-up method, but this method won't allow you to find B and C. As two unknown constants remain, you should find them by equating coefficients.

Example 12 *Finding partial fractions when there is a quadratic factor*

Find the partial fraction expansion of the rational expression $\dfrac{x-5}{(x-2)(3x^2-2x+1)}$.

Solution

Write down the form of the partial fraction expansion of $\dfrac{x-5}{(x-2)(3x^2-2x+1)}$. First check that the quadratic expression $3x^2-2x+1$ cannot be factorised by making sure that $b^2-4ac<0$.

Since

$$(-2)^2 - 4\times 3\times 1 = 4 - 12 = -8 < 0,$$

the quadratic expression $3x^2-2x+1$ cannot be factorised. So

$$\frac{x-5}{(x-2)(3x^2-2x+1)} = \frac{A}{x-2} + \frac{Bx+C}{3x^2-2x+1},$$

where A, B and C are constants.

Use the cover-up method to find A. To do this, cover up the linear factor $x-2$ in the original rational expression to leave

$$\frac{x-5}{(x-2)(3x^2-2x+1)},$$

and substitute $x=2$ into the uncovered part.

Using the cover-up method with $x=2$ gives

$$A = \frac{2-5}{3\times 2^2 - 2\times 2+1} = \frac{-3}{12-4+1} = \frac{-3}{9} = -\frac{1}{3}.$$

So

$$\frac{x-5}{(x-2)(3x^2-2x+1)} = -\frac{1}{3(x-2)} + \frac{Bx+C}{3x^2-2x+1}.$$

You can't use the cover-up method to find B and C. You could find B and C by substituting values of x, but it's simpler to find them by multiplying both sides of the equation by $(x-2)(3x^2-2x+1)$ and then equating coefficients. In fact, since you know that $A=-\frac{1}{3}$, it's neater to multiply both sides by $3(x-2)(3x^2-2x+1)$ so that all the resulting coefficients are integers.

Multiplying both sides by $3(x-2)(3x^2-2x+1)$ gives

$$3(x-5) = -(3x^2-2x+1) + 3(Bx+C)(x-2).$$

Expand the brackets, then collect terms in x^2, terms in x and constant terms.

That is,

$$\begin{aligned}3x-15 &= -(3x^2-2x+1) + 3(Bx^2-2Bx+Cx-2C)\\ &= -(3x^2-2x+1) + (3Bx^2-6Bx+3Cx-6C)\\ &= (3B-3)x^2 + (-6B+3C+2)x + (-6C-1).\end{aligned}$$

Equate coefficients in the equation

$$3x-15 = (3B-3)x^2 + (-6B+3C+2)x + (-6C-1)$$

to find B and C. You can compare the terms in x^2, the terms in x and the constant terms. You need to carry out only two of these three possible comparisons, so you should choose the simplest two. In this particular case, comparing terms in x is the most difficult since the coefficient of x on the right-hand side is the long expression $-6B+3C+2$, which includes both unknowns B and C. So just compare the terms in x^2 and the constant terms.

Comparing the coefficients of x^2 gives

$$0 = 3B-3, \quad \text{so} \quad 3B = 3.$$

Hence $B=\dfrac{3}{3}=1$. Comparing the constant terms gives

$$-15 = -6C-1, \quad \text{so} \quad 6C = 14.$$

Hence $C=\dfrac{14}{6}=\dfrac{7}{3}$. So

$$\begin{aligned}\frac{x-5}{(x-2)(3x^2-2x+1)} &= -\frac{1}{3(x-2)} + \frac{x+\frac{7}{3}}{3x^2-2x+1}\\ &= -\frac{1}{3(x-2)} + \frac{3x+7}{3(3x^2-2x+1)}.\end{aligned}$$

(Check: when $x=0$, LHS $=\frac{-5}{-2}=\frac{5}{2}$ and RHS $=-\frac{1}{-6}+\frac{7}{3}=\frac{5}{2}$.)

Activity 13 *Finding partial fractions when there is a quadratic factor*

Find the partial fraction expansions of the following rational expressions.

(a) $\dfrac{1}{(x+1)(x^2+1)}$ (b) $\dfrac{x^2+1}{x(2x^2+1)}$ (c) $\dfrac{x-2}{(x+1)(3x^2-x+2)}$

The following box summarises a strategy for finding the partial fraction expansion of a proper rational expression using the methods you've learned.

Strategy:
To find the partial fraction expansion of a proper rational expression without repeated quadratic factors

1. Write down the form of the partial fraction expansion, using a different letter to denote each unknown constant.
   - Each linear factor $ax+b$ that is not repeated gives rise to a partial fraction of the form $\dfrac{A}{ax+b}$, where A is a constant.
   - Each repeated linear factor $(ax+b)^n$ gives rise to n partial fractions of the form
   $$\frac{A_1}{ax+b}+\frac{A_2}{(ax+b)^2}+\cdots+\frac{A_n}{(ax+b)^n},$$
   where $A_1, A_2, \ldots, A_n$ are constants.
   - Each quadratic factor ax^2+bx+c that is not repeated and whose discriminant b^2-4ac is negative gives rise to a partial fraction of the form $\dfrac{Ax+B}{ax^2+bx+c}$, where A and B are constants.
2. Determine as many of the constants as you can by using the cover-up method.
3. - If only one constant remains unknown, then find it by using the method of substituting values.
   - If more than one constant remains unknown, then find them by using the method of equating coefficients.

You've seen that there are a number of methods for finding the partial fractions of a rational expression, and the strategy above represents one coherent procedure for doing so. Bear in mind, though, that this is only a guide. Sometimes you may find it easier to substitute values when the strategy tells you to equate coefficients, or vice versa. And sometimes you may discover shortcuts, such as rearranging the numerator, which give you quicker ways of writing down down the partial fraction expansion.

This strategy doesn't tell you how to deal with rational expressions that have *repeated quadratic factors*, such as the expression

$$\frac{2x-1}{(x+3)(x^2+1)^2},$$

which has two copies of the quadratic factor x^2+1 in its denominator. In fact, the partial fraction expansion for this rational expression is of the form

$$\frac{2x-1}{(x+3)(x^2+1)^2} = \frac{A}{x+3} + \frac{Bx+C}{x^2+1} + \frac{Dx+E}{(x^2+1)^2},$$

where A, B, C, D and E are constants. As you can see from this example, repeated quadratic factors are handled in a similar way to repeated linear factors. However, you won't meet rational expressions with repeated quadratic factors in this module.

You may be wondering about higher degree factors, such as cubic or quartic expressions. It is a remarkable fact that these are never needed in the partial fraction expansions of rational expressions. Look back now at the box on page 21, which gave the general form of the partial fraction expansion of a proper rational expression. This should mean more to you now than when you first met it. You'll see that the only partial fractions needed are those with linear or quadratic factors in their denominators.

The fact that higher-degree factors are not needed is a consequence of the following important theorem: any polynomial expression with real coefficients can be factorised into a product of linear and quadratic expressions with real coefficients. The proof of this result is outside the scope of this module.

2.5 Integration of proper rational expressions

One of the main uses of partial fraction expansions is to give a method for integrating rational functions. Suppose, for example, that you wish to find the indefinite integral

$$\int \frac{1}{x^2+x}\,dx.$$

You can factorise the denominator to give $x^2+x = x(x+1)$, and then find the partial fraction expansion of the integrand using the cover-up method. You obtain

$$\frac{1}{x(x+1)} = \frac{1}{x} - \frac{1}{x+1}.$$

Now you can integrate these two partial fractions using standard techniques, and thus find the original integral. Here's another example.

Example 13 *Integrating a proper rational expression using partial fractions*

Find the integral $\displaystyle\int \frac{1}{2x^3+x}\,dx$.

Solution

Write down the form of the partial fraction expansion of $\dfrac{1}{2x^3+x}$. You need to factorise the denominator first.

We have $2x^3+x = x(2x^2+1)$. Since

$$0^2 - 4\times 2\times 1 = -8 < 0,$$

the quadratic expression $2x^2+1$ cannot be factorised. So

$$\frac{1}{2x^3+x} = \frac{1}{x(2x^2+1)} = \frac{A}{x} + \frac{Bx+C}{2x^2+1},$$

where A, B and C are constants.

Use the cover-up method to find A.

Using the cover-up method with $x=0$ gives

$$A = \frac{1}{1} = 1.$$

So

$$\frac{1}{2x^3+x} = \frac{1}{x} + \frac{Bx+C}{2x^2+1}.$$

To find B and C, multiply both sides of the equation by $x(2x^2+1)$ and then equate coefficients.

Multiplying both sides by $x(2x^2+1)$ gives

$$\begin{aligned}1 &= (2x^2+1) + (Bx+C)x\\ &= (2x^2+1) + (Bx^2+Cx)\\ &= (B+2)x^2 + Cx + 1.\end{aligned}$$

Comparing coefficients of x^2 gives

$$0 = B+2, \quad \text{so} \quad B = -2.$$

Comparing coefficients of x gives $C=0$. So

$$\frac{1}{2x^3+x} = \frac{1}{x} - \frac{2x}{2x^2+1}.$$

(Check: when $x=1$, LHS $=\frac{1}{3}$ and RHS $= 1-\frac{2}{3} = \frac{1}{3}$.)

Use the partial fraction expansion to find the integral.

Hence

$$\begin{aligned}\int \frac{1}{2x^3+x}\,\mathrm{d}x &= \int \left(\frac{1}{x} - \frac{2x}{2x^2+1}\right)\mathrm{d}x \\ &= \int \frac{1}{x}\,\mathrm{d}x - \int \frac{2x}{2x^2+1}\,\mathrm{d}x.\end{aligned}$$

The first integral on the right-hand side is a standard one. The second integral on the right-hand side is suitable for a substitution, because the derivative of the denominator $2x^2+1$ is $4x$, which is 'nearly' equal to the numerator $2x$.

The first integral is

$$\int \frac{1}{x}\,\mathrm{d}x = \ln|x| + c.$$

For the second integral, let $u = 2x^2+1$; then $\dfrac{\mathrm{d}u}{\mathrm{d}x} = 4x$. So

$$\begin{aligned}\int \frac{2x}{2x^2+1}\,\mathrm{d}x &= \tfrac{1}{2}\int \left(\frac{1}{2x^2+1}\right)(4x)\,\mathrm{d}x \\ &= \tfrac{1}{2}\int \frac{1}{u}\,\mathrm{d}u\end{aligned}$$

This is now a standard integral in u, so evaluate it and substitute back for u in terms of x.

$$\begin{aligned}&= \tfrac{1}{2}\ln|u| + c \\ &= \tfrac{1}{2}\ln|2x^2+1| + c.\end{aligned}$$

Now subtract the second integral from the first to give the solution. We have used the usual symbol c for the arbitrary constant in both integrals, but of course the constant can take different values in each case, so there will still be an arbitrary constant when we subtract the second integral from the first. We may as well continue to use the symbol c for this arbitrary constant.

So

$$\begin{aligned}\int \frac{1}{2x^3+x}\,\mathrm{d}x &= \ln|x| - \tfrac{1}{2}\ln|2x^2+1| + c \\ &= \tfrac{1}{2}\times 2\ln|x| - \tfrac{1}{2}\ln|2x^2+1| + c\end{aligned}$$

Remember the logarithm law $r\ln x = \ln(x^r)$. In particular, $2\ln|x| = \ln(|x|^2)$.

$$= \tfrac{1}{2}\ln(|x|^2) - \tfrac{1}{2}\ln|2x^2+1| + c$$

Notice that $|x|^2 = x^2$ and that $2x^2 + 1$ is always positive.

$$= \tfrac{1}{2}\ln(x^2) - \tfrac{1}{2}\ln(2x^2 + 1) + c$$

Remember the logarithm law $\ln a - \ln b = \ln(a/b)$. In particular, this law shows that $\ln(x^2) - \ln(2x^2 + 1) = \ln\left(\dfrac{x^2}{2x^2 + 1}\right)$.

$$= \tfrac{1}{2}\ln\left(\frac{x^2}{2x^2 + 1}\right) + c.$$

Before you try some similar examples yourself, here's something that you may find helpful. When you expand an integrand using partial fractions as demonstrated in Example 13, you often find that one or more of the resulting partial fractions is of a particular type, namely that its numerator is a constant multiple of the derivative of its denominator. For instance, the 'second integral' in Example 13 is of this type.

You can always integrate such a fraction by using substitution. However, the working for this always follows a similar pattern, and you may like to shorten it slightly by remembering the following formula.

$$\int \frac{f'(x)}{f(x)}\,\mathrm{d}x = \ln|f(x)| + c$$

For example, you can use this formula to find the second integral in Example 13 as follows:

$$\int \frac{2x}{2x^2 + 1}\,\mathrm{d}x = \tfrac{1}{2}\int \frac{4x}{2x^2 + 1}\,\mathrm{d}x = \tfrac{1}{2}\ln|2x^2 + 1| + c.$$

To see why the formula in the box is true, substitute $u = f(x)$ to evaluate the integral on the left-hand side. Then $\mathrm{d}u/\mathrm{d}x = f'(x)$, which gives

$$\begin{aligned}
\int \frac{f'(x)}{f(x)}\,\mathrm{d}x &= \int \frac{1}{f(x)} f'(x)\,\mathrm{d}x \\
&= \int \frac{1}{u}\,\mathrm{d}u \\
&= \ln|u| + c \\
&= \ln|f(x)| + c.
\end{aligned}$$

You can use this formula in part (d) of the next activity, or you can just use integration by substitution in the usual way, as is done in the solution.

Activity 14 *Integrating using partial fractions*

Find the following integrals.

(a) $\displaystyle\int \frac{x}{(x+5)^2}\,dx$ (b) $\displaystyle\int \frac{1}{(x-4)(x-2)}\,dx$

(c) $\displaystyle\int \frac{1}{x(x-1)(2x-1)}\,dx$ (d) $\displaystyle\int \frac{3x-1}{(x+1)(3x^2+1)}\,dx$

You'll have more opportunities to practise integrating rational functions in the next section, after you've learned how to find the partial fraction expansions of *improper* rational expressions.

3 Partial fractions of improper rational expressions

In the previous section, you learned how to find partial fraction expansions of *proper* rational expressions, that is, rational expressions for which the degree of the polynomial expression in the numerator is smaller than the degree of the polynomial expression in the denominator. In this section we consider *improper* rational expressions, such as

$$\frac{x^3+1}{x^2-2x+1} \quad \text{and} \quad \frac{2x+1}{x+2},$$

in which the degree of the numerator is greater than or equal to the degree of the denominator.

We begin by introducing a useful method for writing any improper rational expression as the sum of a polynomial expression and a proper rational expression.

3.1 Polynomial long division

To motivate this method, it helps to look back at the first subsection of Unit 3, which was about dividing integers. As you saw there, when you divide an integer by a positive integer, you obtain a quotient and a remainder. For example, if you divide 38 by 5 you obtain a quotient of 7 and a remainder of 3, and you can write

$$38 = \underset{\substack{\uparrow \\ \text{quotient}}}{7} \times 5 \; + \; \underset{\substack{\uparrow \\ \text{remainder}}}{3}.$$

Multiplying both sides by $\frac{1}{5}$ gives

$$\frac{38}{5} = 7 + \frac{3}{5}.$$

It's a similar story for polynomial expressions. For example, you can 'divide' the polynomial expression $x^3 + 1$ by the polynomial expression $x^2 - 2x + 1$ to obtain a quotient and remainder as follows:

$$x^3 + 1 = \underset{\substack{\uparrow \\ \text{quotient}}}{(x+2)}(x^2 - 2x + 1) \; + \; \underset{\substack{\uparrow \\ \text{remainder}}}{(3x - 1)}.$$

You can check that this equation is correct by simplifying the right-hand side. You'll see shortly precisely how you can obtain this equation by 'division'. Notice that the remainder $3x - 1$ has smaller degree than the dividing polynomial $x^2 - 2x + 1$.

Multiplying both sides of the above equation by $1/(x^2 - 2x + 1)$ gives

$$\underbrace{\frac{x^3 + 1}{x^2 - 2x + 1}}_{\substack{\text{improper rational} \\ \text{expression}}} = \underbrace{x + 2}_{\substack{\text{polynomial} \\ \text{expression}}} + \underbrace{\frac{3x - 1}{x^2 - 2x + 1}}_{\substack{\text{proper rational} \\ \text{expression}}}.$$

In fact, you obtain similar equations whenever you 'divide' one polynomial expression by another, as long as the dividing expression is not the constant 0 (since division by zero is not defined). This result is summarised in the following box.

The division theorem for polynomial expressions

Suppose that $a(x)$ and $b(x)$ are polynomial expressions, and $b(x)$ is not the expression 0. Then there are unique polynomial expressions $q(x)$ and $r(x)$ such that

$$a(x) = q(x)b(x) + r(x),$$

where the degree of $r(x)$ is less than the degree of $b(x)$.

The expressions $q(x)$ and $r(x)$ are called the **quotient** and **remainder**, respectively, on dividing $a(x)$ by $b(x)$.

If you multiply both sides of the equation $a(x) = q(x)b(x) + r(x)$ by $1/b(x)$, then you obtain

$$\frac{a(x)}{b(x)} = q(x) + \frac{r(x)}{b(x)}.$$

So if $a(x)/b(x)$ is an improper rational expression, then because the degree of $r(x)$ is less than the degree of $b(x)$, this equation shows you that you can write $a(x)/b(x)$ as the sum of a polynomial expression $q(x)$ and a proper rational expression $r(x)/b(x)$.

In the next example you'll see how to find the quotient and remainder on dividing one polynomial expression by another. The procedure is called **polynomial long division**; it is a similar procedure to integer long division, but uses polynomial expressions instead of integers. Polynomial long division is easier to demonstrate than to describe in writing, so you may find it particularly helpful to watch the tutorial clip for this example.

Example 14 *Dividing polynomial expressions*

Find the quotient and remainder on dividing $a(x)$ by $b(x)$ for each of the following pairs of polynomial expressions.

(a) $a(x) = 2x^2 + x + 1$, $b(x) = x - 1$

(b) $a(x) = x^3 + 1$, $b(x) = x^2 - 2x + 1$

Solution

(a) Write down the polynomial expressions using the usual notation for integer long division.

$$x - 1 \,\big)\overline{\,2x^2 + \;x + 1\,}$$

Find an expression of the form 'constant × x^n' that, when multiplied by the divisor $x - 1$, gives a polynomial expression with the same highest power term as $\textcircled{2x^2} + x + 1$ (the circled term). The answer is $2x$, because $2x \times (x - 1) = \textcircled{2x^2} - 2x$. Write this expression $2x$ at the top, in the x column, and write the product $2x^2 - 2x$ at the bottom, making sure that each term is in the appropriate column.

$$\begin{array}{r|l} & \phantom{2x^2 +{}} 2x \\ \cline{2-2} x - 1 & 2x^2 + x + 1 \\ & 2x^2 - 2x \end{array}$$

Subtract the polynomial expression $2x^2 - 2x$ in the third line from the expression $2x^2 + x + 1$ in the second line, and write the answer at the bottom.

$$\begin{array}{r|l} & \phantom{2x^2 +{}} 2x \\ \cline{2-2} x - 1 & 2x^2 + x + 1 \\ & \underline{2x^2 - 2x} \\ & \phantom{2x^2 +{}} 3x + 1 \end{array}$$

Now repeat the process, this time dividing the new expression $3x + 1$ just obtained by the same divisor $x - 1$. Once again, find an expression of the form 'constant × x^n' that, when multiplied by the divisor $x - 1$, gives a polynomial expression with the same highest power term as $\textcircled{3x} + 1$. The answer is 3 (that is, $3 \times x^0$), because $3 \times (x - 1) = \textcircled{3x} - 3$. Write this expression 3 at the top, in the constant term column, and write the product $3x - 3$ at the bottom, making sure that each term is in the appropriate column.

$$\begin{array}{r|l} & \phantom{2x^2 +{}} 2x + 3 \\ \cline{2-2} x - 1 & 2x^2 + x + 1 \\ & \underline{2x^2 - 2x} \\ & \phantom{2x^2 +{}} 3x + 1 \\ & \phantom{2x^2 +{}} 3x - 3 \end{array}$$

Subtract the polynomial expression $3x - 3$ in the fifth line from the expression $3x + 1$ in the fourth line, and write the answer at the bottom.

$$\begin{array}{r|l} & \phantom{2x^2 +{}} 2x + 3 \\ \cline{2-2} x - 1 & 2x^2 + x + 1 \\ & \underline{2x^2 - 2x} \\ & \phantom{2x^2 +{}} 3x + 1 \\ & \phantom{2x^2 +{}} \underline{3x - 3} \\ & \phantom{2x^2 + 3x +{}} 4 \end{array}$$

The result of this subtraction is the polynomial expression 4 at the bottom. This expression has lower degree than the divisor $x - 1$, so the division procedure terminates. The quotient is the polynomial expression at the top, and the remainder is the expression at the bottom.

So the quotient is $2x + 3$ and the remainder is 4.

Check your answer, by making sure that the equation $a(x) = q(x)b(x) + r(x)$ is satisfied, where $q(x)$ is the quotient and $r(x)$ is the remainder. To do this, calculate $q(x)b(x) + r(x)$, and check that it equals $a(x)$.

(Check: $(2x + 3)(x - 1) + 4 = (2x^2 + x - 3) + 4 = 2x^2 + x + 1$.)

(b) Write down the polynomial expressions using the usual notation for integer long division. To ensure that matching powers of x appear in the same column, it helps to write $x^3 + 1$ as $x^3 + 0x^2 + 0x + 1$.

$$x^2 - 2x + 1 \;\big)\; x^3 + 0x^2 + 0x + 1$$

Find an expression of the form 'constant $\times$ x^n' that, when multiplied by the divisor $x^2 - 2x + 1$, gives a polynomial expression with the same highest power term as $\textcircled{x^3} + 1$. The answer is x, because $x \times (x^2 - 2x + 1) = \textcircled{x^3} - 2x^2 + x$. Write this expression x at the top, in the x column, and write the product $x^3 - 2x^2 + x$ at the bottom, making sure that each term is in the appropriate column.

$$\begin{array}{r|l} & \phantom{x^3 + 0x^2 + {}} x \\ \hline x^2 - 2x + 1 & x^3 + 0x^2 + 0x + 1 \\ & x^3 - 2x^2 + x \end{array}$$

Subtract the polynomial expression in the third line from the expression above it.

$$\begin{array}{r|l} & \phantom{x^3 + 0x^2 + {}} x \\ \hline x^2 - 2x + 1 & x^3 + 0x^2 + 0x + 1 \\ & \underline{x^3 - 2x^2 + x\phantom{{}+1}} \\ & \;\; 2x^2 - x + 1 \end{array}$$

Now repeat the process, this time dividing the new expression $2x^2 - x + 1$ just obtained by the same divisor $x^2 - 2x + 1$. The highest power term of $2x^2 - x + 1$ is $2x^2$, so the next expression of the form 'constant $\times\ x^n$' that you need is 2, because $2 \times (x^2 - 2x + 1) = 2x^2 - 4x + 2$.

$$\begin{array}{r|l}
 & \phantom{x^3 + 0x^2 +{}} x + 2 \\ \cline{2-2}
x^2 - 2x + 1 & x^3 + 0x^2 + 0x + 1 \\
 & x^3 - 2x^2 + x \\ \cline{2-2}
 & \phantom{x^3 +{}} 2x^2 - x + 1 \\
 & \phantom{x^3 +{}} 2x^2 - 4x + 2
\end{array}$$

Subtract the fifth line from the fourth line.

$$\begin{array}{r|l}
 & \phantom{x^3 + 0x^2 +{}} x + 2 \\ \cline{2-2}
x^2 - 2x + 1 & x^3 + 0x^2 + 0x + 1 \\
 & x^3 - 2x^2 + x \\ \cline{2-2}
 & \phantom{x^3 +{}} 2x^2 - x + 1 \\
 & \phantom{x^3 +{}} 2x^2 - 4x + 2 \\ \cline{2-2}
 & \phantom{x^3 + 0x^2 +{}} 3x - 1
\end{array}$$

The result of this subtraction is the polynomial expression $3x - 1$ at the bottom. This expression has lower degree than the divisor $x^2 - 2x + 1$, so the division procedure terminates. The quotient is the polynomial expression at the top, and the remainder is the expression at the bottom.

So the quotient is $x + 2$ and the remainder is $3x - 1$.

Check that the equation $a(x) = q(x)b(x) + r(x)$ is satisfied.

(Check:

$$\begin{aligned}
(x+2)(x^2 - 2x + 1) + (3x - 1) &= (x^3 - 3x + 2) + (3x - 1) \\
&= x^3 + 1.)
\end{aligned}$$

Notice that the degree of the quotient on dividing a polynomial expression $a(x)$ by another polynomial expression $b(x)$ is equal to the degree of $a(x)$ minus the degree of $b(x)$. For example, you've just seen that the quotient on dividing $x^3 + 1$ by $x^2 - 2x + 1$ is $x + 2$, and the degrees 3, 2 and 1 of these three polynomial expressions satisfy $3 - 2 = 1$.

The next activity gives you a chance to practise polynomial long division. Remember that when you have an expression such as $x^2 + 1$ you should write it as $x^2 + 0x + 1$ to help ensure that matching powers of x appear in the same column.

Activity 15 *Dividing polynomial expressions*

Find the quotient and remainder on dividing $a(x)$ by $b(x)$ for each of the following pairs of polynomial expressions.

(a) $a(x) = 2x + 1,\ b(x) = x + 2$

(b) $a(x) = x^2 - 3,\ b(x) = x - 3$

(c) $a(x) = x^2 + x,\ b(x) = 2x^2 + x + 1$

(d) $a(x) = x^3 - x^2 + 1,\ b(x) = x^2 + 1$

(e) $a(x) = x^3,\ b(x) = x - 1$

You can also use the computer algebra system to obtain the output of polynomial long division, which is useful for checking your answers.

Activity 16 *Using the computer algebra system to divide polynomial expressions*

Work through Section 6.2 of the *Computer algebra guide*, where you'll learn how to use the computer algebra system to divide polynomial expressions.

3.2 Polynomial long division and partial fractions

Given an improper rational expression, you can use polynomial long division to find the quotient and remainder on dividing the numerator of the improper rational expression by the denominator. You can then use the equation

$$\frac{a(x)}{b(x)} = q(x) + \frac{r(x)}{b(x)}$$

to write the improper rational expression as the sum of a polynomial expression and a proper rational expression. Finally, you can write the proper rational expression as a sum of its partial fractions using the methods you learned in Section 2. The resulting sum is called the **partial fraction expansion** of the improper rational expression.

For instance, in Example 14(b) you saw that

$$\frac{x^3 + 1}{x^2 - 2x + 1} = x + 2 \quad + \quad \frac{3x - 1}{x^2 - 2x + 1},$$

and the partial fraction expansion of the proper rational expression on the right-hand side is

$$\frac{3x - 1}{x^2 - 2x + 1} = \frac{3}{x - 1} + \frac{2}{(x - 1)^2},$$

which you can check by adding the expressions on the right (notice that $x^2 - 2x + 1 = (x-1)^2$). So the partial fraction expansion of the improper rational expression $\dfrac{x^3+1}{x^2-2x+1}$ is

$$\frac{x^3+1}{x^2-2x+1} = x+2 \quad + \quad \frac{3}{x-1} + \frac{2}{(x-1)^2}.$$

The strategy for finding partial fraction expansions of improper rational expressions is summarised below.

Strategy:
To find the partial fraction expansion of an improper rational expression

1. Use polynomial long division to write

   improper rational expression = polynomial expression + proper rational expression

2. Find the partial fraction expansion of the proper rational expression in the usual way.

Example 15 *Finding partial fraction expansions of improper rational expressions*

Find the partial fraction expansions of the following rational expressions.

(a) $\dfrac{x^2}{(2x+1)(x+1)}$ (b) $\dfrac{2x^3-x-1}{3x^2+1}$

Solution

(a) The rational expression is improper, so use polynomial long division to write

improper rational expression = polynomial expression + proper rational expression

To do this, first expand the denominator.

We have

$$\frac{x^2}{(2x+1)(x+1)} = \frac{x^2}{2x^2+3x+1}.$$

Apply polynomial long division to divide x^2 by $2x^2+3x+1$.

$$\begin{array}{r|rrr} & & & \tfrac{1}{2} \\ 2x^2+3x+1 & x^2+ & 0x & +0 \\ & x^2+ & \tfrac{3}{2}x & +\tfrac{1}{2} \\ \hline & & -\tfrac{3}{2}x & -\tfrac{1}{2} \end{array}$$

So the quotient on dividing x^2 by $2x^2+3x+1$ is $\frac{1}{2}$ and the remainder is $-\frac{3}{2}x-\frac{1}{2}$.

There's no need to check this answer now unless you wish to do so, as you'll carry out a check at the end.

You can now write the improper rational expression as the sum of a polynomial expression and a proper rational expression by observing that

$$x^2 = \text{quotient} \times (2x^2+3x+1) + \text{remainder},$$

which gives

$$\frac{x^2}{2x^2+3x+1} = \text{quotient} + \frac{\text{remainder}}{2x^2+3x+1}.$$

Remember that $2x^2+3x+1=(2x+1)(x+1)$.

Hence

$$\begin{aligned}\frac{x^2}{(2x+1)(x+1)} &= \frac{1}{2} + \frac{-\frac{3}{2}x-\frac{1}{2}}{(2x+1)(x+1)} \\ &= \frac{1}{2} - \frac{3x+1}{2(2x+1)(x+1)}.\end{aligned}$$

Now find the partial fraction expansion of the proper rational expression $\dfrac{3x+1}{2(2x+1)(x+1)}$.

We have

$$\frac{3x+1}{2(2x+1)(x+1)} = \frac{A}{2x+1} + \frac{B}{x+1}.$$

Using the cover-up method with $x=-\frac{1}{2}$ gives

$$A = \frac{3\times\left(-\frac{1}{2}\right)+1}{2\left(\left(-\frac{1}{2}\right)+1\right)} = \frac{-\frac{1}{2}}{1} = -\frac{1}{2}.$$

Using the cover-up method with $x=-1$ gives

$$B = \frac{3\times(-1)+1}{2(2\times(-1)+1)} = \frac{-2}{-2} = 1.$$

So

$$\frac{3x+1}{2(2x+1)(x+1)} = -\frac{1}{2(2x+1)} + \frac{1}{x+1}.$$

Combine the results to give the full partial fraction expansion. Don't forget the minus sign before the proper rational expression.

Hence

$$\frac{x^2}{(2x+1)(x+1)} = \frac{1}{2} + \frac{1}{2(2x+1)} - \frac{1}{x+1}.$$

Check your answer. As usual with partial fraction expansions, a suitable check is to make sure that both sides are equal when $x = 0$.

(Check: when $x = 0$, LHS $= 0$ and RHS $= \frac{1}{2} + \frac{1}{2} - 1 = 0$.)

(b) The rational expression is improper, so use polynomial long division to write

$$\text{improper rational expression} = \text{polynomial expression} + \text{proper rational expression}$$

To apply polynomial long division, write $3x^2 + 1$ as $3x^2 + 0x + 1$, and write $2x^3 - x - 1$ as $2x^3 + 0x^2 - x - 1$.

$$\begin{array}{r|l} & \qquad\qquad\quad \tfrac{2}{3}x \\ 3x^2 + 0x + 1 & 2x^3 + 0x^2 - \; x \; - 1 \\ & \underline{2x^3 + 0x^2 + \tfrac{2}{3}x} \\ & \qquad\qquad -\tfrac{5}{3}x - 1 \end{array}$$

So the quotient on dividing $2x^3 - x - 1$ by $3x^2 + 1$ is $\frac{2}{3}x$ and the remainder is $-\frac{5}{3}x - 1$.

You can now write the improper rational expression as the sum of a polynomial expression and a proper rational expression.

Hence

$$\frac{2x^3 - x - 1}{3x^2 + 1} = \frac{2x}{3} + \frac{-\frac{5}{3}x - 1}{3x^2 + 1} = \frac{2x}{3} - \frac{5x + 3}{3(3x^2 + 1)}.$$

The expression $\dfrac{5x+3}{3(3x^2+1)}$ is already a partial fraction – it can't be split up further, because the quadratic factor $3x^2 + 1$ in the denominator cannot be factorised.

This is the required partial fraction expansion because the quadratic expression $3x^2 + 1$ cannot be factorised (since $0^2 - 4 \times 3 \times 1 = -12 < 0$).

Check your answer.

(Check: when $x = 0$, LHS $= \frac{-1}{1} = -1$ and RHS $= 0 - \frac{3}{3} = -1$.)

Activity 17 *Finding partial fraction expansions of improper rational expressions*

Find the partial fraction expansions of the following rational expressions.

(a) $\dfrac{2x^2}{x^2-1}$ (b) $\dfrac{3x^2-1}{2x^2+1}$ (c) $\dfrac{x^3+1}{2x-1}$ (d) $\dfrac{x^3}{(x-1)(x+3)}$

Sometimes you may find that you can write an improper rational expression as the sum of a polynomial expression and a proper rational expression without using polynomial long division, particularly if the numerator and denominator have the same degree. For example, in part (a) of the preceding activity you can write

$$\frac{2x^2}{x^2-1}=\frac{2x^2-2+2}{x^2-1}=\frac{2(x^2-1)+2}{x^2-1}=2+\frac{2}{x^2-1}.$$

If you notice a shorter method such as this, then use it. You'll see more examples of this kind in later activities.

3.3 Integration of improper rational expressions

So far in this section you've seen how to write any improper rational expression as the sum of a polynomial expression and a proper rational expression. Since you know how to integrate polynomial expressions, and you can integrate proper rational expressions using the techniques of the previous section, you now also have a method for integrating improper rational expressions. This method is demonstrated in the following example.

Example 16 *Integrating an improper rational expression*

Find the integral $\displaystyle\int \frac{2x^2+1}{(x-1)^2}\,dx$.

Solution

The rational expression in the integrand is improper, so apply polynomial long division to divide the numerator by the denominator. To do this, first expand the denominator.

We have

$$\frac{2x^2+1}{(x-1)^2}=\frac{2x^2+1}{x^2-2x+1}.$$

Now apply polynomial long division.

$$\begin{array}{r|l} & 2 \\ \hline x^2-2x+1 & 2x^2+0x+1 \\ & 2x^2-4x+2 \\ \hline & 4x-1 \end{array}$$

So the quotient on dividing $2x^2+1$ by x^2-2x+1 is 2 and the remainder is $4x-1$.

Write the improper rational expression as the sum of a polynomial expression and a proper rational expression.

Hence

$$\frac{2x^2+1}{(x-1)^2} = 2 + \frac{4x-1}{(x-1)^2}.$$

Alternatively, you could have rearranged the numerator to obtain this result, as in the example at the end of Subsection 3.2. Since

$$2(x-1)^2 = 2(x^2-2x+1) = 2x^2-4x+2,$$

we have

$$2(x-1)^2 + 4x - 1 = 2x^2 - 4x + 2 + 4x - 1 = 2x^2 + 1,$$

so

$$\frac{2x^2+1}{(x-1)^2} = \frac{2(x-1)^2+4x-1}{(x-1)^2} = 2 + \frac{4x-1}{(x-1)^2}.$$

A similar method can be used to find the partial fraction expansion of the proper rational expression $\dfrac{4x-1}{(x-1)^2}$.

We have

$$\begin{aligned}\frac{4x-1}{(x-1)^2} &= \frac{4x-4+4-1}{(x-1)^2} \\ &= \frac{4(x-1)+3}{(x-1)^2} \\ &= \frac{4}{x-1} + \frac{3}{(x-1)^2}.\end{aligned}$$

Alternatively, you could have used the techniques of Section 2. Now write down the full partial fraction expansion.

Hence

$$\frac{2x^2+1}{(x-1)^2} = 2 + \frac{4}{x-1} + \frac{3}{(x-1)^2}.$$

(Check: when $x=0$, LHS $= \frac{1}{1} = 1$ and RHS $= 2 + \frac{4}{-1} + \frac{3}{1} = 1$.)

Use the partial fraction expansion to find the integral.

So

$$\begin{aligned}\int \frac{2x^2+1}{(x-1)^2}\,dx &= \int \left(2+\frac{4}{x-1}+\frac{3}{(x-1)^2}\right) dx\\ &= \int 2\,dx + \int \frac{4}{x-1}\,dx + \int \frac{3}{(x-1)^2}\,dx\\ &= \int 2\,dx + 4\int \frac{1}{x-1}\,dx + 3\int (x-1)^{-2}\,dx\end{aligned}$$

All three integrals are standard integrals that have been modified by multiplying by constant factors and by using functions of linear expressions.

$$\begin{aligned}&= 2x + 4\ln|x-1| - 3(x-1)^{-1} + c\\ &= 2x + 4\ln|x-1| - \frac{3}{x-1} + c.\end{aligned}$$

Activity 18 *Integrating improper rational expressions*

Find the following integrals.

(a) $\displaystyle\int \frac{x-1}{x+1}\,dx$ (b) $\displaystyle\int \frac{x^2}{4x^2+1}\,dx$ (c) $\displaystyle\int \frac{x^2}{(x+1)(x+2)}\,dx$

It's possible to integrate *any* rational expression by finding the partial fraction expansion of the expression, and then integrating each of the partial fractions.

However, this may not always be the *best* way of integrating a rational expression. For example, consider the integral

$$\int \frac{2x}{x^2-1}\,dx.$$

You could find this integral by first finding the partial fraction expansion of the integrand, but an easier method is to use the substitution $u = x^2 - 1$. Then $\dfrac{du}{dx} = 2x$, and

$$\int \frac{2x}{x^2-1}\,dx = \int \frac{1}{u}\,du = \ln|u| + c = \ln|x^2-1| + c.$$

For most rational expressions, however, there is no shortcut similar to the one used in this example, and integrating by using the partial fraction expansion is the best approach. Indeed, there's no harm in using that method even for those few cases where there is a quicker alternative strategy.

4 Graphs of rational functions

In MST124, you saw how to sketch the graph of a cubic function by finding its stationary points and determining their type. The graphs of cubic functions, and in fact all polynomial functions, consist of one 'piece', in the sense that they can be drawn in one continuous line without lifting your pen from the paper.

This is not always the case for graphs of rational functions that are not polynomial functions. For example, the graph of the function $f(x) = 1/x$ shown in Figure 5 has two 'pieces'. To sketch the graph of a rational function that may have several pieces, you need a strategy that tells you the location and rough shape of each piece. Such a strategy is described in this section.

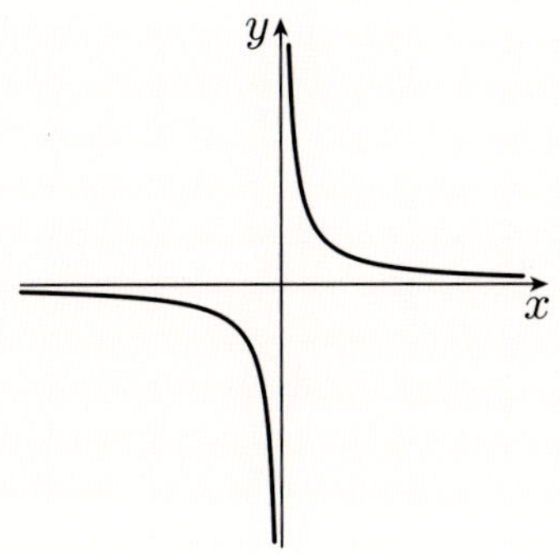

Figure 5 The graph of $f(x) = \dfrac{1}{x}$

4.1 Features of graphs of rational functions

The strategy we'll use to sketch the graph of a rational function is to first determine several features of the function and its graph, and then combine these features to give a complete sketch of the graph. In this subsection we'll go through these features one by one, and in the next subsection you'll see how to combine them to sketch a graph. To illustrate this approach, we'll use the rational function

$$f(x) = \frac{1}{x^2 - 1}$$

in many of the examples.

Domain

When asked to sketch the graph of *any* function, you should first work out the domain of the function; that is, the set of allowed input values for the function. Usually when you are given a rational function there is no mention of a domain, in which case you should assume that the domain is the largest possible set of values for which the function makes sense. For example, the rational function

$$f(x) = \frac{1}{x}$$

makes sense unless $x = 0$, because you cannot divide by 0. In interval notation, its domain is therefore $(-\infty, 0) \cup (0, \infty)$. More generally, the domain of a rational function consists of all real numbers except those for which the denominator of the rational function is 0.

Here's another example.

Example 17 *Finding the domain of a rational function*

Find the domain of the rational function $f(x) = \dfrac{1}{x^2-1}$. Express your answer using interval notation.

Solution

The domain consists of all real numbers except those for which the denominator of $f(x)$ is 0.

The denominator of $f(x)$ is 0 when $x^2 - 1 = 0$; that is, when $x^2 = 1$. So the domain consists of all real numbers other than -1 and 1.

Express the domain using interval notation.

Hence the domain is $(-\infty, -1) \cup (-1, 1) \cup (1, \infty)$.

Activity 19 *Finding the domains of rational functions*

Find the domains of the following rational functions. Express your answers using interval notation.

(a) $f(x) = \dfrac{x}{x^2-4}$ (b) $f(x) = \dfrac{2}{x^2+2}$ (c) $f(x) = \dfrac{1}{(x+1)^3}$

Intercepts

Once you know the domain of the rational function whose graph you wish to sketch, you should then work out the points at which the graph meets the axes. The value of y at which the graph meets the y-axis is called the **y-intercept**. The y-intercept is the value of f at the input value $x = 0$; that is, $f(0)$. Since functions have exactly one output value for each input value, there is only one y-intercept, unless 0 is not in the domain of the function, in which case there are no y-intercepts.

The values of x at which the graph meets the x-axis are called the **x-intercepts**. These are the values of x such that $f(x) = 0$. There may be several of these, or only one, or none at all.

Example 18 *Finding the intercepts of a rational function*

Find the intercepts of the rational function $f(x) = \dfrac{1}{x^2 - 1}$.

Solution

Find the y-intercept first, which is given by $f(0)$.

The y-intercept is

$$f(0) = \frac{1}{0^2 - 1} = -1.$$

Now find the x-intercepts. These are the values of x for which $f(x) = 0$.

The equation

$$\frac{1}{x^2 - 1} = 0$$

has no solutions, so there are no x-intercepts.

Activity 20 *Finding the intercepts of rational functions*

Find the intercepts of the following rational functions.

(a) $f(x) = \dfrac{x^2 - 1}{2x^3 + 1}$ (b) $f(x) = \dfrac{x}{x^2 + 1}$ (c) $f(x) = \dfrac{x^2 + 5}{x + 1}$

Stationary points and intervals on which a function is increasing or decreasing

The next feature of your function that you should determine in order to sketch its graph is where it is increasing, decreasing or stationary. To do this, you must differentiate the function.

A **stationary point** of a function f is a point at which the gradient of the graph of f is zero. The stationary points of f can be found by solving the equation $f'(x) = 0$. Both the x-coordinate of the point and the point itself are known as a stationary point.

Away from the stationary points, the function behaves according to the following criterion.

Increasing/decreasing criterion

If $f'(x)$ is positive for all x in an interval I, then f is increasing on I.

If $f'(x)$ is negative for all x in an interval I, then f is decreasing on I.

To find the intervals on which f is increasing or decreasing, you should create a *table of signs* for $f'(x)$. Tables of signs, and the other ideas used in this subsection, were covered in detail in MST124 Units 3 and 6.

The table of signs for $f'(x)$ not only tells you where f is increasing or decreasing, it also enables you to determine the nature of the stationary points of f using the *first derivative test*, which is summarised in the box below.

First derivative test (for determining the nature of a stationary point of a function f)

If there are open intervals immediately to the left and right of a stationary point such that

- $f'(x)$ is positive on the left interval and negative on the right interval, then the stationary point is a local maximum
- $f'(x)$ is negative on the left interval and positive on the right interval, then the stationary point is a local minimum
- $f'(x)$ is positive on both intervals or negative on both intervals, then the stationary point is a horizontal point of inflection.

Let's demonstrate all this with an example.

Example 19 *Working out where a rational function is increasing, decreasing or stationary*

Consider the rational function $f(x) = \dfrac{1}{x^2 - 1}$.

(a) Find the coordinates of the stationary points of f.

(b) Determine the intervals on which f is increasing or decreasing.

(c) Determine whether each stationary point of f is a local maximum, a local minimum or a horizontal point of inflection.

Solution

(a) Differentiate f using the chain rule.

We have

$$f(x) = \frac{1}{x^2 - 1} = (x^2 - 1)^{-1},$$

so, by the chain rule,

$$f'(x) = (-1) \times (2x) \times (x^2 - 1)^{-2} = \frac{-2x}{(x^2 - 1)^2}.$$

The stationary points of f are the values of x for which $f'(x) = 0$.

Multiplying both sides of the equation $f'(x) = 0$ by $(x^2 - 1)^2$ gives

$$-2x = 0.$$

Hence the only stationary point of f is 0.

The *coordinates* of the stationary point are $(0, f(0))$.

Since

$$f(0) = \frac{1}{-1} = -1,$$

the coordinates of the stationary point are $(0, -1)$.

(b) Construct a table of signs for $f'(x)$ to help you find the intervals on which $f'(x)$ is negative or positive. Include column headings for the stationary points of f (the values where $f'(x) = 0$) and the values where $f'(x)$ is not defined, as well as column headings for the intervals to the left and right of, and between, these values. In the row headings, write the numerator and denominator of $f'(x)$, and then $f'(x)$ itself. The numerator has one factor in this example; if a numerator has more than one factor, then split the numerator over several rows by writing each factor in a separate row heading. The denominator is never negative because it is a square, so it is simpler not to split it into factors.

In each of the rows for the numerator and denominator, enter $+$, $-$ or 0 according to whether the expression for that row is positive, negative or zero, respectively, for values of x in that column. Then use these entries to complete the row for $f'(x)$, entering $*$ where it is not defined because of division by 0.

x	$(-\infty,-1)$	-1	$(-1,0)$	0	$(0,1)$	1	$(1,\infty)$
$-2x$	$+$	$+$	$+$	0	$-$	$-$	$-$
$(x^2-1)^2$	$+$	0	$+$	$+$	$+$	0	$+$
$f'(x)$	$+$	$*$	$+$	0	$-$	$*$	$-$

Hence f is increasing on the intervals $(-\infty,-1)$ and $(-1,0)$, and f is decreasing on the intervals $(0,1)$ and $(1,\infty)$.

(c) The table tells you the sign of $f'(x)$ to the left and right of the stationary point, so use the first derivative test to determine its nature.

Since $f'(x)$ is positive to the left and negative to the right of the stationary point 0, we deduce that 0 is a local maximum of f.

When filling in the table of signs for $f'(x)$, don't forget to put a $*$ in the row for $f'(x)$ in each column where $f'(x)$ is not defined. For rational functions, $f'(x)$ is undefined at the same values of x at which $f(x)$ is undefined, though this is not true of all functions.

In the preceding example, the denominator $(x^2-1)^2$ of $f'(x)$ is never negative, because it is the square of an expression. It follows that $f'(x)$ always has the same sign as its numerator $-2x$, where it is defined. This gives you a quicker way of completing the last row of the table of signs. You can use a similar observation to help you complete tables of signs for derivatives of other rational functions.

In the example, you found the coordinates of the stationary point to be $(0,-1)$. Then, when calculating the table of signs, the symbols $(-1,0)$ and $(0,1)$ were used to represent intervals. This is a clash of notation, but it is common usage and the meaning is usually clear from the context. In practice, if you set out your work carefully, then it's unlikely you'll mix up the two meanings.

Activity 21 *Working out where a rational function is increasing, decreasing or stationary*

Consider the rational function $f(x) = \dfrac{x^2}{x+1}$.

(a) Find the coordinates of the stationary points of f.

(b) Determine the intervals on which f is increasing or decreasing.

(c) Determine whether each stationary point of f is a local maximum, a local minimum or a horizontal point of inflection.

Asymptotic behaviour

If you trace your pen tip along one of the pieces of the graph of a rational function, then you can continue indefinitely in either direction. The **asymptotic behaviour** of the graph is the shape of the traces that you leave as you run your pen further and further along each piece. There are two types of asymptotic behaviour for rational functions, which we consider in turn.

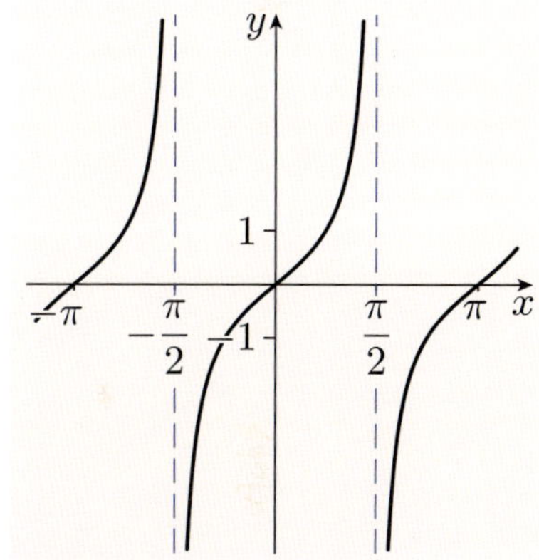

Figure 6 The graph of $y = \tan x$

Asymptotic behaviour at vertical asymptotes

You may recall that an **asymptote** of a graph is a line that the graph approaches arbitrarily closely as you trace your pen tip further and further along it away from the origin. For example, the lines with equations $x = \pi/2$ and $x = -\pi/2$ are asymptotes of the graph of the tangent function, shown in Figure 6. The asymptotes of the graph of the tangent function are called **vertical asymptotes** because they are vertical lines.

Suppose now that f is a rational function that is not defined at the value a, because the denominator of $f(x)$ is zero when x is a. As x gets close to but not equal to a, the value $f(x)$ becomes large in magnitude, so the vertical line with equation $x = a$ is a vertical asymptote of the graph of f. For example, you saw earlier that the function

$$f(x) = \frac{1}{x^2 - 1}$$

is defined for all real numbers except -1 and 1. If x is close to but not equal to one of these numbers, then $f(x)$ is large in magnitude. Hence the vertical lines with equations $x = -1$ and $x = 1$ are vertical asymptotes of the graph of this function. Near to a vertical asymptote, the graph of a rational function has one of the four shapes shown in Figure 7. In graph (a) of that figure, f is increasing to the left of the asymptote and decreasing to the right of the asymptote. In (b), f is increasing on both

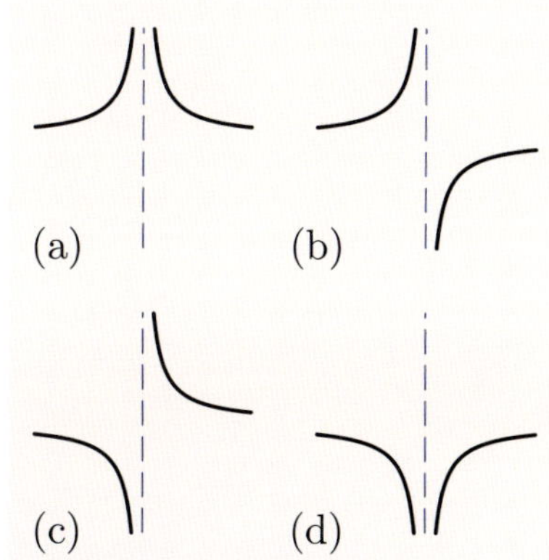

Figure 7 The behaviour of the graph to the left and right of a vertical asymptote

the left and the right. In (c), f is decreasing on both sides, and in (d) f is decreasing on the left and increasing on the right. Since the values of $f'(x)$ tell you where f is increasing or decreasing, you can use the table of signs of $f'(x)$ to deduce which of the four shapes (a), (b), (c) or (d) the graph has near a vertical asymptote.

For example, consider again the function $f(x) = \dfrac{1}{x^2-1}$. Earlier you saw that its derivative has the following table of signs.

x	$(-\infty,-1)$	-1	$(-1,0)$	0	$(0,1)$	1	$(1,\infty)$
$-2x$	$+$	$+$	$+$	0	$-$	$-$	$-$
$(x^2-1)^2$	$+$	0	$+$	$+$	$+$	0	$+$
$f'(x)$	$+$	$*$	$+$	0	$-$	$*$	$-$

From the table, you can see that $f'(x)$ is positive to the left and to the right of the vertical asymptote $x=-1$. It follows that f is increasing to the left and right of $x=-1$, so its graph near that asymptote has the shape shown in Figure 7(b). Also, $f'(x)$ is negative to the left and to the right of the vertical asymptote $x=1$, so f is decreasing to the left and right of $x=1$, and its graph near that asymptote has the shape shown in Figure 7(c).

Activity 22 *Finding asymptotic behaviour near vertical asymptotes*

Each of the following rational functions has a vertical asymptote with equation $x=0$, and no other vertical asymptotes. For each function, create a table of signs for its derivative, and work out which of the four sketches in Figure 7 represents the behaviour of the function near the asymptote.

(a) $f(x) = \dfrac{1}{x}$ (b) $f(x) = -\dfrac{1}{x}$ (c) $f(x) = \dfrac{1}{x^2}$ (d) $f(x) = -\dfrac{1}{x^2}$

Asymptotic behaviour as $x \to \infty$ and as $x \to -\infty$

Let's now look at the other type of asymptotic behaviour, which is about the behaviour of a rational function f as you travel arbitrarily far from the origin along the x-axis. The behaviour of $f(x)$ as you travel arbitrarily far to the right along the x-axis is described as the behaviour of $f(x)$ as x **tends to infinity**. The phrase 'x tends to infinity' is represented symbolically by $x \to \infty$. Similarly, the behaviour of $f(x)$ as you travel arbitrarily far to the left along the x-axis is described as the behaviour of $f(x)$ as x **tends to minus infinity**, and this phrase is represented by $x \to -\infty$.

There are several possible types of asymptotic behaviour of a rational function f as $x \to \infty$ and as $x \to -\infty$. The possibilities for the behaviour as $x \to \infty$ are listed below, and those as $x \to -\infty$ are similar. You'll see shortly how to work out which type of behaviour arises for any given rational function.

- The value of $f(x)$ may approach some constant number a as x tends to infinity. In this case we say that $f(x)$ *tends to a as x tends to infinity*, and we write this as

$$f(x) \to a \quad \text{as} \quad x \to \infty.$$

- The value of $f(x)$ may become arbitrarily large in magnitude and positive as x tends to infinity. In this case we say that $f(x)$ *tends to infinity as x tends to infinity*, and we write this as

$$f(x) \to \infty \quad \text{as} \quad x \to \infty.$$

- The value of $f(x)$ may become arbitrarily large in magnitude and negative as x tends to infinity. In this case we say that $f(x)$ *tends to minus infinity as x tends to infinity*, and we write this as

$$f(x) \to -\infty \quad \text{as} \quad x \to \infty.$$

We use similar notation for behaviour as $x \to -\infty$. For example, we can write '$f(x) \to \infty$ as $x \to -\infty$'.

To illustrate how to determine the behaviour of a rational function as $x \to \infty$ and as $x \to -\infty$, consider the function

$$f(x) = \frac{2x}{x^2+2}.$$

The term in a polynomial expression with the highest power of x is called the **dominant term**. You can see the dominant terms in the numerator and denominator of $f(x)$ circled below:

$$f(x) = \frac{\textcircled{2x}}{\textcircled{x^2}+2}.$$

When the magnitude of x is large, the dominant terms in the numerator and denominator of a rational function govern the behaviour of the function, because the other terms are small in comparison. It follows that the function behaves in a similar way to the simpler function obtained by ignoring all other terms. In our example, when the magnitude of x is large, f behaves like the simpler function

$$g(x) = \frac{2x}{x^2} = \frac{2}{x}.$$

The behaviour of this expression $g(x)$ is easier to understand than that of $f(x)$: you can see that

$$g(x) \to 0 \quad \text{as} \quad x \to \infty, \quad \text{and} \quad g(x) \to 0 \quad \text{as} \quad x \to -\infty.$$

It follows that

$$f(x) \to 0 \quad \text{as} \quad x \to \infty, \quad \text{and} \quad f(x) \to 0 \quad \text{as} \quad x \to -\infty.$$

The graph of this function f is shown in Figure 8. The horizontal line with equation $y = 0$ (the x-axis) is an asymptote of the graph because the graph approaches it arbitrarily closely (on both the extreme left and right). A horizontal line that is an asymptote is called a **horizontal asymptote**.

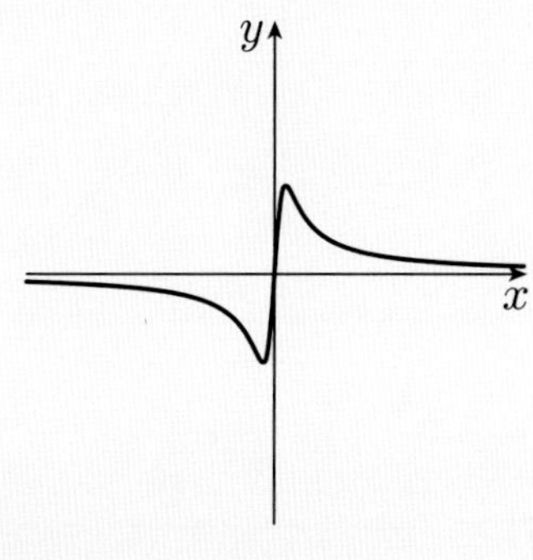

Figure 8 The graph of $f(x) = \dfrac{2x}{x^2+2}$

Reasoning in a similar way, you can obtain the following more general observation about asymptotic behaviour (you'll see another example in Example 20).

> If the degree of the numerator of the rational expression $f(x)$ is less than or equal to the degree of the denominator, then there is a constant number a such that
>
> $$f(x) \to a \quad \text{as} \quad x \to \infty, \quad \text{and} \quad f(x) \to a \quad \text{as} \quad x \to -\infty,$$
>
> and the graph of f has a horizontal asymptote with equation $y = a$.
>
> If $f(x)$ is a proper rational expression, then $a = 0$.

As another example of asymptotic behaviour, consider the function

$$f(x) = \frac{x^5 - 3x^4 + 1}{2x^2 + x}.$$

If we ignore all terms other than the dominant terms in the numerator and denominator of $f(x)$, then we obtain the function

$$g(x) = \frac{x^5}{2x^2} = \frac{x^3}{2}.$$

Since f behaves in a similar way to g as x tends to infinity and as x tends to minus infinity, we deduce that

$$f(x) \to \infty \quad \text{as} \quad x \to \infty, \quad \text{and} \quad f(x) \to -\infty \quad \text{as} \quad x \to -\infty.$$

In fact, by reasoning in a similar way you can see that if the degree of the numerator of a rational expression $f(x)$ is greater than the degree of the denominator, then $f(x)$ tends to either infinity or minus infinity as x tends to infinity and as x tends to minus infinity.

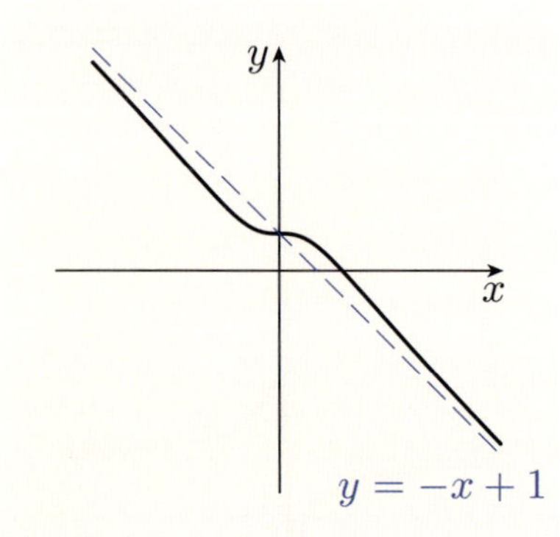

Figure 9 The graph of $f(x) = \dfrac{-x^3 + x^2 + 2}{x^2 + 2}$

Finally, let's consider one particular class of rational functions a little more carefully: those for which the degree of the numerator is exactly one more than the degree of the denominator. For example, consider the function

$$f(x) = \frac{-x^3 + x^2 + 2}{x^2 + 2},$$

whose numerator has degree 3 and denominator has degree 2. You can see that the graph of this function, shown in Figure 9, approaches the graph of a straight line on the far left and right. Such a line is therefore an asymptote of the graph, and because it is sloping it is called a **slant asymptote**.

> If the degree of the numerator of the rational expression $f(x)$ is one more than the degree of the denominator, then the graph of f has a slant asymptote.

You can determine the equation of the slant asymptote of a function of the type considered here by using polynomial long division. For example, using polynomial long division you can write the expression $f(x)$ whose graph is shown in Figure 9 as the sum of a polynomial expression and a proper rational expression:

$$f(x) = -x + 1 + \frac{2x}{x^2+2}.$$

As you saw earlier, the proper rational expression tends to 0 as $x \to \infty$ and as $x \to -\infty$, which implies that the value of $f(x)$ approaches the value of $-x+1$ as $x \to \infty$ and as $x \to -\infty$. In other words, the line $y = -x + 1$ is an asymptote of f.

Example 20 *Determining asymptotic behaviour as $x \to \infty$ and as $x \to -\infty$*

For each of the following functions, determine the asymptotic behaviour as $x \to \infty$ and as $x \to -\infty$, and give the equations of any horizontal or slant asymptotes.

(a) $f(x) = \dfrac{3x^3 + x}{2x^3 - 1}$ (b) $f(x) = \dfrac{-x^3 + 1}{x^2 + 1}$

Solution

(a) Find the asymptotic behaviour by using the dominant terms in the numerator and denominator of $f(x)$.

Ignoring all terms other than the dominant terms in the numerator and denominator of $f(x)$ gives

$$g(x) = \frac{3x^3}{2x^3} = \frac{3}{2}.$$

Since $f(x)$ has the same asymptotic behaviour as $x \to \infty$ and as $x \to -\infty$ as $g(x)$, we see that

$$f(x) \to \tfrac{3}{2} \quad \text{as} \quad x \to \infty, \quad \text{and} \quad f(x) \to \tfrac{3}{2} \quad \text{as} \quad x \to -\infty.$$

Since $f(x)$ approaches a constant number as x tends to infinity and as x tends to minus infinity, its graph has a horizontal asymptote.

So the graph of f has a horizontal asymptote with equation $y = \frac{3}{2}$.

(b) The degree of the numerator of $f(x)$ is one more than the degree of the denominator, so the graph of f has a slant asymptote. Use polynomial long division to write $f(x)$ as the sum of a polynomial expression and a proper rational expression.

$$\begin{array}{r|l} & -x \\ \hline x^2+0x+1 & -x^3+0x^2+0x+1 \\ & -x^3+0x^2-x \\ \cline{2-2} & x+1 \end{array}$$

So the quotient is $-x$ and the remainder is $x+1$.

(Check: $-x(x^2+1)+(x+1) = -x^3 - x + x + 1 = -x^3 + 1$.)

It follows that

$$f(x) = -x + \frac{x+1}{x^2+1}.$$

The proper rational expression tends to 0 as $x \to \infty$ and as $x \to -\infty$, so the value of $f(x)$ approaches the value of the polynomial expression as $x \to \infty$ and as $x \to -\infty$. The polynomial expression gives the equation of the slant asymptote.

Hence

$$f(x) \to -\infty \quad \text{as} \quad x \to \infty, \quad \text{and} \quad f(x) \to \infty \quad \text{as} \quad x \to -\infty.$$

The graph of f has a slant asymptote with equation $y = -x$.

Activity 23 *Determining asymptotic behaviour as $x \to \infty$ and as $x \to -\infty$*

For each of the following functions, determine the asymptotic behaviour as $x \to \infty$ and as $x \to -\infty$, and give the equations of any horizontal or slant asymptotes.

(a) $f(x) = \dfrac{4x^2-1}{2x^3+1}$ (b) $f(x) = \dfrac{4x^2-1}{2x^2+1}$ (c) $f(x) = \dfrac{4x^3-1}{2x^2+1}$

(d) $f(x) = \dfrac{4x^3-1}{-2x^2+1}$

Even and odd functions

The two graphs in Figure 10 both have 'symmetrical' features. The graph on the left is unchanged by reflection in the y-axis, and the graph on the right is unchanged by a rotation of angle 180° about the origin. They are examples of an *even function* and an *odd function*, respectively.

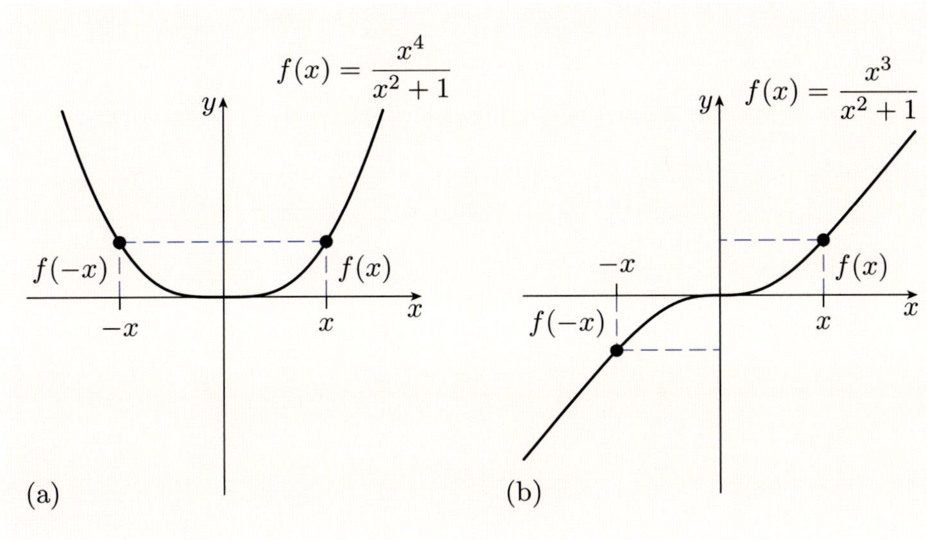

Figure 10 (a) An even function (b) an odd function

From the graph of $f(x) = \dfrac{x^4}{x^2+1}$ on the left you can see that $f(-x)$ and $f(x)$ are equal for all values of x, which you can check:

$$f(-x) = \frac{(-x)^4}{(-x)^2+1} = \frac{x^4}{x^2+1} = f(x).$$

In contrast, from the graph of $f(x) = \dfrac{x^3}{x^2+1}$ on the right you can see that $f(-x)$ and $-f(x)$ are equal for all values of x, which you can also check:

$$f(-x) = \frac{(-x)^3}{(-x)^2+1} = \frac{-x^3}{x^2+1} = -f(x).$$

This gives us the following simpler way of saying what even and odd functions are.

Even and odd functions

A function f is an **even function** if $f(-x) = f(x)$ for all x in the domain of f.

A function f is an **odd function** if $f(-x) = -f(x)$ for all x in the domain of f.

You've probably met these concepts before, perhaps when studying the trigonometric functions, where you'll have seen that cosine is an even function and sine is an odd function.

Example 21 *Deciding whether functions are even or odd functions*

Which of the following rational functions are even or odd functions?

(a) $f(x) = \dfrac{1}{x^2 - 1}$ (b) $f(x) = \dfrac{1}{x - 1}$

Solution

(a) Work out $f(-x)$ and see whether it's the same as $f(x)$ or $-f(x)$.

Since

$$f(-x) = \frac{1}{(-x)^2 - 1} = \frac{1}{x^2 - 1} = f(x),$$

f is an even function.

(b) We have

$$f(-x) = \frac{1}{(-x) - 1} = -\frac{1}{x + 1},$$

so it seems that f is neither an even nor an odd function. To demonstrate this, you only need to find one value of x such that $f(-x)$ is not equal to either $f(x)$ or $-f(x)$.

Since $f(2) = 1$ and $f(-2) = -1/3$, f is neither an even function nor an odd function.

Activity 24 *Deciding whether functions are even or odd functions*

Which of the following rational functions are even or odd functions?

(a) $f(x) = \dfrac{x^2}{x^2 + 2}$ (b) $f(x) = \dfrac{x}{x^2 + 2}$ (c) $f(x) = \dfrac{x}{(x + 2)^2}$

Other features

Using the features of a rational function that you've met so far, you can sketch its graph, as you'll see in the next subsection. However, sometimes you may find it helpful to work out some other features of the function before you sketch its graph, or you may use these other features to check that your sketch is correct. Here are three such features.

Coordinates of individual points on the graph

Sometimes it's useful to plot particular points that lie on the graph of your function. This can be a handy quick check to make sure part of your graph is where it should be.

Intervals on which the function is positive or negative

You've already created a table of signs for the derivative of the function, but you can create one for the function itself. This helps you to verify that your graph is correctly located relative to the x-axis.

Second derivative

It may be time consuming to work out the second derivative of your function, but to do so can be useful to improve the accuracy of your sketch or to check the nature of the stationary points.

In MST124 Unit 6 you saw that, on an interval where the second derivative is positive, the graph of a function is *concave up* (think 'curved upwards'), and on an interval where the second derivative is negative, the graph is *concave down* (think 'curved downwards'). So you could consider drawing up a table of signs for the second derivative of your function to better appreciate the shape of its graph.

You can also use the second derivative test as a check on the nature of the stationary points. This test says that a stationary point of a function is a local maximum if the second derivative at that point is negative, and a local minimum if the second derivative at that point is positive. Remember, though, that if the second derivative is zero at a stationary point, this tells you nothing about the nature of the stationary point. In such cases, you must determine the nature of the stationary point using the first derivative test.

4.2 Sketching graphs of rational functions

In the previous subsection you learned how to determine a number of features of the graph of a given rational function. Here you'll see how to combine these features to sketch the graph. Remember that in sketching a graph you are not trying to determine its precise shape – you can use the computer algebra system to do that. Rather, a sketch is meant to capture the important features of the graph, namely the features that you use to create the graph.

Let's sketch the graph of the rational function

$$f(x) = \frac{1}{x^2 - 1}$$

that was used in several of the earlier examples. You saw that this function has domain $(-\infty, -1) \cup (-1, 1) \cup (1, \infty)$, so the graph has vertical asymptotes with equations $x = -1$ and $x = 1$; these are the first things you should draw when sketching your graph, as shown in Figure 11.

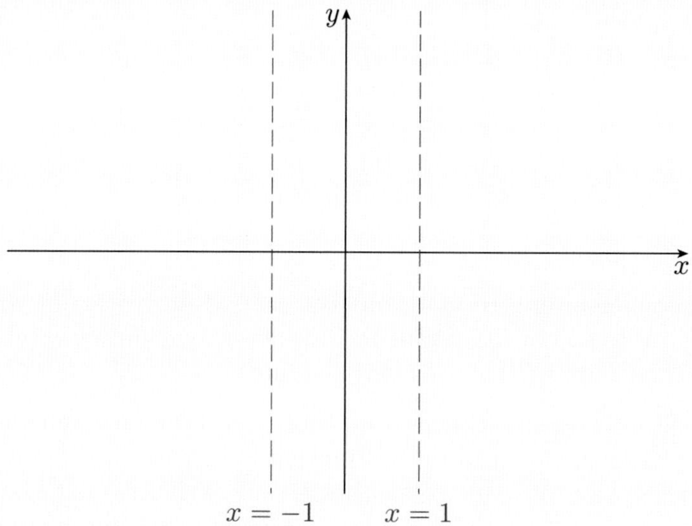

Figure 11 Vertical asymptotes of the graph of $f(x) = \dfrac{1}{x^2 - 1}$

Next you should mark the intercepts on the graph. You've seen that the y-intercept is $(0, -1)$, and that there are no x-intercepts. So mark a point at position $(0, -1)$, and label it.

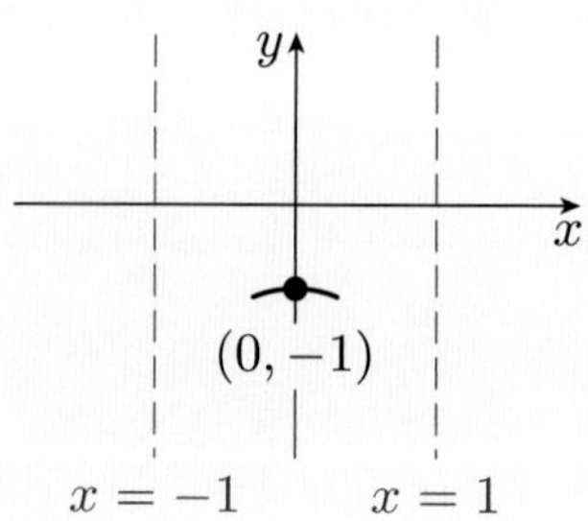

Figure 12 The stationary point is a local maximum

After this you should determine the coordinates of the stationary points, and a table of signs for $f'(x)$ (these were given in Example 19). There is a single stationary point with coordinates $(0, -1)$, which is the point where the graph cuts the y-axis, and it's a local maximum. Mark the stationary point on your graph (it's there already) and draw a small curve through it, as shown in Figure 12, to indicate that it's a local maximum.

Now use the table of signs to find the asymptotic behaviour of the function near the vertical asymptotes. Since $f'(x)$ is positive to the left and right of $x = -1$, and negative to the left and right of $x = 1$, you see that the behaviour of the graph near these asymptotes is as shown in Figure 13.

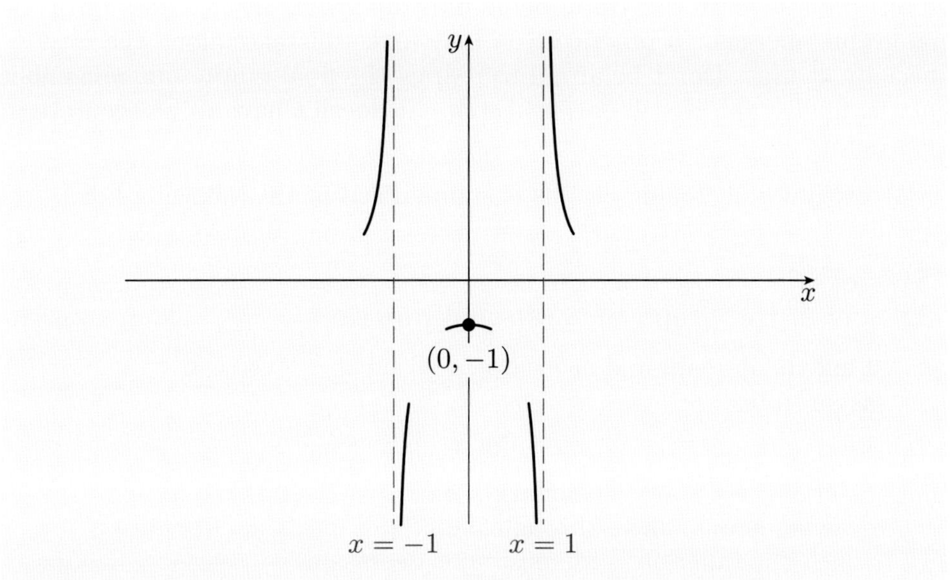

Figure 13 Asymptotic behaviour near the vertical asymptotes

Since $f(x)$ is a proper rational expression, it follows that $f(x) \to 0$ as $x \to \infty$, and $f(x) \to 0$ as $x \to -\infty$, and the graph of f has a horizontal asymptote with equation $y = 0$. Using these facts you can extend the parts of the graph you've drawn so far to give a complete sketch, making sure that you don't include any more stationary points or points of intersection with the axes. Remember that, because f is an even function, the graph should be unchanged by reflection in the y-axis. The final sketch is shown in Figure 14.

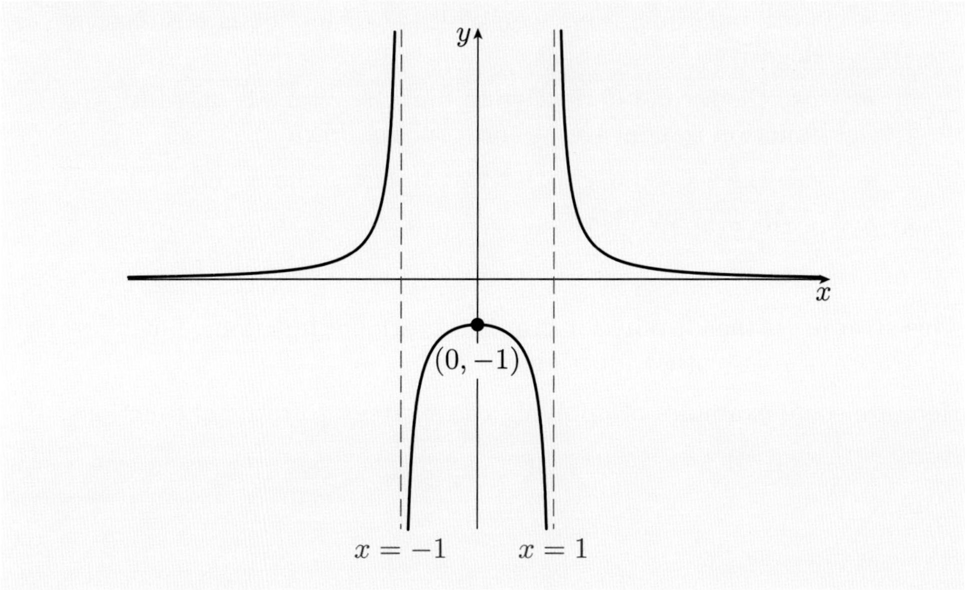

Figure 14 The graph of $f(x) = \dfrac{1}{x^2 - 1}$

The explanation above makes the process of sketching a graph seem like a smooth process, with the graph being built up gradually in stages until the final graph emerges. In practice, you may make mistakes along the way, especially at first. Don't be afraid to redraw the final graph, but remember that the final graph is still only a sketch – it doesn't have to be accurate in every detail!

The strategy for sketching graphs is summarised in the following box.

Strategy: To sketch the graph of a rational function

1. Find the domain and then draw and label the vertical asymptotes.
2. Find and label the x- and y-intercepts, if any.
3. Find and label any stationary points, indicating their type by drawing small curves through them, and find the intervals on which the function is increasing or decreasing.
4. Sketch the shape of the graph near the vertical asymptotes.
5. Work out the asymptotic behaviour as $x \to \infty$ and as $x \to -\infty$, and draw and label any horizontal or slant asymptotes. Sketch the shape of the graph near these asymptotes, making sure that you don't introduce any unwanted stationary points or points of intersection with the asymptotes.
6. Check whether the function is even or odd, or neither.
7. In addition to these steps you can also
   - plot particular points on the graph
   - work out the intervals on which the function is positive or negative
   - use the second derivative to find the intervals on which the function is 'concave up' or 'concave down'
   - use the second derivative test to check the nature of stationary points.

This strategy is meant only for graphs of rational functions, but it works for graphs of many other functions too.

Here are some examples of applying the strategy to rational functions.

Example 22 *Sketching graphs of rational functions*

Sketch the graphs of the following rational functions.

(a) $f(x) = \dfrac{x}{x^2+1}$ (b) $f(x) = \dfrac{x^2-3x+3}{x-1}$

Solution

(a) First work out the domain of the function. Since the denominator x^2+1 is always positive, there are no vertical asymptotes.

The domain of f is $\mathbb{R}$, and there are no vertical asymptotes.

Find the intercepts and mark them on the graph. Begin with the y-intercept, which is given by $f(0)$.

The y-intercept is $f(0) = 0$.

Now find the x-intercepts, if there are any. These are the values of x that satisfy $f(x) = 0$.

The equation $f(x) = 0$ is

$$\frac{x}{x^2+1} = 0.$$

Multiplying both sides of this equation by x^2+1 gives $x = 0$. So the only x-intercept is 0.

Differentiate f to find the stationary points and the intervals on which f is increasing or decreasing.

By the quotient rule,

$$f'(x) = \frac{(x^2+1)\times 1 - (2x)\times x}{(x^2+1)^2} = \frac{(x^2+1)-2x^2}{(x^2+1)^2} = \frac{-x^2+1}{(x^2+1)^2}.$$

Now work out the stationary points by solving the equation $f'(x) = 0$.

Multiplying both sides of the equation $f'(x) = 0$ by $(x^2+1)^2$ gives

$$-x^2+1 = 0, \quad \text{so} \quad x^2 = 1.$$

So the stationary points of f are at $x = -1$ and $x = 1$.

Find the coordinates of these stationary points, and mark them on the graph.

Since

$$f(-1) = \frac{-1}{(-1)^2+1} = -\frac{1}{2} \quad \text{and} \quad f(1) = \frac{1}{1^2+1} = \frac{1}{2},$$

the coordinates of the stationary points are $\left(-1, -\tfrac{1}{2}\right)$ and $\left(1, \tfrac{1}{2}\right)$.

Create a table of signs for $f'(x)$ and determine the intervals on which f is increasing or decreasing. Since the denominator $(x^2+1)^2$ is positive, $f'(x)$ has the same sign as the numerator $-x^2+1$.

The tables of signs for $f'(x)$ is as follows.

x	$(-\infty,-1)$	-1	$(-1,1)$	1	$(1,\infty)$
$-x^2+1$	$-$	0	$+$	0	$-$
$(x^2+1)^2$	$+$	$+$	$+$	$+$	$+$
$f'(x)$	$-$	0	$+$	0	$-$

Hence f is decreasing on the intervals $(-\infty,-1)$ and $(1,\infty)$, and f is increasing on the interval $(-1,1)$.

Apply the first derivative test to determine the nature of the stationary points. Draw a small curve on the graph through each stationary point to indicate its type.

Since $f'(x)$ is negative to the left and positive to the right of the stationary point -1, it follows that -1 is a local minimum of f.

Since $f'(x)$ is positive to the left and negative to the right of the stationary point 1, it follows that 1 is a local maximum of f.

Find the asymptotic behaviour of the function. There are no vertical asymptotes, so you only need to consider the behaviour of $f(x)$ as $x\to\infty$ and as $x\to-\infty$.

Since $f(x)$ is a proper rational expression, it follows that $f(x)\to 0$ as $x\to\infty$, and $f(x)\to 0$ as $x\to-\infty$, and the graph of f has a horizontal asymptote with equation $y=0$.

Check whether the function is even or odd, or neither.

Since

$$f(-x)=\frac{-x}{(-x)^2+1}=-\frac{x}{x^2+1}=-f(x),$$

f is an odd function.

Finish sketching the graph of f. The graph crosses the axes at the point $(0,0)$, and at no other points. There is a local minimum at $\left(-1,-\frac{1}{2}\right)$ and a local maximum at $\left(1,\frac{1}{2}\right)$. The table of signs tells you where f is increasing and decreasing. The graph approaches the line with equation $y=0$ as x tends to infinity and x tends to minus infinity. This line is a horizontal asymptote, but there's no need to make any extra markings on the graph for this asymptote as it coincides with the x-axis. As f is an odd function, its graph is unchanged by a rotation of angle 180° about the origin.

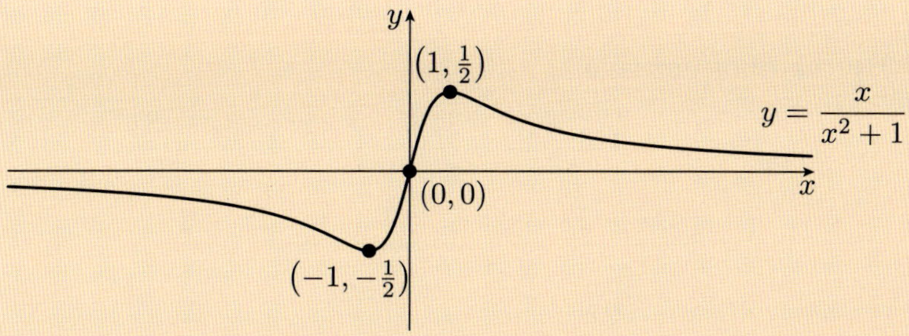

(b) First work out the domain of the function. It consists of all real numbers apart from those exceptional values for which the denominator of the function is 0. Draw a vertical asymptote through each exceptional value.

The denominator of $f(x)$ is 0 when $x = 1$, so the domain of f is $(-\infty, 1) \cup (1, \infty)$. The line $x = 1$ is a vertical asymptote of the graph of f.

Find the intercepts and mark them on the graph. Begin with the y-intercept, which is given by $f(0)$.

The y-intercept is $f(0) = \dfrac{3}{-1} = -3$.

Now find the x-intercepts, if there are any. These are the points x that satisfy $f(x) = 0$.

The equation $f(x) = 0$ is

$$\frac{x^2 - 3x + 3}{x - 1} = 0.$$

Multiplying both sides of this equation by $x - 1$ gives $x^2 - 3x + 3 = 0$. The discriminant of the quadratic $x^2 - 3x + 3$ is

$$(-3)^2 - 4 \times 1 \times 3 = 9 - 12 = -3 < 0.$$

It follows that the equation $x^2 - 3x + 3 = 0$ has no solutions, so there are no x-intercepts.

Differentiate f to find the stationary points and the intervals on which f is increasing or decreasing.

By the quotient rule,

$$f'(x) = \frac{(x-1)\times(2x-3) - 1\times(x^2-3x+3)}{(x-1)^2}$$
$$= \frac{(2x^2-2x-3x+3)-(x^2-3x+3)}{(x-1)^2}$$
$$= \frac{x^2-2x}{(x-1)^2}$$

Factorise the numerator: doing so will help you find the stationary points and the intervals where $f'(x)$ is increasing or decreasing.

$$= \frac{x(x-2)}{(x-1)^2}.$$

Now work out the stationary points by solving the equation $f'(x) = 0$.

Multiplying both sides of the equation $f'(x) = 0$ by $(x-1)^2$ gives

$$x(x-2) = 0.$$

So the stationary points of f are at $x = 0$ and $x = 2$.

Find the coordinates of these stationary points, and mark them on the graph.

Since

$$f(0) = \frac{3}{-1} = -3 \quad \text{and} \quad f(2) = \frac{2^2 - 3\times 2 + 3}{2-1} = 1,$$

the coordinates of the stationary points are $(0, -3)$ and $(2, 1)$.

Create a table of signs for $f'(x)$ and determine the intervals on which f is increasing or decreasing. Include one row for each factor in the numerator. Remember to show $*$ in any column where $f'(x)$ is not defined.

The tables of signs for $f'(x)$ is as follows.

x	$(-\infty, 0)$	0	$(0,1)$	1	$(1,2)$	2	$(2,\infty)$
x	$-$	0	$+$	$+$	$+$	$+$	$+$
$x-2$	$-$	$-$	$-$	$-$	$-$	0	$+$
$(x-1)^2$	$+$	$+$	$+$	0	$+$	$+$	$+$
$f'(x)$	$+$	0	$-$	$*$	$-$	0	$+$

Hence f is increasing on the intervals $(-\infty, 0)$ and $(2, \infty)$, and f is decreasing on the intervals $(0, 1)$ and $(1, 2)$.

Apply the first derivative test to determine the nature of the stationary points. Draw a small curve on the graph through each stationary point to indicate its type.

Since $f'(x)$ is positive to the left and negative to the right of the stationary point 0, it follows that 0 is a local maximum of f.

Since $f'(x)$ is negative to the left and positive to the right of the stationary point 2, it follows that 2 is a local minimum of f.

Find the asymptotic behaviour of the function. Since $f'(x)$ is negative to the left and right of the vertical asymptote $x = 1$, draw decreasing asymptotic curves to the left and right of the line $x = 1$ (the left one will be towards the bottom of the graph, and the right one towards the top). To work out the behaviour of $f(x)$ as $x \to \infty$ and as $x \to -\infty$, use polynomial long division because the degree of the numerator of $f(x)$ is one more than the degree of the denominator, so the graph of f has a slant asymptote.

$$\begin{array}{r|rr}
 & x & -2 \\ \hline
x-1 & x^2 - & 3x + 3 \\
 & x^2 - & x \\ \hline
 & & -2x + 3 \\
 & & -2x + 2 \\ \hline
 & & 1
\end{array}$$

(Check: $(x-1)(x-2)+1 = x^2 - 3x + 2 + 1 = x^2 - 3x + 3$.)

It follows that

$$f(x) = x - 2 + \frac{1}{x-1}.$$

Hence

$$f(x) \to \infty \quad \text{as} \quad x \to \infty, \quad \text{and} \quad f(x) \to -\infty \quad \text{as} \quad x \to -\infty,$$

and the graph of f has a slant asymptote with equation $y = x - 2$.

Check whether the function is even or odd, or neither.

Since

$$f(2) = \frac{2^2 - 3 \times 2 + 3}{2 - 1} = 1$$

and

$$f(-2) = \frac{(-2)^2 - 3 \times (-2) + 3}{(-2) - 1} = -\frac{13}{3},$$

we see that $f(-2)$ is not equal to either $f(2)$ or $-f(2)$, so f is neither even nor odd.

Finish sketching the graph of f. There is a vertical asymptote with equation $x = 1$, and a slant asymptote with equation $y = x - 2$. The graph crosses the y-axis at the point $(0, -3)$, and it doesn't cross the x-axis. There is a local maximum at $(0, -3)$ and a local minimum at $(2, 1)$. The table of signs tells you where f is increasing and decreasing. The function f is decreasing on either side of the vertical asymptote. Also, the graph of f approaches (but never crosses) the slant asymptote as x tends to infinity and as x tends to minus infinity.

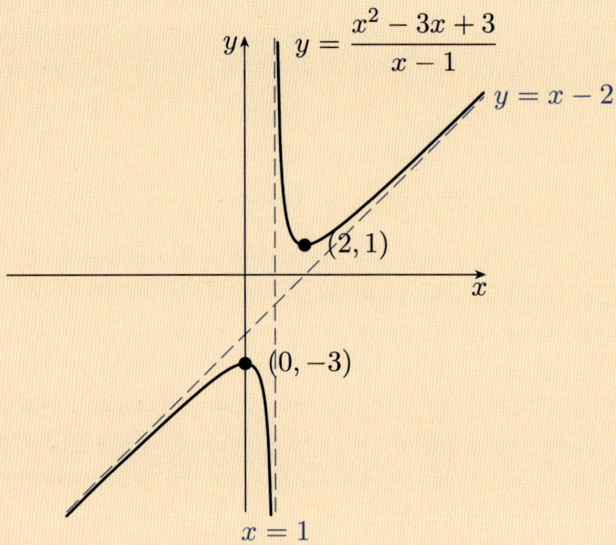

Remember that once you've sketched a graph you can check that it's of the right shape using the computer algebra system.

Here are some graphs for you to sketch.

Activity 25 *Sketching graphs of rational functions*

Sketch the graphs of the following rational functions.

(a) $f(x) = \dfrac{1}{x^2 + 1}$ (b) $f(x) = \dfrac{3x - 5}{x - 2}$ (c) $f(x) = \dfrac{3x}{x^2 - 4}$

(d) $f(x) = \dfrac{x^2}{x + 1}$

Witch of Agnesi

The graph of the rational function

$$f(x) = \frac{1}{x^2 + 1}$$

that you sketched in the last activity is known as the 'Witch of Agnesi', after the Italian mathematician Maria Agnesi, who studied the curve. The term 'witch' is used because of a mistake in an English translation of Agnesi's celebrated two-volume work *Instituzioni analitiche ad uso della gioventù italiana*, which was published in 1748 (volume I) and 1749 (volume II). This work was one of the most complete accounts of calculus available in the mid-eighteenth century, and is considered to be the first text to deal with both differentiation and integration.

Maria Agnesi (1718–1799)

5 More integration methods

In this section you'll learn about strategies for integrating expressions that involve trigonometric functions. You'll also see some cunning trigonometric substitutions that enable you to tackle tricky-looking integrals such as

$$\int \sqrt{9 - x^2}\, dx.$$

At the end of the section, some of these ideas are applied to derive the well-known formula for the area of a circle.

5.1 Integrating trigonometric expressions

As you saw in MST124, you can sometimes integrate an expression that involves trigonometric functions by first using a trigonometric identity to rewrite the expression in a different form. The idea is to rewrite it in a form that allows you to use one of the standard integrals, or to use a technique that you've met, such as integration by substitution.

In this subsection you'll see some examples of the sorts of trigonometric expressions that you can integrate in this way, and how to deal with them.

Integrands of the form $\sin(mx)\cos(nx)$

You can integrate any trigonometric expression of the form $\sin(mx)\cos(nx)$, where m and n are integers (possibly negative), by using one of the trigonometric identities below. These identities can also be found in the *Handbook*.

Product to sum identities

$$\sin A \sin B = \tfrac{1}{2}\cos(A-B) - \tfrac{1}{2}\cos(A+B)$$
$$\cos A \cos B = \tfrac{1}{2}\cos(A+B) + \tfrac{1}{2}\cos(A-B)$$
$$\sin A \cos B = \tfrac{1}{2}\sin(A+B) + \tfrac{1}{2}\sin(A-B)$$

Here's an example.

Example 23 *Integrating an expression of the form* $\sin(mx)\cos(nx)$

Find the integral

$$\int \sin(3x)\cos(4x)\,\mathrm{d}x.$$

Solution

Use the identity $\sin A \cos B = \frac{1}{2}\sin(A+B) + \frac{1}{2}\sin(A-B)$ with $A = 3x$ and $B = 4x$.

$$\begin{aligned}\int \sin(3x)\cos(4x)\,\mathrm{d}x &= \int \left(\tfrac{1}{2}\sin(3x+4x) + \tfrac{1}{2}\sin(3x-4x)\right)\mathrm{d}x\\ &= \tfrac{1}{2}\int (\sin(7x) + \sin(-x))\,\mathrm{d}x\end{aligned}$$

Use the fact that sine is an odd function.

$$\begin{aligned}&= \tfrac{1}{2}\int (\sin(7x) - \sin x)\,\mathrm{d}x\\ &= \tfrac{1}{2}\left(-\tfrac{1}{7}\cos(7x) + \cos x\right) + c\\ &= \tfrac{1}{2}\cos x - \tfrac{1}{14}\cos(7x) + c\end{aligned}$$

Activity 26 *Integrating expressions of the form* $\sin(mx)\cos(nx)$

Find the following integrals.

(a) $\displaystyle\int \sin(6x)\sin(4x)\,\mathrm{d}x$ (b) $\displaystyle\int \cos x\cos(8x)\,\mathrm{d}x$

(c) $\displaystyle\int \sin(-3x)\cos(5x)\,\mathrm{d}x$

Integrands of the form $\sin^m x \cos^n x$

It is usually more difficult to integrate expressions of the form $\sin^m x \cos^n x$ than it is to integrate expressions of the form $\sin(mx)\cos(nx)$. Here you'll learn about techniques for integrating $\sin^m x \cos^n x$ when m and n are non-negative integers.

If one of m or n is *odd*, then you can use the trigonometric identity

$$\sin^2 x + \cos^2 x = 1$$

to rewrite the expression $\sin^m x \cos^n x$ in one of the forms $f(\sin x)\cos x$ or $f(\cos x)\sin x$, where f is a function that you can integrate. Then you can use integration by substitution. This process is illustrated in the next example.

Example 24 *Integrating expressions of the form $\sin^m x \cos^n x$ when one of m or n is odd*

Find the following integrals.

(a) $\displaystyle\int \cos^5 x \,\mathrm{d}x$ (b) $\displaystyle\int \sin^3 x \cos^2 x \,\mathrm{d}x$

Solution

(a) The integrand is an odd power of $\cos x$. Separate out one factor $\cos x$, and write it at the end. Express the remaining power of $\cos x$ in terms of $\cos^2 x$.

$$\int \cos^5 x \,\mathrm{d}x = \int (\cos^2 x)^2 \cos x \,\mathrm{d}x$$

Use the identity $\sin^2 x + \cos^2 x = 1$ to express $\cos^2 x$ in terms of $\sin^2 x$.

$$= \int (1 - \sin^2 x)^2 \cos x \,\mathrm{d}x$$

The integrand is now of the form $f(\sin x)\cos x$, so use integration by substitution.

Let $u = \sin x$; then $\dfrac{\mathrm{d}u}{\mathrm{d}x} = \cos x$. The integral becomes

$$\begin{aligned}\int (1-u^2)^2 \,\mathrm{d}u &= \int (1 - 2u^2 + u^4)\,\mathrm{d}u \\ &= u - \tfrac{2}{3}u^3 + \tfrac{1}{5}u^5 + c \\ &= \sin x - \tfrac{2}{3}\sin^3 x + \tfrac{1}{5}\sin^5 x + c.\end{aligned}$$

(b) The integrand contains an odd power of $\sin x$. Separate out one factor $\sin x$, and write it at the end. Express the remaining power of $\sin x$ in terms of $\sin^2 x$ (here the remaining power of $\sin x$ is just $\sin^2 x$, so you don't need to do anything more).

$$\int \sin^3 x \cos^2 x \, dx = \int \sin^2 x \cos^2 x (\sin x) \, dx$$

Use the identity $\sin^2 x + \cos^2 x = 1$ to express $\sin^2 x$ in terms of $\cos^2 x$.

$$= \int (1 - \cos^2 x) \cos^2 x (\sin x) \, dx$$

The integrand is now of the form $f(\cos x) \sin x$, so use integration by substitution. First you need a further small rearrangement.

$$= -\int (1 - \cos^2 x) \cos^2 x (-\sin x) \, dx$$

Let $u = \cos x$; then $\dfrac{du}{dx} = -\sin x$. The integral becomes

$$\begin{aligned} -\int (1 - u^2) u^2 \, du &= -\int (u^2 - u^4) \, du \\ &= \int (u^4 - u^2) \, du \\ &= \tfrac{1}{5}u^5 - \tfrac{1}{3}u^3 + c \\ &= \tfrac{1}{5}\cos^5 x - \tfrac{1}{3}\cos^3 x + c. \end{aligned}$$

Activity 27 *Integrating expressions of the form $\sin^m x \cos^n x$ when one of m or n is odd*

Find the following integrals.

(a) $\int \cos^3 x \, dx$ (b) $\int \sin^5 x \, dx$ (c) $\int \sin^2 x \cos^3 x \, dx$

When m and n are both even integers, you cannot integrate $\sin^m x \cos^n x$ by using the method demonstrated in the example above. Instead, there is an alternative method, which uses the half-angle identities given below. These identities can also be found in the *Handbook*.

Half-angle identities

$$\sin^2 x = \tfrac{1}{2}(1 - \cos(2x))$$
$$\cos^2 x = \tfrac{1}{2}(1 + \cos(2x))$$

Example 25 *Integrating expressions of the form* $\sin^m x \cos^n x$ *when* m *and* n *are even*

Find the following integrals.

(a) $\displaystyle\int \sin^2 x \, dx$ (b) $\displaystyle\int \cos^4 x \, dx$

Solution

(a) Use the half-angle identity for sine.

By the half-angle identity for sine,

$$\begin{aligned}\int \sin^2 x \, dx &= \int \tfrac{1}{2}(1 - \cos(2x)) \, dx \\ &= \tfrac{1}{2}\int (1 - \cos(2x)) \, dx \\ &= \tfrac{1}{2}\left(x - \tfrac{1}{2}\sin(2x)\right) + c \\ &= \tfrac{1}{2}x - \tfrac{1}{4}\sin(2x) + c.\end{aligned}$$

(b) Express the integrand in terms of $\cos^2 x$, and then use the half-angle identity for cosine.

By the half-angle identity for cosine,

$$\begin{aligned}\int \cos^4 x \, dx &= \int (\cos^2 x)^2 \, dx \\ &= \int \left(\tfrac{1}{2}(1 + \cos(2x))\right)^2 dx \\ &= \tfrac{1}{4}\int (1 + \cos(2x))^2 \, dx \\ &= \tfrac{1}{4}\int (1 + 2\cos(2x) + \cos^2(2x)) \, dx.\end{aligned}$$

Now express the term $\cos^2(2x)$ in a form that you can integrate, by using the half-angle identity for cosine with x replaced by $2x$.

By the half-angle identity for cosine again, the integral becomes

$$\begin{aligned}
&\tfrac{1}{4}\int \left(1 + 2\cos(2x) + \tfrac{1}{2}(1 + \cos(4x))\right)\,\mathrm{d}x \\
&= \tfrac{1}{8}\int (2 + 4\cos(2x) + 1 + \cos(4x))\,\mathrm{d}x \\
&= \tfrac{1}{8}\int (3 + 4\cos(2x) + \cos(4x))\,\mathrm{d}x \\
&= \tfrac{1}{8}(3x + 4 \times \tfrac{1}{2}\sin(2x) + \tfrac{1}{4}\sin(4x)) + c \\
&= \tfrac{3}{8}x + \tfrac{1}{4}\sin(2x) + \tfrac{1}{32}\sin(4x) + c.
\end{aligned}$$

There is another identity that is helpful in integrating some expressions of the form $\sin^m x \cos^n x$. To obtain this identity, recall the double-angle identity $\sin(2x) = 2\sin x \cos x$. Dividing both sides by 2 and swapping sides gives the identity below.

$$\sin x \cos x = \tfrac{1}{2}\sin(2x).$$

This helpful identity can be used, for example, to find

$$\int \sin x \cos x\,\mathrm{d}x.$$

You can also use it in part (c) of the next activity.

Activity 28 *Integrating expressions of the form $\sin^m x \cos^n x$ when m and n are even*

Find the following integrals.

(a) $\int \cos^2 x\,\mathrm{d}x$ (b) $\int \sin^4 x\,\mathrm{d}x$ (c) $\int \sin^2 x \cos^2 x\,\mathrm{d}x$

Here's a summary of the methods you've just seen.

Strategy:

To find $\int \sin^m x \cos^n x \, dx$ (where m and n are non-negative integers)

- If the power of $\sin x$ is odd, then separate out one factor $\sin x$ and use the identity $\sin^2 x + \cos^2 x = 1$ to express the remaining power of $\sin x$ in terms of $\cos x$. Then use integration by substitution.
- If the power of $\cos x$ is odd, then separate out one factor $\cos x$ and use the identity $\sin^2 x + \cos^2 x = 1$ to express the remaining power of $\cos x$ in terms of $\sin x$. Then use integration by substitution.
- If the powers of $\sin x$ and $\cos x$ are both even, then use the half-angle identities. The identity $\sin x \cos x = \frac{1}{2}\sin(2x)$ is also sometimes helpful.

When the powers of $\sin x$ and $\cos x$ are both odd, you can use either the method for an odd power of $\sin x$ or the method for an odd power of $\cos x$.

Note also that, when the powers of $\sin x$ and $\cos x$ are both even, applying the half-angle identities gives you a combination of more expressions of the form $\sin^m x \cos^n x$, where m and n may be odd or even. You then have to apply the strategy described in the box to each such expression again, as you saw in Example 25(b), where the half-angle identity for cosine was applied twice.

In the next activity you're asked to find the area of a region enclosed by the graphs of two trigonometric expressions.

Activity 29 *Integrating trigonometric expressions to find an area*

Find the area of the shaded region shown below that is bounded by the graphs of the expressions $\sin^2 x$ and $\cos^2 x$ between $x = -\pi/4$ and $x = \pi/4$.

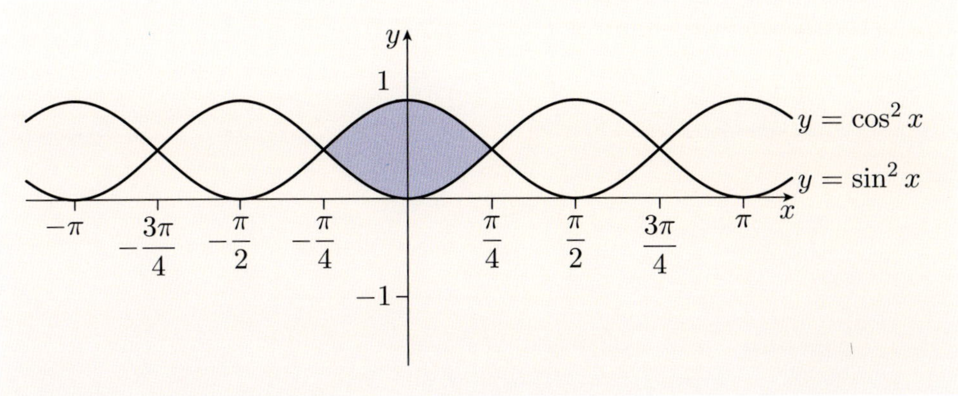

Hint: find the area between the graph of $\cos^2 x$ and the x-axis from $-\pi/4$ to $\pi/4$, and subtract from this the area between the graph of $\sin^2 x$ and the x-axis from $-\pi/4$ to $\pi/4$.

Integrands involving tan, cosec, sec or cot

The same techniques that you've learned for integrating expressions involving sin and cos can often also be used for integrating expressions involving tan, cosec, sec or cot, because you can write those four functions in terms of sin and cos using

$$\tan x = \frac{\sin x}{\cos x}, \quad \operatorname{cosec} x = \frac{1}{\sin x}, \quad \sec x = \frac{1}{\cos x} \quad \text{and} \quad \cot x = \frac{\cos x}{\sin x}.$$

Part (a) of the next example illustrates this procedure.

In part (b) of the example you'll see that sometimes it's better to use a suitable trigonometric identity to find an integral involving tan, cosec, sec or cot, rather than writing the integrand in terms of sin and cos.

Example 26 *Integrating expressions that involve tan, cosec, sec or cot*

Find the following integrals.

(a) $\displaystyle\int \frac{\tan x}{\sec^2 x}\,dx$ (b) $\displaystyle\int \tan^2 x\,dx$

Solution

(a) Write the integrand $\dfrac{\tan x}{\sec^2 x}$ in terms of $\sin x$ and $\cos x$, and then simplify the resulting expression.

$$\begin{aligned}\int \frac{\tan x}{\sec^2 x}\,dx &= \int \frac{\sin x/\cos x}{1/\cos^2 x}\,dx \\ &= \int \sin x \cos x\,dx\end{aligned}$$

Apply the identity $\sin x \cos x = \frac{1}{2}\sin(2x)$.

By the identity $\sin x \cos x = \frac{1}{2}\sin(2x)$, the integral becomes

$$\begin{aligned}\int \tfrac{1}{2}\sin(2x)\,dx &= \tfrac{1}{2}\int \sin(2x)\,dx \\ &= \tfrac{1}{2} \times \left(-\tfrac{1}{2}\cos(2x)\right) + c \\ &= -\tfrac{1}{4}\cos(2x) + c.\end{aligned}$$

(b) You could write the integrand $\tan^2 x$ in terms of $\sin x$ and $\cos x$; however, it is difficult to integrate the resulting expression using the techniques you've learned so far. Instead, recall the identity $\tan^2 x + 1 = \sec^2 x$, which tells you that you can write the integral as a sum of standard integrals.

By the identity $\tan^2 x = \sec^2 x - 1$,

$$\begin{aligned}\int \tan^2 x \, dx &= \int (\sec^2 x - 1) \, dx \\ &= \int \sec^2 x \, dx - \int 1 \, dx \\ &= \tan x - x + c.\end{aligned}$$

Activity 30 *Integrating expressions that involve tan, cosec, sec or cot*

Find the following integrals.

(a) $\displaystyle\int \tan x \, dx$ (b) $\displaystyle\int \frac{\cot x}{\operatorname{cosec} x \sec x} \, dx$ (c) $\displaystyle\int \cot^2 x \, dx$

Hint for part (a): use the substitution $u = \cos x$.

5.2 Trigonometric substitutions

When you revised integration by substitution in Section 1, you met integrals whose integrands were not of the form

f(something) × the derivative of the something,

but which could nevertheless be integrated by applying suitable substitutions. Here you'll learn about a particular class of integrals of this type, each of which can be found by substituting the variable x in the integrand with a trigonometric function in the variable u. This sort of substitution is called a **trigonometric substitution**.

Trigonometric substitutions can be useful when you have an integrand that involves one of the expressions

$$a^2 - x^2, \quad x^2 - a^2 \quad \text{or} \quad a^2 + x^2,$$

where x is the variable of the integrand, and a is a constant. For example, the integrals

$$\int \sqrt{3^2 - x^2} \, dx, \quad \int \frac{\sqrt{x^2 - 4^2}}{x} \, dx \quad \text{and} \quad \int \frac{1}{(1 + x^2)^2} \, dx$$

can all be found using trigonometric substitutions. You'll notice that the first two of these integrals involve the square-root operation $\sqrt{}$. This is a feature of many integrals that can be found using a trigonometric substitution.

In this subsection, you'll use three different trigonometric substitutions. These substitutions make use of the following three standard identities, each of which is a minor rearrangement of one of the Pythagorean identities, which you can find in the *Handbook*.

$$1 - \sin^2 u = \cos^2 u$$
$$\sec^2 u - 1 = \tan^2 u$$
$$1 + \tan^2 u = \sec^2 u$$

When you wish to make a trigonometric substitution, the table below tells you which substitution to apply, and the identity that you'll need once you've carried out the substitution (the way in which you should use the identity will become clear shortly).

Table of trigonometric substitutions

Expression	Substitution	Identity
$a^2 - x^2$	$x = a\sin u$	$1 - \sin^2 u = \cos^2 u$
$x^2 - a^2$	$x = a\sec u$	$\sec^2 u - 1 = \tan^2 u$
$a^2 + x^2$	$x = a\tan u$	$1 + \tan^2 u = \sec^2 u$

Most of the substitutions that you've met so far have been of the form

$$u = \text{expression in } x.$$

In contrast, the substitutions in the table of trigonometric substitutions have the form

$$x = \text{expression in } u.$$

Because of this, you have to calculate the derivative $\mathrm{d}x/\mathrm{d}u$ rather than $\mathrm{d}u/\mathrm{d}x$, and you'll also need to rearrange the substitution you've made to express u in terms of x. Apart from these changes, the method of substitution is similar, as you'll see in the next example.

Example 27 *Integrating using trigonometric substitutions*

Find the following integrals.

(a) $\displaystyle\int \sqrt{9-x^2}\,\mathrm{d}x$ (b) $\displaystyle\int \frac{1}{x\sqrt{x^2-1}}\,\mathrm{d}x$

Solution

(a) The integrand involves the expression $9-x^2$, which is 3^2-x^2, so try the substitution $x = 3\sin u$.

Let $x = 3\sin u$; then $\dfrac{\mathrm{d}x}{\mathrm{d}u} = 3\cos u$. Also, rearranging the equation $x = 3\sin u$ gives $u = \sin^{-1}(x/3)$.

Imagine 'cross-multiplying' in the equation $\dfrac{\mathrm{d}x}{\mathrm{d}u} = 3\cos u$ to obtain $\mathrm{d}x = (3\cos u)\,\mathrm{d}u$.

So

$$\begin{aligned}\int \sqrt{9-x^2}\,\mathrm{d}x &= \int \sqrt{9-(3\sin u)^2}\,(3\cos u)\,\mathrm{d}u\\ &= 3\int (\cos u)\sqrt{3^2-3^2\sin^2 u}\,\mathrm{d}u\\ &= 9\int (\cos u)\sqrt{1-\sin^2 u}\,\mathrm{d}u\end{aligned}$$

Use the identity $1-\sin^2 u = \cos^2 u$.

$$\begin{aligned}&= 9\int (\cos u)\sqrt{\cos^2 u}\,\mathrm{d}u\\ &= 9\int \cos^2 u\,\mathrm{d}u.\end{aligned}$$

Remember that to integrate $\cos^2 u$ you should apply the identity $\cos^2 u = \frac{1}{2}(1+\cos(2u))$.

Using the half-angle identity for cosine, the integral becomes

$$\begin{aligned}9\int \tfrac{1}{2}(1+\cos(2u))\,\mathrm{d}u &= \tfrac{9}{2}\int (1+\cos(2u))\,\mathrm{d}u\\ &= \tfrac{9}{2}\left(u+\tfrac{1}{2}\sin(2u)\right)+c\\ &= \tfrac{9}{2}u+\tfrac{9}{4}\sin(2u)+c\end{aligned}$$

Substitute back for u in terms of x.

$$= \tfrac{9}{2}\sin^{-1}(x/3)+\tfrac{9}{4}\sin(2\sin^{-1}(x/3))+c.$$

(b) The integrand involves the expression $x^2 - 1$, so try the substitution $x = \sec u$. You'll need the derivative of $\sec u$, which is in the *Handbook* (or you can work it out).

Let $x = \sec u$; then $\dfrac{dx}{du} = \sec u \tan u$.

Also, rearranging the equation $x = \sec u$ gives $u = \sec^{-1} x$.

Imagine 'cross-multiplying' in the equation $\dfrac{dx}{du} = \sec u \tan u$ to obtain $dx = (\sec u \tan u)\,du$.

So

$$\begin{aligned}\int \frac{1}{x\sqrt{x^2-1}}\,dx &= \int \frac{1}{(\sec u)\sqrt{\sec^2 u - 1}}(\sec u \tan u)\,du \\ &= \int \frac{\tan u}{\sqrt{\sec^2 u - 1}}\,du\end{aligned}$$

Use the identity $\sec^2 u - 1 = \tan^2 u$.

$$\begin{aligned}&= \int \frac{\tan u}{\sqrt{\tan^2 u}}\,du \\ &= \int \frac{\tan u}{\tan u}\,du \\ &= \int 1\,du \\ &= u + c\end{aligned}$$

Substitute back for u in terms of x.

$$= \sec^{-1} x + c.$$

In the following activity, you'll integrate one integrand of each of the types shown in the table of trigonometric substitutions.

Activity 31 *Integrating using trigonometric substitutions*

Find the following integrals.

(a) $\displaystyle\int \frac{x^2}{\sqrt{1-x^2}}\,dx$ (b) $\displaystyle\int \frac{\sqrt{x^2-16}}{x}\,dx$ (c) $\displaystyle\int \frac{1}{(1+x^2)^2}\,dx$

The solutions to the preceding example and activity involved composing trigonometric functions with inverse trigonometric functions. For instance, the solution to Activity 31(a) was

$$\tfrac{1}{2}\sin^{-1} x - \tfrac{1}{4}\sin(2\sin^{-1} x) + c,$$

and the second term in this expression involves such a composite. It's possible to state expressions of this type in a different form, without trigonometric functions or inverse trigonometric functions. Let's see how to do this for the expression just given. The activity uses the substitution $x = \sin u$, which gives $u = \sin^{-1} x$, so

$$\sin(2\sin^{-1} x) = \sin(2u).$$

Using the identities $\sin(2u) = 2\sin u \cos u$ and $\cos^2 u = 1 - \sin^2 u$, you obtain

$$\begin{aligned}\tfrac{1}{4}\sin(2\sin^{-1} x) &= \tfrac{1}{4}\sin(2u)\\ &= \tfrac{1}{2}\sin u\cos u\\ &= \tfrac{1}{2}\sin u\sqrt{1-\sin^2 u}\\ &= \tfrac{1}{2}x\sqrt{1-x^2}.\end{aligned}$$

So you can write the solution to Activity 31(a) in the alternative form

$$\tfrac{1}{2}\sin^{-1} x - \tfrac{1}{2}x\sqrt{1-x^2} + c.$$

Due to the extra work involved, we won't write solutions in this form in future. However, if you use a computer to check an integral, and the computer's answer looks different from yours, then the explanation above may be the reason. In these circumstances, you can quickly check whether the answers are in fact identical by using a computer to plot the graphs of both.

In the next activity, you'll use trigonometric substitutions to find two of the integrals from the table of standard indefinite integrals.

Activity 32 *Integrating using trigonometric substitutions to obtain two of the standard integrals*

Use trigonometric substitutions to establish the following.

(a) $\displaystyle\int \frac{1}{\sqrt{1-x^2}}\,dx = \sin^{-1} x + c$

(b) $\displaystyle\int \frac{1}{1+x^2}\,dx = \tan^{-1} x + c$

Sometimes you have to rearrange an integrand to put it in a form suitable for a trigonometric substitution. The methods you should use are illustrated by the next example.

Example 28 *Rearranging integrals before using trigonometric substitutions*

Find the following integrals.

(a) $\displaystyle\int \frac{\sqrt{25x^2-1}}{x^3}\,dx$ (b) $\displaystyle\int \frac{1}{(x^2-2x+2)^{3/2}}\,dx$

Solution

(a) The expression $25x^2-1$ is not in a form suitable for a trigonometric substitution. However, if you write it as

$$25x^2-1 = 25\left(x^2-\frac{1}{25}\right) = 25\left(x^2-\frac{1}{5^2}\right),$$

then the last expression in the brackets is of a suitable form.

Let $x=\frac{1}{5}\sec u$; then $\dfrac{dx}{du}=\frac{1}{5}\sec u\tan u$.

Also, rearranging the equation $x=\frac{1}{5}\sec u$ gives $u=\sec^{-1}(5x)$.

Imagine 'cross-multiplying' in the equation $\dfrac{dx}{du}=\frac{1}{5}\sec u\tan u$ to obtain $dx=\left(\frac{1}{5}\sec u\tan u\right)du$.

So

$$\begin{aligned}\int \frac{\sqrt{25x^2-1}}{x^3}\,dx &= \int \frac{\sqrt{25\left(\frac{1}{5}\sec u\right)^2-1}}{\left(\frac{1}{5}\sec u\right)^3}\left(\tfrac{1}{5}\sec u\tan u\right)du\\ &= \frac{\frac{1}{5}}{\left(\frac{1}{5}\right)^3}\int \frac{\sqrt{\sec^2 u-1}}{\sec^3 u}\sec u\tan u\,du\\ &= 25\int \frac{\sqrt{\sec^2 u-1}}{\sec^2 u}\tan u\,du\end{aligned}$$

Use the identity $\sec^2 u-1=\tan^2 u$.

$$\begin{aligned}&= 25\int \frac{\sqrt{\tan^2 u}}{\sec^2 u}\tan u\,du\\ &= 25\int \frac{\tan^2 u}{\sec^2 u}\,du\\ &= 25\int \sin^2 u\,du.\end{aligned}$$

Remember that to integrate $\sin^2 u$ you should apply the identity $\sin^2 u = \frac{1}{2}(1 - \cos(2u))$.

By the half-angle identity for sine, the integral becomes

$$\begin{aligned} 25\int \tfrac{1}{2}(1-\cos(2u))\,\mathrm{d}u &= \tfrac{25}{2}\int (1-\cos(2u))\,\mathrm{d}u \\ &= \tfrac{25}{2}\left(u - \tfrac{1}{2}\sin(2u)\right) + c \\ &= \tfrac{25}{2}u - \tfrac{25}{4}\sin(2u) + c \\ &= \tfrac{25}{2}\sec^{-1}(5x) - \tfrac{25}{4}\sin(2\sec^{-1}(5x)) + c. \end{aligned}$$

(b) Complete the square in the quadratic expression to put the integrand into a form suitable for a trigonometric substitution.

We have

$$x^2 - 2x + 2 = (x-1)^2 - 1 + 2 = (x-1)^2 + 1.$$

If the quadratic expression was $x^2 + 1$, then you would apply the substitution $x = \tan u$. In fact, the quadratic expression is $(x-1)^2 + 1$, so instead try $x - 1 = \tan u$, or, equivalently, $x = 1 + \tan u$.

Let $x = 1 + \tan u$; then $\dfrac{\mathrm{d}x}{\mathrm{d}u} = \sec^2 u$.

Also, rearranging the equation $x = 1 + \tan u$ gives $x - 1 = \tan u$, so $u = \tan^{-1}(x-1)$.

Imagine 'cross-multiplying' in the equation $\dfrac{\mathrm{d}x}{\mathrm{d}u} = \sec^2 u$ to obtain $\mathrm{d}x = (\sec^2 u)\,\mathrm{d}u$.

So

$$\begin{aligned} \int \frac{1}{(x^2-2x+2)^{3/2}}\,\mathrm{d}x &= \int \frac{1}{((x-1)^2+1)^{3/2}}\,\mathrm{d}x \\ &= \int \frac{1}{(\tan^2 u + 1)^{3/2}}(\sec^2 u)\,\mathrm{d}u \\ &= \int \frac{\sec^2 u}{(\tan^2 u + 1)^{3/2}}\,\mathrm{d}u \end{aligned}$$

Use the identity $\tan^2 u + 1 = \sec^2 u$.

$$\begin{aligned} &= \int \frac{\sec^2 u}{(\sec^2 u)^{3/2}}\,\mathrm{d}u \\ &= \int \frac{1}{\sec u}\,\mathrm{d}u \\ &= \int \cos u\,\mathrm{d}u \\ &= \sin u + c \\ &= \sin(\tan^{-1}(x-1)) + c. \end{aligned}$$

Activity 33 *Rearranging integrals before using trigonometric substitutions*

Find the following integrals.

(a) $\displaystyle\int \frac{1}{x^2\sqrt{1-4x^2}}\,\mathrm{d}x$ (b) $\displaystyle\int \frac{1}{(x+1)\sqrt{(x+1)^2-1}}\,\mathrm{d}x$

(c) $\displaystyle\int \frac{1}{10+6x+x^2}\,\mathrm{d}x$

Sometimes integrals that can be found by using a trigonometric substitution can also be integrated by other methods, such as partial fractions. As you develop your toolbox of integration techniques you'll come to notice multiple ways of integrating expressions, and you should use whichever technique is simplest.

5.3 Finding the area of a circle using integration

In this short subsection, you'll see how to use a trigonometric substitution to find a definite integral that gives the area of a circle in terms of its radius. Of course, you know a formula for the area of a circle in terms of its radius already – but you may not know how to obtain this formula by using integration.

Let's consider a circle of radius r, such as that shown in the Cartesian plane in Figure 15.

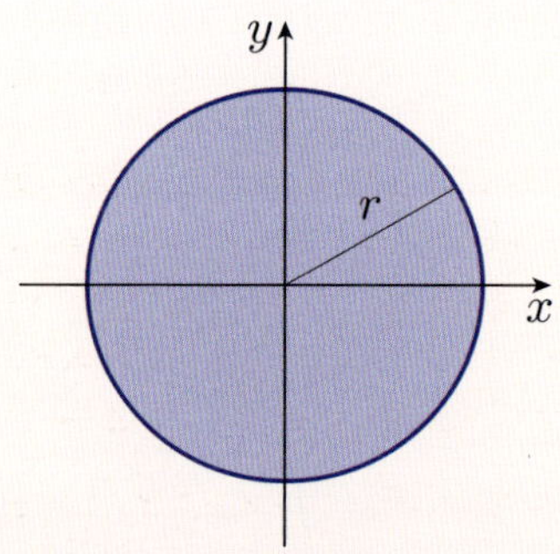

Figure 15 A circle of radius r

In order to work out the area of this circle, we focus on the sector of the circle in the top-right quadrant, shown in Figure 16.

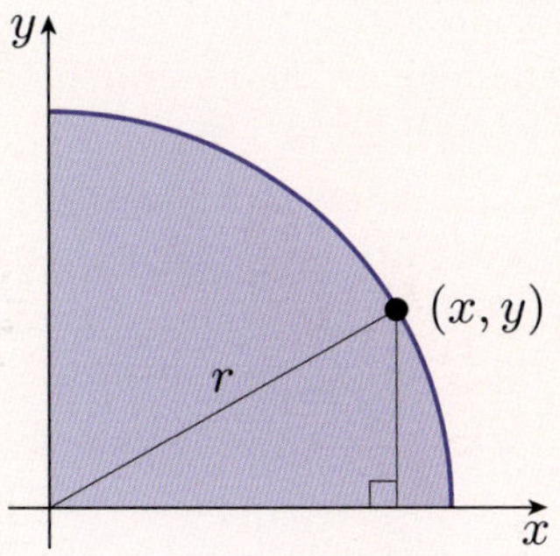

Figure 16 The sector of the circle in the top-right quadrant

As you saw in MST124, the equation of the circle of radius r with centre at the origin is

$$x^2 + y^2 = r^2.$$

So $y^2 = r^2 - x^2$. Since y is positive in the top-right quadrant, the equation of the part of the circle in that quadrant is

$$y = \sqrt{r^2 - x^2}.$$

Therefore the area of the sector is

$$\int_0^r \sqrt{r^2 - x^2}\,\mathrm{d}x.$$

Activity 34 *Finding the area of a circle*

Evaluate the definite integral

$$\int_0^r \sqrt{r^2 - x^2}\,\mathrm{d}x,$$

and hence obtain the formula for the area of a circle of radius r.

Hint: use the substitution $x = r \sin u$.

Depending on your study programme, in further modules you may learn how to use integration to measure other physical quantities, such as volumes and surface areas of three-dimensional objects.

Banach–Tarski paradox

The subject known as **measure theory** is concerned with the deeper properties of integration. In 1924, the Polish mathematician Stefan Banach and the Polish-American mathematician and philosopher Alfred Tarski, who both worked on measure theory, made a curious observation, which today is called the **Banach–Tarski paradox**. They noticed that it is possible, in an abstract sense, to divide a three-dimensional solid sphere into a finite number of parts (five will suffice) and then reassemble those parts to form two identical copies of the original sphere. Although it is of course impossible to do this in a practical sense, it's not really a paradox: each of the 'parts' is a highly abstract infinite collection of points that are disconnected from one another.

A variant on Banach and Tarski's observation is the **pea and the Sun paradox**, which says that, in an abstract sense, you can divide a pea into a (very large) finite number of parts and then reassemble those parts to form a pea the size of the Sun.

6 Hyperbolic functions

This section is about an important class of functions called the *hyperbolic functions*, which share many properties with the trigonometric functions. After meeting several helpful identities, and learning how to differentiate and integrate hyperbolic functions, you'll see how these functions can be used to give us yet more methods of integration.

6.1 Sinh, cosh and tanh

Let's begin by introducing two functions whose study will occupy most of this section, called **sinh** and **cosh**. The word 'sinh' is pronounced either as 'shine' or as 'sinsh' (where the 'i' in 'sinsh' is spoken either like the 'i' in 'integer', or like the 'i' in 'line'). The word 'cosh' is pronounced as it is spelled. These functions are defined using the exponential function, as follows.

$$\sinh x = \tfrac{1}{2}(e^x - e^{-x})$$

$$\cosh x = \tfrac{1}{2}(e^x + e^{-x})$$

The equations above show that each of the functions sinh and cosh takes any real number as an input value, and outputs another real number.

They are sometimes called **hyperbolic sine** and **hyperbolic cosine**, respectively, because they are closely related to the trigonometric functions sine and cosine, as you'll see as you work through this section. Unlike sine and cosine, however, the variable x in the functions sinh and cosh is not interpreted as an angle. The reason for the term 'hyperbolic' will be explained later, after you've learned about an important identity involving sinh and cosh.

You can use a computer or a calculator to find values of sinh and cosh. The buttons you need to press to find these values vary between different calculators. Sometimes there is a button labelled 'hyp' that provides access to the hyperbolic functions.

Activity 35 *Finding values of sinh and cosh*

Work out the following values of sinh and cosh. You shouldn't need a calculator for parts (a) and (b). In parts (c) to (f), give your answers to five decimal places.

(a) $\sinh 0$ (b) $\cosh 0$ (c) $\sinh(10)$ (d) $\cosh(10)$

(e) $\sinh(-10)$ (f) $\cosh(-10)$

Activity 36 *Working out where sinh and cosh are positive and negative*

(a) Show that $\sinh x$ is positive if x is positive, and negative if x is negative.

(b) Show that $\cosh x$ is positive for all values of x.

Hint for part (a): remember that $f(x) = e^x$ is an increasing function.

Hyperbolic functions and trigonometric functions

If you have studied complex numbers (for example, in MST124 Unit 12), then you may have encountered the formulas

$$\sin x = \frac{1}{2i}(e^{ix} - e^{-ix})$$
$$\cos x = \frac{1}{2}(e^{ix} + e^{-ix}),$$

where the complex number i is a square root of -1. From these formulas, you can see the connection between hyperbolic functions and trigonometric functions, because

$$\sinh(ix) = \frac{1}{2}(e^{ix} - e^{-ix}) = i \times \frac{1}{2i}(e^{ix} - e^{-ix}) = i \sin x,$$

and

$$\cosh(ix) = \frac{1}{2}(e^{ix} + e^{-ix}) = \cos x.$$

Keeping these relationships in mind may help you understand the material in this section, particularly the part about hyperbolic identities. However, don't worry if you haven't met complex numbers before, as they won't be used in the main text.

You can get a good idea of what the graphs of sinh and cosh look like by first sketching the graphs of $y = e^x$, $y = e^{-x}$ and $y = -e^{-x}$, as shown in Figure 17.

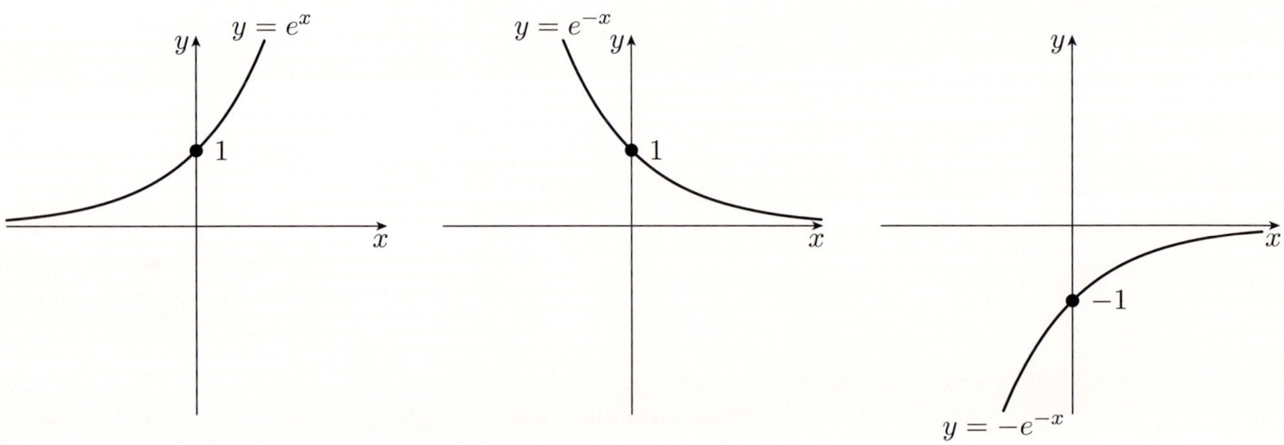

Figure 17 Graphs of exponential functions

If you add the expressions e^x and $-e^{-x}$, then divide by 2, you obtain $\sinh x$. So $\sinh x$ is obtained by 'taking the average' of e^x and $-e^{-x}$.

Its graph is shown in Figure 18.

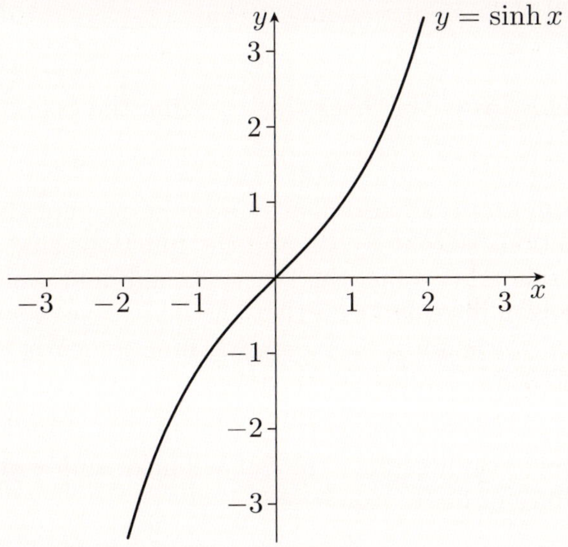

Figure 18 The graph of sinh

If you 'take the average' of the expressions $y = e^x$ and $y = e^{-x}$, then you obtain $\cosh x$. Its graph is shown in Figure 19.

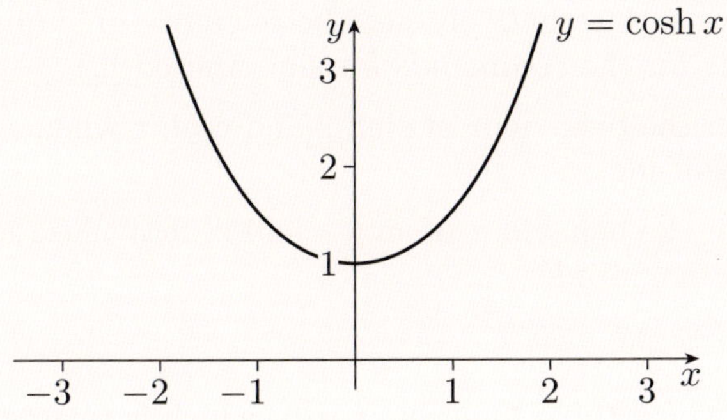

Figure 19 The graph of cosh

Figure 20 A hanging chain takes the shape of a catenary

The shape of the graph of cosh is sometimes called a **catenary**; it is the shape assumed by a hanging chain that is fixed at each end (see Figure 20).

The graphs of sinh and cosh display some of the similarities that sinh and cosh have with sine and cosine. For example, if you rotate the graph of sinh through 180° about the origin, then it is left unchanged. This implies that, like sine, sinh is an odd function, so it satisfies

$$\sinh(-x) = -\sinh x$$

for every value of x. You can check this by using the definition of sinh:

$$\sinh(-x) = \tfrac{1}{2}(e^{-x} - e^{-(-x)}) = \tfrac{1}{2}(e^{-x} - e^{x}) = -\sinh x.$$

The graph of cosh is also symmetrical, in that if you reflect it in the y-axis, then it is left unchanged. This implies that, like cosine, cosh is an even function, so it satisfies

$$\cosh(-x) = \cosh x$$

for every value of x. You can check this by using the definition of cosh:

$$\cosh(-x) = \tfrac{1}{2}(e^{-x} + e^{-(-x)}) = \tfrac{1}{2}(e^{-x} + e^{x}) = \cosh x.$$

The graphs of sinh and cosh also display some important differences between the functions sinh and cosh and the functions sine and cosine. For example, unlike sine and cosine, the functions sinh and cosh are not periodic. In fact, you'll see later on that the derivative of $\sinh x$ is positive for every value of x, so sinh is an increasing function. You'll also see that the derivative of $\cosh x$ is positive whenever x belongs to the interval $(0, \infty)$, so cosh is an increasing function on that interval.

In the next activity you'll explore the behaviour of $\sinh x$ and $\cosh x$ when x takes values of large magnitude.

Activity 37 *Comparing the graphs of sinh and cosh*

(a) Using the computer algebra system, plot the graphs of $\sinh x$, $\cosh x$ and $\frac{1}{2}e^{x}$ on the same axes.

(You can plot the graphs of $\sinh x$ and $\cosh x$ by using the formulas for these functions. Alternatively, see the reference guide in the *Computer algebra guide* for the commands for sinh and cosh.)

(b) Comment on the behaviour of $\sinh x$ and $\cosh x$ when x is positive and of large magnitude.

(c) Comment on the behaviour of $\sinh x$ and $\cosh x$ when x is negative and of large magnitude.

Let's now introduce a third function, **tanh**, which is related to sinh and cosh in the same way that the trigonometric function tan is related to sin and cos. (The word 'tanh' is pronounced either as 'than' or 'tansh', where the 'th' in 'than' is spoken like the 'th' in 'thistle'.)

$$\tanh x = \frac{\sinh x}{\cosh x}$$

The function tanh is sometimes called **hyperbolic tangent**. Like the other hyperbolic functions, it takes any real number as an input value, and outputs another real number. You'll recall that the trigonometric expression $\tan x$ is not defined for those values of x for which $\cos x = 0$ (because you can't divide by 0); however, tanh doesn't suffer from this problem as $\cosh x$ is never equal to 0.

By writing $\sinh x$ and $\cosh x$ in terms of e^x, you can give a different formula for tanh:

$$\tanh x = \frac{\sinh x}{\cosh x} = \frac{\frac{1}{2}(e^x - e^{-x})}{\frac{1}{2}(e^x + e^{-x})} = \frac{e^x - e^{-x}}{e^x + e^{-x}}.$$

$$\tanh x = \frac{e^x - e^{-x}}{e^x + e^{-x}}$$

The next activity invites you to express this formula for tanh in another way.

Activity 38 *Finding another formula for tanh*

Show that

$$\tanh x = \frac{e^{2x} - 1}{e^{2x} + 1}$$

for all values of x.

The graph of tanh is shown in Figure 21.

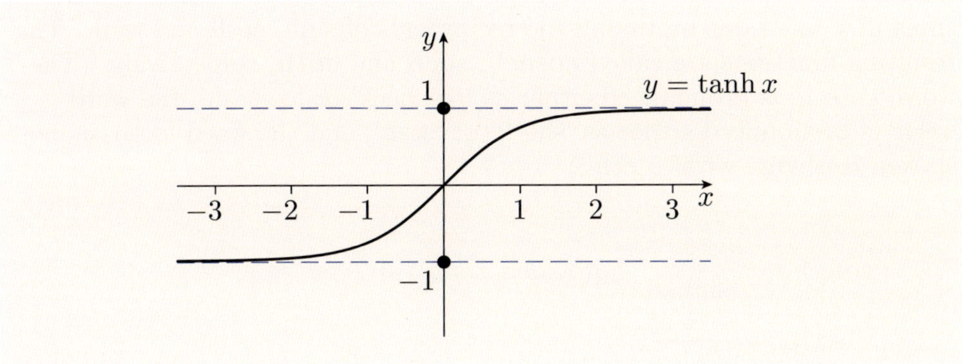

Figure 21 The graph of tanh

The graph appears to show that $-1 < \tanh x < 1$ for all values of x. To see that this is indeed so, first observe that, because e^{2x} is always positive, we have

$$-e^{2x} - 1 < e^{2x} - 1 < e^{2x} + 1,$$

for all values of x. If you now divide throughout by the expression $e^{2x} + 1$, then you obtain

$$-1 < \frac{e^{2x} - 1}{e^{2x} + 1} < 1.$$

As you saw in Activity 38, the middle expression is equal to $\tanh x$, which proves that $-1 < \tanh x < 1$.

It also appears from Figure 21 that the line $y = 1$ is a horizontal asymptote of the graph of $\tanh x$: as $x \to \infty$ the graph approaches but never reaches this line. This is indeed so because, for positive values of x of large magnitude, the expression e^{-x} is close to 0, so using the formula

$$\tanh x = \frac{e^x - e^{-x}}{e^x + e^{-x}},$$

you can see that $\tanh x$ is close to 1. In a similar way, you can see that the line $y = -1$ is another horizontal asymptote of the graph of tanh.

Later on you'll prove that the derivative of $\tanh x$ is positive for all values of x, which tells you that tanh is an increasing function.

Activity 39 *Establishing properties of tanh*

(a) Work out $\tanh 0$ without using a calculator.

(b) Show that $\tanh x$ is positive if x is positive, and negative if x is negative.

(c) Show that tanh is an odd function.

Just as you can define the functions cosecant, secant and cotangent by taking the reciprocals of sine, cosine and tangent, so you can also define three new functions by taking the reciprocals of sinh, cosh and tanh. The resulting functions are called **cosech**, **sech** and **coth**, respectively. (The word 'cosech' is pronounced either as 'co-sheck' or 'co-sesh', the word 'sech' is pronounced either as 'sheck' or 'sesh', and the word 'coth' is spoken to rhyme with 'moth'.)

$$\operatorname{cosech} x = \frac{1}{\sinh x} \quad (\text{provided } x \neq 0)$$
$$\operatorname{sech} x = \frac{1}{\cosh x}$$
$$\coth x = \frac{1}{\tanh x} \quad (\text{provided } x \neq 0)$$

The functions cosech and coth are defined only when $x \neq 0$, because when $x = 0$ both $\sinh x$ and $\tanh x$ equal 0, and it is not possible to divide by 0.

Together the functions sinh, cosh, tanh, cosech, sech and coth are called the **hyperbolic functions**. In this module, the only hyperbolic functions that you'll work with are sinh, cosh and tanh; you may use the other three functions if you study further modules on calculus.

6.2 Inverse hyperbolic functions

You've learned that sinh is an increasing function such that $\sinh x \to \infty$ as $x \to \infty$, and $\sinh x \to -\infty$ as $x \to -\infty$. It follows that sinh is a one-to-one function with domain $\mathbb{R}$ and image set $\mathbb{R}$. You saw in MST124 that any one-to-one function has an inverse function; that is, a function that 'undoes' the effect of the original function.

Inverse sinh function

The **inverse sinh function** $\sinh^{-1}$ is the function with domain $\mathbb{R}$ and rule

$$\sinh^{-1} x = y,$$

where y is the real number such that $\sinh y = x$.

Take care using the notation $\sinh^{-1} x$: remember that it is *not* the same as $(\sinh x)^{-1}$, which is the reciprocal of $\sinh x$ (namely $\operatorname{cosech} x$). This notation can be confusing because, in contrast, $\sinh^2 x$ *does* mean $(\sinh x)^2$. The conventions about writing powers and inverse functions of hyperbolic functions are the same as those used for the trigonometric functions.

You can draw the graph of the inverse sinh function by reflecting the graph of sinh in the line $y = x$, as shown in Figure 22, where both axes have the same scale.

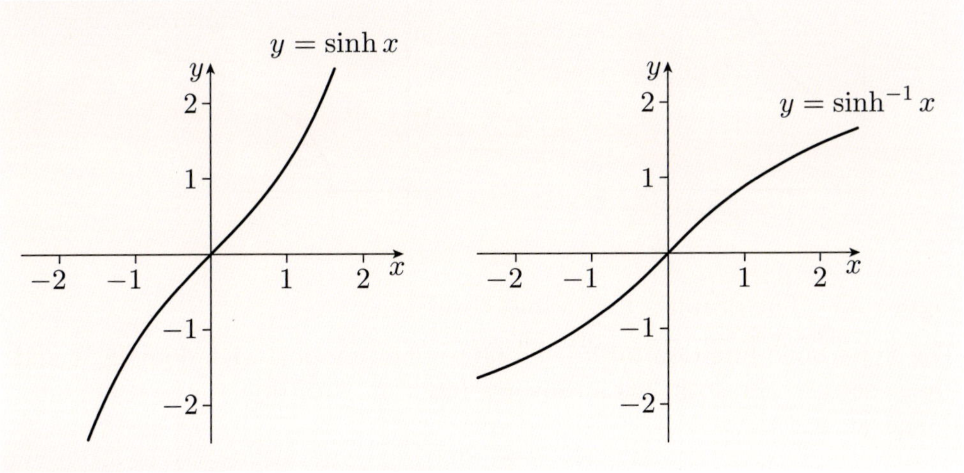

Figure 22 The graphs of sinh and $\sinh^{-1}$

Unlike sinh, cosh is not a one-to-one function because $\cosh x = \cosh(-x)$ for any value of x. However, if you restrict the domain of cosh to the interval $[0, \infty)$, then it is an increasing function. It follows that cosh is a one-to-one function on the domain $[0, \infty)$. Since $\cosh 0 = 1$, and $\cosh x \to \infty$ as $x \to \infty$, the image set of cosh when restricted to the domain $[0, \infty)$ is $[1, \infty)$. So cosh has an inverse function with domain $[1, \infty)$ and image set $[0, \infty)$.

Inverse cosh function

The **inverse cosh function** $\cosh^{-1}$ is the function with domain $[1, \infty)$ and rule

$$\cosh^{-1} x = y,$$

where y is the number in the interval $[0, \infty)$ such that $\cosh y = x$.

You can draw the graph of the inverse cosh function by reflecting the graph of cosh, with domain restricted to $[0, \infty)$, in the line $y = x$. The graphs of $y = \cosh x$ and $y = \cosh^{-1} x$ are shown alongside each other on axes with the same scale in Figure 23.

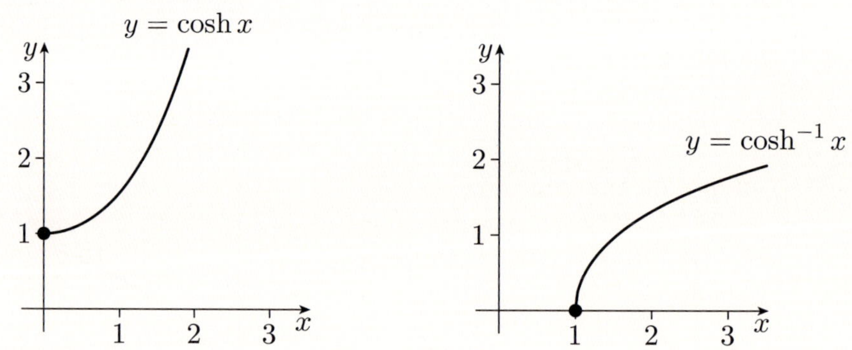

Figure 23 The graphs of cosh and $\cosh^{-1}$

The hyperbolic function tanh is a one-to-one function with domain $\mathbb{R}$ and image set $(-1, 1)$, so it has an inverse function with domain $(-1, 1)$ and image set $\mathbb{R}$.

Inverse tanh function

The **inverse tanh function** $\tanh^{-1}$ is the function with domain $(-1, 1)$ and rule

$$\tanh^{-1} x = y,$$

where y is the real number such that $\tanh y = x$.

You can draw the graph of the inverse tanh function by reflecting the graph of tanh in the line $y = x$. The graphs of $y = \tanh x$ and $y = \tanh^{-1} x$ are shown on axes with the same scale in Figure 24.

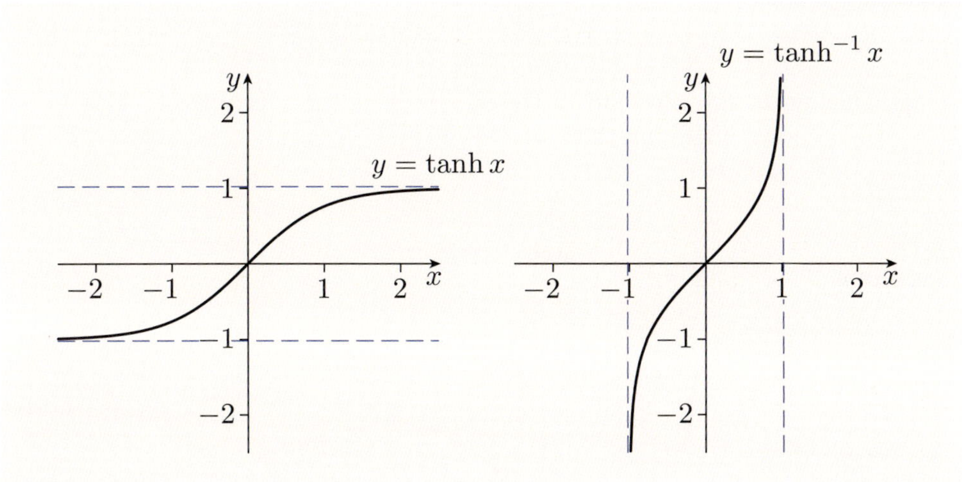

Figure 24 The graphs of tanh and $\tanh^{-1}$

The inverse sinh, inverse cosh and inverse tanh functions are known as the **inverse hyperbolic functions**. In other texts you may see them called arsinh, arcosh and artanh, respectively, or arcsinh, arccosh and arctanh. Some calculators and computers use the names INV SINH, INV COSH, INV TANH or asinh, acosh, atanh.

You can use a calculator to find values of the inverse hyperbolic functions. For example, a calculator gives $\sinh^{-1}(0.5) = 0.481\,211\ldots$. When using a calculator, make sure that the input values you enter are allowed, or the calculator is likely to give you an error message. For instance, you shouldn't ask your calculator to work out $\cosh^{-1}(0.5)$ because the domain of $\cosh^{-1}$ is $[1, \infty)$, so $\cosh^{-1}(0.5)$ is not defined.

Activity 40 *Calculating values of inverse hyperbolic functions*

Which of the following values are defined? For the values that are defined, give the value to five decimal places.

(a) $\sinh^{-1} 0$ (b) $\cosh^{-1} 0$ (c) $\tanh^{-1} 0$

(d) $\sinh^{-1} 1$ (e) $\cosh^{-1} 1$ (f) $\tanh^{-1} 1$

Tractrix

The curve that is formed from the graph of the equation

$$y = \cosh^{-1}\left(\frac{1}{x}\right) - \sqrt{1 - x^2}$$

together with its reflection in the x-axis is called a **tractrix**. This curve is shown in Figure 25.

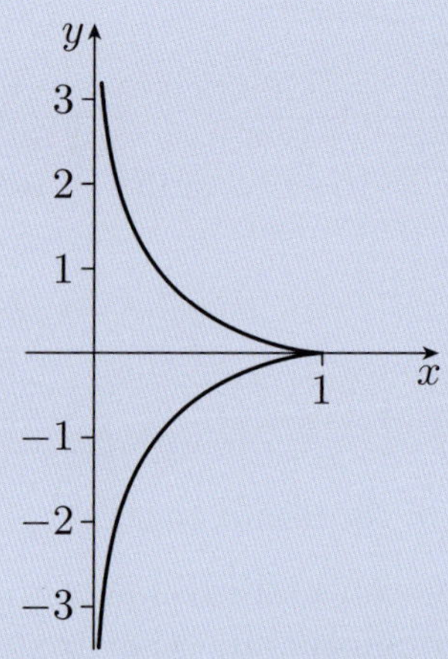

Figure 25 A tractrix

The word 'tractrix' is derived from the Latin verb 'trahere', which means to pull or drag. This terminology is used because of the following physical situation in which a tractrix arises. Think of the right-hand half of the Cartesian plane as a canal and the y-axis as the tow path alongside the canal. Imagine a person standing at $(0, 0)$ holding one end of a taut rope, the other end of which is attached to a small boat at the point $(1, 0)$. The canal is still. The person then walks along the tow path, vertically down the y-axis, pulling the boat in such a way that the rope remains taut. The path in the water traced by the boat is the bottom half of the tractrix.

6.3 Hyperbolic identities

Like the trigonometric functions, the hyperbolic functions satisfy a number of identities, which are called **hyperbolic identities**. In this subsection you'll meet a selection of hyperbolic identities, all of which should seem familiar, as each one has a trigonometric identity counterpart.

You've met the following three identities already; they tell us that sinh and tanh are odd functions, and that cosh is an even function.

Symmetry identities

$$\sinh(-x) = -\sinh x$$
$$\cosh(-x) = \cosh x$$
$$\tanh(-x) = -\tanh x$$

The most important identity you'll encounter here is a hyperbolic version of the trigonometric Pythagorean identity $\sin^2 x + \cos^2 x = 1$. In the trigonometric version of this identity, the expressions $\sin^2 x$ and $\cos^2 x$ represent $(\sin x)^2$ and $(\cos x)^2$, respectively. In the same way, $(\sinh x)^2$ and $(\cosh x)^2$ are usually written as $\sinh^2 x$ and $\cosh^2 x$, as mentioned earlier.

We'll call the new identity a **hyperbolic Pythagorean identity**, by analogy with the trigonometric Pythagorean identities (though this terminology is not universal). To obtain it, first observe that

$$\cosh x + \sinh x = \tfrac{1}{2}(e^x + e^{-x}) + \tfrac{1}{2}(e^x - e^{-x}) = e^x$$

and

$$\cosh x - \sinh x = \tfrac{1}{2}(e^x + e^{-x}) - \tfrac{1}{2}(e^x - e^{-x}) = e^{-x}.$$

So

$$(\cosh x + \sinh x)(\cosh x - \sinh x) = e^x e^{-x}.$$

Using the usual formula for a difference of two squares, the left-hand side of this equation is $\cosh^2 x - \sinh^2 x$. The right-hand side is 1. This gives the following identity.

A hyperbolic Pythagorean identity

$$\cosh^2 x - \sinh^2 x = 1$$

The term 'hyperbolic' is used for hyperbolic functions because you can use sinh and cosh to describe points on a hyperbola. The way in which this is done is similar to how sine and cosine are defined using points on the unit circle (see Subsection 2.1 of Unit 1). Indeed, sine and cosine are sometimes referred to as 'circular' functions. You studied hyperbolas in Unit 4. To understand the connection between sinh, cosh and hyperbolas, consider the hyperbola shown in Figure 26, which is given by the equation $x^2 - y^2 = 1$.

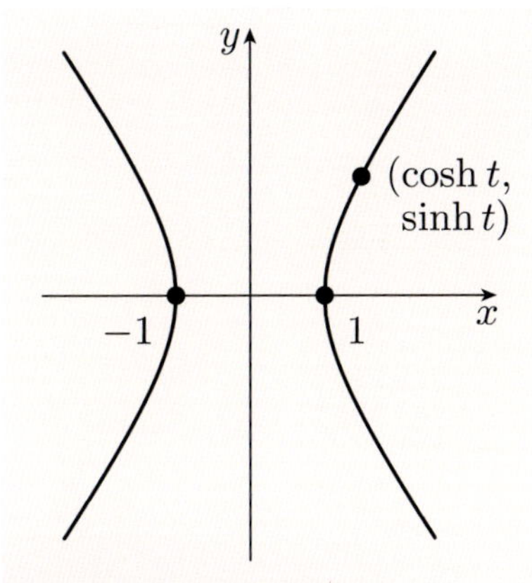

Figure 26 The graph of $x^2 - y^2 = 1$

For any real number t, the point $(\cosh t, \sinh t)$ must lie on the hyperbola because it satisfies $\cosh^2 t - \sinh^2 t = 1$. In fact, the point lies on the right-hand branch of the hyperbola because $\cosh t$ is positive; you can write any point on the right-hand branch of the hyperbola in that form. Points on the left-hand branch of the hyperbola can be written in the form $(-\cosh t, \sinh t)$. Thus we have found a parametrisation of the hyperbola shown in Figure 26, which is an alternative to the standard parametrisation you met in Unit 4.

So you see that points on a hyperbola are given by $(\pm\cosh t, \sinh t)$, just as points on the unit circle are given by $(\cos t, \sin t)$. In fact, just as any ellipse in standard position has a parametrisation of the form $(a\cos t, b\sin t)$, so any hyperbola in standard position has a parametrisation of the form $(\pm a\cosh t, b\sinh t)$.

The strong relationship between hyperbolic identities and trigonometric identities is described by **Osborn's rule**. This rule says that, if you have an identity involving sine and cosine, then you can transform it to an identity involving sinh and cosh by replacing each sine with sinh, each cosine with cosh, and whenever there is a term in the identity involving a product of two sine terms, you should change the sign of that term.

For example, let's transform the trigonometric identity $\sin^2 x + \cos^2 x = 1$ to a hyperbolic identity using Osborn's rule. To do this, replace sin with sinh and cos with cosh, and then change the sign of the term $\sin^2 x$ (which is the product of two sine terms). You obtain

$$-\sinh^2 x + \cosh^2 x = 1,$$

which is equivalent to the hyperbolic Pythagorean identity derived above.

Note that you should only use Osborn's rule as a guide, because there are some exceptional cases for which it fails. For instance, it fails if the trigonometric identity has a term that involves a product of four sines, and it fails for some identities involving expressions of the form $\sin(x + b)$, where b is a constant not equal to 0.

If you apply Osborn's rule to the double-angle identities

$$\sin(2x) = 2\sin x\cos x$$
$$\cos(2x) = \cos^2 x - \sin^2 x,$$

then you obtain the following pair of hyperbolic identities.

Hyperbolic double-variable identities

$$\sinh(2x) = 2\sinh x\cosh x$$
$$\cosh(2x) = \cosh^2 x + \sinh^2 x$$

Let's see why the first of these identities is true; the second identity is considered in the next activity. We have

$$\sinh(2x) = \tfrac{1}{2}(e^{2x} - e^{-2x}) = \tfrac{1}{2}((e^x)^2 - (e^{-x})^2).$$

The expression on the right involves a difference of two squares, which you can write as

$$(e^x)^2 - (e^{-x})^2 = (e^x - e^{-x})(e^x + e^{-x}).$$

So

$$\begin{aligned}\sinh(2x) &= \tfrac{1}{2}(e^x - e^{-x})(e^x + e^{-x})\\ &= 2 \times \tfrac{1}{2}(e^x - e^{-x}) \times \tfrac{1}{2}(e^x + e^{-x})\\ &= 2\sinh x \cosh x.\end{aligned}$$

Activity 41 *Establishing the double-variable identity for cosh*

Prove the identity $\cosh(2x) = \cosh^2 x + \sinh^2 x$.

There are two alternative forms of the double-variable identity for cosh. To obtain these, we rearrange the identity $\cosh^2 x - \sinh^2 x = 1$ to give $\sinh^2 x = \cosh^2 x - 1$ and $\cosh^2 x = 1 + \sinh^2 x$. So

$$\begin{aligned}\cosh(2x) &= \cosh^2 x + \sinh^2 x\\ &= (1 + \sinh^2 x) + \sinh^2 x\\ &= 1 + 2\sinh^2 x\\ &= 2\sinh^2 x + 1\end{aligned}$$

and

$$\begin{aligned}\cosh(2x) &= \cosh^2 x + \sinh^2 x\\ &= \cosh^2 x + (\cosh^2 x - 1)\\ &= 2\cosh^2 x - 1.\end{aligned}$$

Alternative double-variable identities for cosh

$$\cosh(2x) = 2\sinh^2 x + 1$$
$$\cosh(2x) = 2\cosh^2 x - 1$$

These alternative double-variable identities for cosh can be rearranged into the forms below.

Half-variable identities

$$\sinh^2 x = \tfrac{1}{2}(\cosh(2x) - 1)$$
$$\cosh^2 x = \tfrac{1}{2}(\cosh(2x) + 1)$$

You'll need these identities later on when using hyperbolic functions in integration. The description 'half-variable' refers to the fact that these identities are sometimes stated with x and $2x$ replaced by $\frac{1}{2}x$ and x, respectively, as follows:

$$\sinh^2(\tfrac{1}{2}x) = \tfrac{1}{2}(\cosh x - 1)$$
$$\cosh^2(\tfrac{1}{2}x) = \tfrac{1}{2}(\cosh x + 1).$$

Activity 42 *Finding values of sinh and cosh*

Suppose that $\cosh(2x) = 3$. Find the values of $\sinh x$ and $\cosh x$.

You can obtain many other hyperbolic identities by applying Osborn's rule to trigonometric identities. For example, applying Osborn's rule to the angle sum identity for sine gives the following similar-looking identity for sinh:

$$\sinh(A + B) = \sinh A \cosh B + \cosh A \sinh B.$$

You can check that this identity is true by writing each sinh and cosh expression in terms of the exponential function.

A summary of the main hyperbolic identities found in this unit is given in the *Handbook*.

Origin of Osborn's rule

If you are comfortable working with complex numbers, then you can get an idea of why Osborn's rule works by using the formulas

$$\sinh(ix) = i \sin x \quad \text{and} \quad \cosh(ix) = \cos x$$

obtained earlier, where i is a square root of -1.

For example, here's how you can use these formulas to turn the trigonometric identity $\sin^2 x + \cos^2 x = 1$ into the hyperbolic identity $\cosh^2 x - \sinh^2 x = 1$. If you take the square of each side of the formulas above and then use $i^2 = -1$, you obtain

$$\sinh^2(ix) = -\sin^2 x \quad \text{and} \quad \cosh^2(ix) = \cos^2 x.$$

So the usual Pythagorean identity $\cos^2 x + \sin^2 x = 1$ can be written as

$$\cosh^2(ix) - \sinh^2(ix) = 1.$$

Now replace ix by x to obtain the identity

$$\cosh^2 x - \sinh^2 x = 1.$$

You can transform other trigonometric identities in a similar manner.

Osborn's rule is named after a short note by the mathematician George Osborn (1864–1932), quoted in full below, which was published in *The Mathematical Gazette*, Vol. 2, No. 34, (Jul., 1902), p. 189.

109. [D. 6. d.] *Mnemonic for hyperbolic formulae.*

Hyperbolic functions are now so constantly used, that a brief mnemonic for their somewhat confusing formulae may not be unwelcome.

In any Trigonometrical formula for θ, 2θ, 3θ, or θ and ϕ, after changing *sin* to *sinh*, *cos* to *cosh*, etc., change the sign of any term that contains (or implies) a *product of sinhs, e.g.* $\tanh\theta\,\tanh\phi$ implies a product of sinhs,

$$\therefore \tanh(\theta+\phi) = \frac{\tanh\theta + \tanh\phi}{1+\tanh\theta\tanh\phi}.$$

$$\sinh 3\theta = 3\sinh\theta + 4\sinh 3\theta;$$

$$\cosh\theta - \cosh\phi = +2\sinh\frac{\theta+\phi}{2}\sinh\frac{\theta-\phi}{2};$$

and so on. This rule would fail for terms of the 4th degree, but it covers everything that is likely to be required, and is very convenient for teaching purposes. G. OSBORN.

6.4 Differentiating and integrating hyperbolic functions

In this subsection you'll learn how to differentiate and integrate sinh, cosh and tanh. Once you've seen how to do this, you'll be able to differentiate and integrate more complicated hyperbolic expressions by using techniques that you know already, such as the chain rule for differentiation and integration by parts.

Let's start by differentiating $\sinh x$. You can do this immediately by writing sinh in terms of the exponential function, as follows:

$$\begin{aligned}\frac{\mathrm{d}}{\mathrm{d}x}(\sinh x) &= \frac{\mathrm{d}}{\mathrm{d}x}\left(\tfrac{1}{2}(e^x - e^{-x})\right)\\ &= \tfrac{1}{2}(e^x - (-e^{-x}))\\ &= \tfrac{1}{2}(e^x + e^{-x})\\ &= \cosh x.\end{aligned}$$

Similarly,

$$\begin{aligned}\frac{\mathrm{d}}{\mathrm{d}x}(\cosh x) &= \frac{\mathrm{d}}{\mathrm{d}x}\left(\tfrac{1}{2}(e^x + e^{-x})\right)\\ &= \tfrac{1}{2}(e^x - e^{-x})\\ &= \sinh x.\end{aligned}$$

Since integration 'undoes' the effect of differentiation, you see that

$$\int \sinh x \, dx = \cosh x + c \qquad \text{and} \qquad \int \cosh x \, dx = \sinh x + c.$$

You can use these observations about sinh and cosh to differentiate and integrate tanh, in the next activity.

Activity 43 *Differentiating and integrating tanh*

(a) Show that $\dfrac{d}{dx}(\tanh x) = \dfrac{1}{\cosh^2 x}$.

(b) Show that $\displaystyle\int \tanh x \, dx = \ln(\cosh x) + c$.

Hint for part (b): use the substitution $u = \cosh x$.

These observations about derivatives and integrals are summarised in the table below.

Derivatives and integrals of sinh, cosh and tanh

$$\frac{d}{dx}(\sinh x) = \cosh x \qquad \int \sinh x \, dx = \cosh x + c$$

$$\frac{d}{dx}(\cosh x) = \sinh x \qquad \int \cosh x \, dx = \sinh x + c$$

$$\frac{d}{dx}(\tanh x) = \frac{1}{\cosh^2 x} \qquad \int \tanh x \, dx = \ln(\cosh x) + c$$

In the next activity you're asked to show that the derivatives of sinh, cosh and tanh are positive on certain intervals. These properties were used earlier in this section to show that the hyperbolic functions are increasing on those intervals, in order to define inverse functions.

Activity 44 *Finding intervals on which the derivatives of sinh, cosh and tanh are positive.*

(a) Show that the derivatives of $\sinh x$ and $\tanh x$ are positive for all values of x.

(b) Show that the derivative of $\cosh x$ is positive if x is positive and negative if x is negative.

You can integrate many expressions involving hyperbolic functions by using similar methods to those you use to integrate trigonometric expressions. Here's an example.

Example 29 *Integrating an expression involving a hyperbolic function*

Find the integral $\int \sinh^2 x \, dx$.

Solution

Use the half-variable identity for sinh.

By the half-variable identity for sinh,

$$\begin{aligned}\int \sinh^2 x \, dx &= \int \tfrac{1}{2}(\cosh(2x) - 1) \, dx \\ &= \tfrac{1}{2} \int (\cosh(2x) - 1) \, dx \\ &= \tfrac{1}{2}\left(\tfrac{1}{2}\sinh(2x) - x\right) + c \\ &= \tfrac{1}{4}\sinh(2x) - \tfrac{1}{2}x + c.\end{aligned}$$

Activity 45 *Integrating expressions involving hyperbolic functions*

Find the following integrals.

(a) $\int \cosh^2 x \, dx$ (b) $\int \sinh(4x - 7) \, dx$ (c) $\int \sinh x \cosh^2 x \, dx$

6.5 Hyperbolic substitutions

In Subsection 5.2, you learned how trigonometric substitutions can be used to find integrals such as

$$\int \sqrt{9 - x^2} \, dx \quad \text{and} \quad \int \frac{1}{(1 + x^2)^2} \, dx.$$

Sometimes trigonometric substitutions lead to integrands that are difficult to integrate. For example, suppose you wish to find the integral

$$\int \sqrt{1 + x^2} \, dx.$$

As the integrand involves the expression $1 + x^2$, you can apply the substitution $x = \tan u$, so that $\dfrac{dx}{du} = \sec^2 u$, and use the identity $1 + \tan^2 u = \sec^2 u$. The integral becomes

$$\int \sqrt{1 + \tan^2 u} \, (\sec^2 u) \, du = \int \sqrt{\sec^2 u} \, (\sec^2 u) \, du = \int \sec^3 u \, du.$$

The resulting integral is no easier to find than the one you started with.

When a trigonometric substitution leads to a difficult integral, such as the integral of $\sec^3 u$, you can consider an alternative strategy for finding the original integral. With this strategy, you replace the variable x in the integrand with a *hyperbolic* function in the variable u. This sort of substitution is called a **hyperbolic substitution**.

Here you'll learn about two hyperbolic substitutions, which can be used as alternatives to trigonometric substitutions to find integrals that involve one of the expressions

$$x^2 - a^2 \quad \text{or} \quad a^2 + x^2,$$

where x is the variable in the integrand, and a is a constant. Like trigonometric substitutions, hyperbolic substitutions are most useful when the integrand involves the square root of one of these expressions, since it is for such integrands that other methods like finding partial fractions fail.

The hyperbolic substitutions are based on the following pair of identities, each of which is a rearrangement of the identity $\cosh^2 u - \sinh^2 u = 1$.

$$\cosh^2 u - 1 = \sinh^2 u$$
$$1 + \sinh^2 u = \cosh^2 u$$

When you wish to make a hyperbolic substitution, the table below tells you which substitution to apply, and the identity that you'll need once you've carried out the substitution.

Table of hyperbolic substitutions

Expression	Substitution	Identity
$x^2 - a^2$	$x = a\cosh u$	$\cosh^2 u - 1 = \sinh^2 u$
$a^2 + x^2$	$x = a\sinh u$	$1 + \sinh^2 u = \cosh^2 u$

Here are examples of how to apply each of these substitutions.

Example 30 *Integrating using hyperbolic substitutions*

Find the following integrals.

(a) $\displaystyle\int \frac{1}{\sqrt{x^2-9}}\,\mathrm{d}x$ (b) $\displaystyle\int \sqrt{1+x^2}\,\mathrm{d}x$

Solution

(a) The integrand involves the expression x^2-9, which is x^2-3^2, so try the substitution $x = 3\cosh u$.

Let $x = 3\cosh u$; then $\dfrac{\mathrm{d}x}{\mathrm{d}u} = 3\sinh u$.

Also, rearranging the equation $x = 3\cosh u$ gives $u = \cosh^{-1}(x/3)$.

Imagine 'cross-multiplying' in the equation $\dfrac{\mathrm{d}x}{\mathrm{d}u} = 3\sinh u$ to obtain $\mathrm{d}x = (3\sinh u)\,\mathrm{d}u$.

So

$$\begin{aligned}\int \frac{1}{\sqrt{x^2-9}}\,\mathrm{d}x &= \int \frac{1}{\sqrt{(3\cosh u)^2-9}}(3\sinh u)\,\mathrm{d}u\\ &= 3\int \frac{\sinh u}{\sqrt{3^2\cosh^2 u - 3^2}}\,\mathrm{d}u\\ &= \int \frac{\sinh u}{\sqrt{\cosh^2 u - 1}}\,\mathrm{d}u\end{aligned}$$

Use the identity $\cosh^2 u - 1 = \sinh^2 u$.

$$\begin{aligned}&= \int \frac{\sinh u}{\sqrt{\sinh^2 u}}\,\mathrm{d}u\\ &= \int 1\,\mathrm{d}u\\ &= u + c\end{aligned}$$

Substitute back for u in terms of x.

$$= \cosh^{-1}(x/3) + c.$$

(b) The integrand involves the expression $1+x^2$, so try the substitution $x=\sinh u$.

Let $x=\sinh u$; then $\dfrac{dx}{du}=\cosh u$.

Also, rearranging the equation $x=\sinh u$ gives $u=\sinh^{-1} x$.

Imagine 'cross-multiplying' in the equation $\dfrac{dx}{du}=\cosh u$ to obtain $dx=(\cosh u)\,du$.

So

$$\int \sqrt{1+x^2}\,dx = \int \sqrt{1+\sinh^2 u}\,(\cosh u)\,du$$

Use the identity $1+\sinh^2 u=\cosh^2 u$.

$$= \int \sqrt{\cosh^2 u}\,(\cosh u)\,du$$

$$= \int \cosh^2 u\,du$$

To integrate $\cosh^2 u$ you should apply the half-variable identity for cosh.

By the half-variable identity for cosh, the integral becomes

$$\begin{aligned}\int \tfrac{1}{2}(\cosh(2u)+1)\,du &= \tfrac{1}{2}\int (\cosh(2u)+1)\,du\\ &= \tfrac{1}{2}\left(\tfrac{1}{2}\sinh(2u)+u\right)+c\\ &= \tfrac{1}{4}\sinh(2u)+\tfrac{1}{2}u+c\end{aligned}$$

Substitute back for u in terms of x.

$$= \tfrac{1}{4}\sinh(2\sinh^{-1} x)+\tfrac{1}{2}\sinh^{-1} x+c.$$

Activity 46 *Integrating using hyperbolic substitutions*

Find the following integrals.

(a) $\displaystyle\int \frac{1}{\sqrt{4+x^2}}\,dx$ (b) $\displaystyle\int \sqrt{x^2-1}\,dx$ (c) $\displaystyle\int \frac{x^2}{\sqrt{x^2-2}}\,dx$

7 Summary of integration methods

Integration is a rich subject because of the many methods for integrating functions, some of which you've met in this unit. However, the diversity of methods can also make it a difficult topic. You can use the following checklist to guide you in choosing the most suitable technique for integration.

Choosing a method of integration

- Is it a standard integral, or a sum of standard integrals, perhaps modified using constant multiples and linear expressions? If so, then consult the table of standard integrals in the *Handbook*, and use standard rules about modifying and combining integrals.
- Can the integrand be written in the form

  $$f(\text{something}) \times \text{the derivative of the something},$$

  where f is a function that you can integrate? If so, then use integration by substitution. Start by setting the 'something' equal to u.
- Is the integrand of the form

  $$f(x)g(x),$$

  where f is a function that becomes simpler when differentiated, and g is a function that you can integrate? If so, then try integration by parts.
- Is the integrand a rational expression? If so, then find its partial fraction expansion, and integrate the partial fractions separately.
- Does the integrand contain trigonometric functions? If so, then try to find a trigonometric identity to rewrite it in a form that you can integrate.
- Does the integrand contain one of the expressions $a^2 - x^2$, $x^2 - a^2$ or $a^2 + x^2$; in particular, does it contain the square root of one of these expressions? If so, then you may be able to find the integral by using a trigonometric substitution.
- Does a trigonometric substitution still leave you with a difficult integral? If so, and the integrand contains one of the expressions $a^2 - x^2$ or $a^2 + x^2$ (and, in particular, if it contains the square root of one of these expressions), then you could try a hyperbolic substitution instead of a trigonometric substitution.

You can use this checklist to help you with the next activity.

Activity 47 *Choosing a method of integration*

Find the following integrals.

(a) $\int (2x+1)^3 \, dx$ (b) $\int \sin(\sin x) \cos x \, dx$ (c) $\int 2^x \, dx$

(d) $\int (\sin x + \cos x)^2 \, dx$ (e) $\int \frac{1}{x^2 - 3x + 2} \, dx$ (f) $\int \sin^3(3x) \, dx$

(g) $\int \tan^3 x \, dx$ (h) $\int \left(\frac{x}{x+3}\right)^2 dx$ (i) $\int x\sqrt{4 - x^2} \, dx$

(j) $\int \tan^{-1} x \, dx$ (k) $\int \frac{x^3 + 1}{x^2 - x} \, dx$ (l) $\int \frac{x^2}{\sqrt{1 + x^2}} \, dx$

(m) $\int x \ln(x+1) \, dx$

Hint for part (c): write 2^x in the form e^{kx} for some number k which you should determine.

Hint for part (j): write the integrand as $(\tan^{-1} x) \times 1$ and integrate by parts.

Hint for part (m): start by using integration by parts.

Impossible integrals

There are some integrals that you cannot find using any of the standard methods of integration. A prime example is

$$\int e^{-x^2} \, dx.$$

The expression e^{-x^2} certainly has antiderivatives, but, unlike the antiderivatives you've met so far, they cannot be written as combinations of rational, trigonometric, exponential and logarithmic expressions using only the operations $+$, $-$, $\times$, $\div$ and $\sqrt[n]{\ }$. Despite this shortcoming, the integral of e^{-x^2} is an important mathematical tool, particularly in statistics, where it is closely related to the **normal distribution**, which is a rule for measuring probabilities that is much used in science. One of the key properties of the function $y = e^{-x^2}$ is that the total area between its graph and the x-axis (shown in Figure 27) is $\sqrt{\pi}$. This fact is written as

$$\int_{-\infty}^{\infty} e^{-x^2} \, dx = \sqrt{\pi}.$$

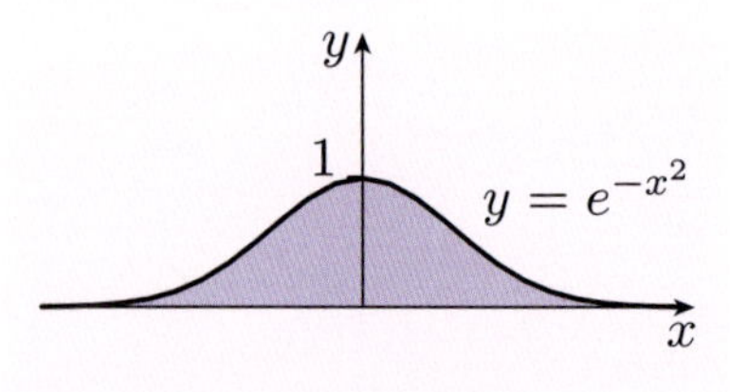

Figure 27 The graph of $y = e^{-x^2}$

The integral in this equation is called the **Gaussian integral**, named after the eminent German mathematician Carl Friedrich Gauss (1777–1855), who developed the theory of the normal distribution.

Learning outcomes

After studying this unit, you should be able to:

- integrate by substitution
- integrate by parts
- find partial fraction expansions
- apply polynomial long division
- integrate rational expressions
- sketch graphs of rational functions
- integrate trigonometric expressions
- use trigonometric substitutions
- define the hyperbolic functions and inverse hyperbolic functions
- understand and use hyperbolic identities
- differentiate and integrate hyperbolic functions
- use hyperbolic substitutions
- identify a suitable method of integration for some types of integrals.

Solutions to activities

Solution to Activity 1

(a)
$$\begin{aligned}\int(3-x)x^2\,dx &= \int(3x^2-x^3)\,dx\\ &= 3\int x^2\,dx-\int x^3\,dx\\ &= 3\times\tfrac{1}{3}x^3-\tfrac{1}{4}x^4+c\\ &= x^3-\tfrac{1}{4}x^4+c.\end{aligned}$$

(b)
$$\int e^{-8x+2}\,dx = -\tfrac{1}{8}e^{-8x+2}+c.$$

(c)
$$\begin{aligned}&\int(\operatorname{cosec} x)(\cot x-3\operatorname{cosec} x)\,dx\\ &= \int(\operatorname{cosec} x\cot x-3\operatorname{cosec}^2 x)\,dx\\ &= \int\operatorname{cosec} x\cot x\,dx-3\int\operatorname{cosec}^2 x\,dx\\ &= -\operatorname{cosec} x-3(-\cot x)+c\\ &= -\operatorname{cosec} x+3\cot x+c.\end{aligned}$$

(d)
$$\begin{aligned}\int\frac{1}{\sqrt{1-9x^2}}\,dx &= \int\frac{1}{\sqrt{1-(3x)^2}}\,dx\\ &= \tfrac{1}{3}\sin^{-1}(3x)+c.\end{aligned}$$

(e)
$$\begin{aligned}&\int\left(\sqrt{x}+\frac{1}{\sqrt{x}}\right)^2\,dx\\ &= \int\left(\left(\sqrt{x}\right)^2+2\left(\sqrt{x}\times\frac{1}{\sqrt{x}}\right)+\left(\frac{1}{\sqrt{x}}\right)^2\right)\,dx\\ &= \int\left(x+2+\frac{1}{x}\right)\,dx\\ &= \int x\,dx+\int 2\,dx+\int\frac{1}{x}\,dx\\ &= \tfrac{1}{2}x^2+2x+\ln|x|+c.\end{aligned}$$

Solution to Activity 2

(a) Let $u=\sin x$; then $\dfrac{du}{dx}=\cos x$. So
$$\begin{aligned}\int e^{\sin x}\cos x\,dx &= \int e^u\,du\\ &= e^u+c\\ &= e^{\sin x}+c.\end{aligned}$$

(b) Let $u=x^2+x+2$; then $\dfrac{du}{dx}=2x+1$. So
$$\begin{aligned}\int(x^2+x+2)^{1/3}(2x+1)\,dx &= \int u^{1/3}\,du\\ &= \tfrac{3}{4}u^{4/3}+c\\ &= \tfrac{3}{4}(x^2+x+2)^{4/3}+c.\end{aligned}$$

(Alternatively, you can make the substitution $u=x^2+x$. This gives an integrand $(u+2)^{1/3}$, which is slightly harder to integrate than $u^{1/3}$.)

(c) Let $u=\tan x$; then $\dfrac{du}{dx}=\sec^2 x$. So
$$\begin{aligned}\int\left(\frac{1}{\sqrt{1-\tan^2 x}}\right)\sec^2 x\,dx &= \int\frac{1}{\sqrt{1-u^2}}\,du\\ &= \sin^{-1}u+c\\ &= \sin^{-1}(\tan x)+c.\end{aligned}$$

Solution to Activity 3

(a) Let $u=x^4$; then $\dfrac{du}{dx}=4x^3$. So
$$\begin{aligned}\int x^3e^{x^4}\,dx &= \int e^{x^4}x^3\,dx\\ &= \tfrac{1}{4}\int e^{x^4}(4x^3)\,dx\\ &= \tfrac{1}{4}\int e^u\,du\\ &= \tfrac{1}{4}e^u+c\\ &= \tfrac{1}{4}e^{x^4}+c.\end{aligned}$$

(b) Let $u=2+\cos x$; then $\dfrac{du}{dx}=-\sin x$. So
$$\begin{aligned}\int\frac{\sin x}{2+\cos x}\,dx &= -\int\left(\frac{1}{2+\cos x}\right)(-\sin x)\,dx\\ &= -\int\frac{1}{u}\,du\\ &= -\ln|u|+c\\ &= -\ln|2+\cos x|+c\\ &= -\ln(2+\cos x)+c,\end{aligned}$$

since $2+\cos x$ is always positive.

(c) Let $u = x^2$; then $\dfrac{du}{dx} = 2x$. So

$$\begin{aligned}\int \frac{x}{1+x^4}\,dx &= \int \left(\frac{1}{1+(x^2)^2}\right) x\,dx\\ &= \tfrac{1}{2}\int \left(\frac{1}{1+(x^2)^2}\right)(2x)\,dx\\ &= \tfrac{1}{2}\int \frac{1}{1+u^2}\,du\\ &= \tfrac{1}{2}\tan^{-1} u + c\\ &= \tfrac{1}{2}\tan^{-1}(x^2) + c.\end{aligned}$$

Solution to Activity 4

(a) Let $u = x+1$; then $\dfrac{du}{dx} = 1$. Also, $x = u-1$. So

$$\begin{aligned}\int x(x+1)^{3/2}\,dx &= \int (u-1)u^{3/2}\,du\\ &= \int \left(u^{5/2} - u^{3/2}\right)du\\ &= \tfrac{2}{7}u^{7/2} - \tfrac{2}{5}u^{5/2} + c\\ &= \tfrac{2}{7}(x+1)^{7/2} - \tfrac{2}{5}(x+1)^{5/2} + c.\end{aligned}$$

(b) Let $u = x-2$; then $\dfrac{du}{dx} = 1$. Also, $x = u+2$, so $x+1 = u+3$. Hence

$$\begin{aligned}\int \frac{x+1}{(x-2)^2}\,dx &= \int \frac{u+3}{u^2}\,du\\ &= \int \left(u^{-1} + 3u^{-2}\right)du\\ &= \ln|u| + 3(-u^{-1}) + c\\ &= \ln|u| - \frac{3}{u} + c\\ &= \ln|x-2| - \frac{3}{x-2} + c.\end{aligned}$$

Solution to Activity 5

(a) Let $u = x^3+1$; then $\dfrac{du}{dx} = 3x^2$.

Putting $x = 0$ gives $u = 1$ and putting $x = 1$ gives $u = 2$. So

$$\begin{aligned}\int_0^1 x^2\sqrt{x^3+1}\,dx &= \tfrac{1}{3}\int_0^1 (x^3+1)^{1/2}\left(3x^2\right)dx\\ &= \tfrac{1}{3}\int_1^2 u^{1/2}\,du\\ &= \tfrac{1}{3}\left[\tfrac{2}{3}u^{3/2}\right]_1^2\\ &= \tfrac{2}{9}\left[u^{3/2}\right]_1^2\\ &= \tfrac{2}{9}(2\sqrt{2}-1).\end{aligned}$$

(b) Let $u = 4x$; then $\dfrac{du}{dx} = 4$.

Putting $x = \pi/16$ gives $u = \pi/4$ and putting $x = \pi/8$ gives $u = \pi/2$. So

$$\begin{aligned}\int_{\pi/16}^{\pi/8} \operatorname{cosec}^2(4x)\,dx &= \tfrac{1}{4}\int_{\pi/16}^{\pi/8} (\operatorname{cosec}^2(4x)) \times 4\,dx\\ &= \tfrac{1}{4}\int_{\pi/4}^{\pi/2} \operatorname{cosec}^2 u\,du\\ &= \tfrac{1}{4}\big[-\cot u\big]_{\pi/4}^{\pi/2}\\ &= -\tfrac{1}{4}(0-1)\\ &= \tfrac{1}{4}.\end{aligned}$$

(You may have noticed that the expression $\operatorname{cosec}^2(4x)$ is of the form f(linear expression), where f is the function given by $f(x) = \operatorname{cosec}^2 x$, and the linear expression is $4x$. The integral of $\operatorname{cosec}^2 x$ is given in the table of standard indefinite integrals, so you can find the indefinite integral of $\operatorname{cosec}^2(4x)$ using the linear expression rule. You obtain

$$\int \operatorname{cosec}^2(4x)\,dx = -\tfrac{1}{4}\cot(4x) + c.$$

Thus an alternative solution is

$$\begin{aligned}\int_{\pi/16}^{\pi/8} \operatorname{cosec}^2(4x)\,dx &= \left[-\tfrac{1}{4}\cot(4x)\right]_{\pi/16}^{\pi/8}\\ &= -\tfrac{1}{4}(\cot(\pi/2) - \cot(\pi/4))\\ &= -\tfrac{1}{4}(0-1)\\ &= \tfrac{1}{4}.)\end{aligned}$$

(c) Let $u = 1+e^x$; then $\dfrac{du}{dx} = e^x$.

Putting $x = 0$ gives $u = 1 + e^0 = 2$ and putting $x = \ln 3$ gives

$$u = 1 + e^{\ln 3} = 1 + 3 = 4.$$

So

$$\begin{aligned}\int_0^{\ln 3} \frac{e^x}{1+e^x}\,dx &= \int_0^{\ln 3} \left(\frac{1}{1+e^x}\right)(e^x)\,dx\\ &= \int_2^4 \frac{1}{u}\,du\\ &= \big[\ln|u|\big]_2^4\\ &= \ln 4 - \ln 2\\ &= \ln\tfrac{4}{2}\\ &= \ln 2.\end{aligned}$$

Solution to Activity 6

(a) Integrating by parts gives

$$\begin{aligned}\int xe^{-3x}\,\mathrm{d}x &= x\left(-\tfrac{1}{3}e^{-3x}\right) - \int 1\times\left(-\tfrac{1}{3}e^{-3x}\right)\mathrm{d}x\\ &= -\tfrac{1}{3}xe^{-3x} + \tfrac{1}{3}\int e^{-3x}\,\mathrm{d}x\\ &= -\tfrac{1}{3}xe^{-3x} + \tfrac{1}{3}\left(-\tfrac{1}{3}e^{-3x}\right) + c\\ &= -\tfrac{1}{3}xe^{-3x} - \tfrac{1}{9}e^{-3x} + c\\ &= -\tfrac{1}{9}e^{-3x}(3x+1) + c.\end{aligned}$$

(b) Integrating by parts gives

$$\begin{aligned}\int x^4\ln x\,\mathrm{d}x &= \int(\ln x)x^4\,\mathrm{d}x\\ &= (\ln x)\times\left(\tfrac{1}{5}x^5\right) - \int x^{-1}\times\left(\tfrac{1}{5}x^5\right)\mathrm{d}x\\ &= \tfrac{1}{5}x^5\ln x - \tfrac{1}{5}\int x^4\,\mathrm{d}x\\ &= \tfrac{1}{5}x^5\ln x - \tfrac{1}{5}\left(\tfrac{1}{5}x^5\right) + c\\ &= \tfrac{1}{5}x^5\ln x - \tfrac{1}{25}x^5 + c\\ &= \tfrac{1}{25}x^5(5\ln x - 1) + c.\end{aligned}$$

(c) Integrating by parts gives

$$\begin{aligned}&\int x(x+1)^{1/2}\,\mathrm{d}x\\ &= x\left(\tfrac{2}{3}(x+1)^{3/2}\right) - \int 1\times\left(\tfrac{2}{3}(x+1)^{3/2}\right)\mathrm{d}x\\ &= \tfrac{2}{3}x(x+1)^{3/2} - \tfrac{2}{3}\int(x+1)^{3/2}\,\mathrm{d}x\\ &= \tfrac{2}{3}x(x+1)^{3/2} - \tfrac{2}{3}\left(\tfrac{2}{5}(x+1)^{5/2}\right) + c\\ &= \tfrac{2}{3}x(x+1)^{3/2} - \tfrac{4}{15}(x+1)^{5/2} + c.\end{aligned}$$

Solution to Activity 7

(a)
$$\begin{aligned}\frac{2}{x+2} + \frac{1}{x-1} &= \frac{2(x-1)}{(x+2)(x-1)} + \frac{x+2}{(x+2)(x-1)}\\ &= \frac{2(x-1)+(x+2)}{(x+2)(x-1)}\\ &= \frac{(2x-2)+(x+2)}{(x+2)(x-1)}\\ &= \frac{3x}{(x+2)(x-1)}.\end{aligned}$$

(b)
$$\begin{aligned}&\frac{9}{x+1} + \frac{x+4}{x^2+1}\\ &= \frac{9(x^2+1)}{(x+1)(x^2+1)} + \frac{(x+4)(x+1)}{(x+1)(x^2+1)}\\ &= \frac{9(x^2+1)+(x+4)(x+1)}{(x+1)(x^2+1)}\\ &= \frac{(9x^2+9)+(x^2+5x+4)}{(x+1)(x^2+1)}\\ &= \frac{10x^2+5x+13}{(x+1)(x^2+1)}.\end{aligned}$$

(c)
$$\begin{aligned}&\frac{3}{x} - \frac{1}{x+4} - \frac{1}{(x+4)^2}\\ &= \frac{3(x+4)^2}{x(x+4)^2} - \frac{x(x+4)}{x(x+4)^2} - \frac{x}{x(x+4)^2}\\ &= \frac{3(x+4)^2 - x(x+4) - x}{x(x+4)^2}\\ &= \frac{3(x^2+8x+16) - (x^2+4x) - x}{x(x+4)^2}\\ &= \frac{2x^2+19x+48}{x(x+4)^2}.\end{aligned}$$

Solution to Activity 9

(a) We have

$$\frac{x-3}{(x-1)(x+1)} = \frac{A}{x-1} + \frac{B}{x+1},$$

where A and B are constants. Multiplying both sides by $(x-1)(x+1)$ and collecting terms gives

$$\begin{aligned} x-3 &= A(x+1) + B(x-1) \\ &= (A+B)x + (A-B). \end{aligned}$$

Comparing coefficients of the terms in x and the constant terms gives

$$A + B = 1$$

$$A - B = -3.$$

Adding these equations gives

$$2A = -2, \quad \text{so} \quad A = -1.$$

Substituting $A = -1$ into the first equation $A + B = 1$ then gives

$$B = 1 - A = 1 - (-1) = 2.$$

Hence

$$\begin{aligned} \frac{x-3}{(x-1)(x+1)} &= \frac{-1}{x-1} + \frac{2}{x+1} \\ &= \frac{2}{x+1} - \frac{1}{x-1}. \end{aligned}$$

(Check: when $x = 0$, LHS $= \frac{-3}{(-1)\times 1} = 3$ and RHS $= \frac{2}{1} - \frac{1}{-1} = 3$.)

(b) We have

$$\frac{5}{x(2x+1)} = \frac{A}{x} + \frac{B}{2x+1},$$

where A and B are constants. Multiplying both sides by $x(2x+1)$ and collecting terms gives

$$\begin{aligned} 5 &= A(2x+1) + Bx \\ &= (2A+B)x + A. \end{aligned}$$

Comparing coefficients of the terms in x and the constant terms gives

$$\begin{aligned} 2A + B &= 0 \\ A &= 5. \end{aligned}$$

Substituting $A = 5$ into the first equation $2A + B = 0$ then gives

$$B = -2A = -2 \times 5 = -10.$$

Hence

$$\begin{aligned} \frac{5}{x(2x+1)} &= \frac{5}{x} + \frac{-10}{2x+1} \\ &= \frac{5}{x} - \frac{10}{2x+1}. \end{aligned}$$

(Check: here we cannot use $x = 0$ as a check, because the factor x occurs in the denominator of the expression, so use $x = 1$.
When $x = 1$, LHS $= \frac{5}{(2\times 1)+1} = \frac{5}{3}$
and RHS $= \frac{5}{1} - \frac{10}{(2\times 1)+1} = \frac{5}{3}$.)

Solution to Activity 10

(a) We have

$$\frac{x-2}{(x-1)(x-3)} = \frac{A}{x-1} + \frac{B}{x-3},$$

where A and B are constants. Multiplying both sides by $(x-1)(x-3)$ gives

$$x - 2 = A(x-3) + B(x-1).$$

Choosing $x = 1$ gives

$$\begin{aligned} 1 - 2 &= A \times (1-3) \\ -1 &= -2A, \end{aligned}$$

so $A = \frac{1}{2}$.

Choosing $x = 3$ gives

$$\begin{aligned} 3 - 2 &= B \times (3-1) \\ 1 &= 2B, \end{aligned}$$

so $B = \frac{1}{2}$.

Hence

$$\begin{aligned} \frac{x-2}{(x-1)(x-3)} &= \frac{\frac{1}{2}}{x-1} + \frac{\frac{1}{2}}{x-3} \\ &= \frac{1}{2(x-1)} + \frac{1}{2(x-3)}. \end{aligned}$$

(Check: when $x = 0$, LHS $= \frac{-2}{3} = -\frac{2}{3}$
and RHS $= \frac{1}{-2} + \frac{1}{-6} = -\frac{2}{3}$.)

(b) We have

$$\frac{-7x-11}{(x+2)(x+1)(x-1)} = \frac{A}{x+2} + \frac{B}{x+1} + \frac{C}{x-1},$$

where A, B and C are constants. Multiplying both sides by $(x+2)(x+1)(x-1)$ gives

$$\begin{aligned}-7x-11 &= A(x+1)(x-1)\\ &\quad + B(x+2)(x-1) + C(x+2)(x+1).\end{aligned}$$

Choosing $x=-2$ gives

$$\begin{aligned}-7\times(-2)-11 &= A\times(-2+1)(-2-1)\\ 3 &= A\times(-1)\times(-3)\\ 1 &= A,\end{aligned}$$

so $A=1$.

Choosing $x=-1$ gives

$$\begin{aligned}-7\times(-1)-11 &= B\times(-1+2)(-1-1)\\ -4 &= B\times 1\times(-2)\\ 2 &= B,\end{aligned}$$

so $B=2$.

Choosing $x=1$ gives

$$\begin{aligned}-7\times 1-11 &= C\times(1+2)(1+1)\\ -18 &= C\times 3\times 2\\ -18 &= 6C,\end{aligned}$$

so $C = \dfrac{-18}{6} = -3.$

Hence

$$\frac{-7x-11}{(x+2)(x+1)(x-1)} = \frac{1}{x+2} + \frac{2}{x+1} - \frac{3}{x-1}.$$

(Check: when $x=0$, LHS $= \frac{-11}{-2} = \frac{11}{2}$ and RHS $= \frac{1}{2} + 2 - \frac{3}{-1} = \frac{11}{2}$.)

Solution to Activity 11

(a) We have

$$\frac{x}{(x+1)(3x+2)} = \frac{A}{x+1} + \frac{B}{3x+2},$$

where A and B are constants. Using the cover-up method with $x=-1$ gives

$$A = \frac{-1}{3\times(-1)+2} = \frac{-1}{-1} = 1.$$

Using the cover-up method with $x = -\frac{2}{3}$ gives

$$B = \frac{-\frac{2}{3}}{-\frac{2}{3}+1} = \frac{-\frac{2}{3}}{\frac{1}{3}} = -2.$$

So

$$\frac{x}{(x+1)(3x+2)} = \frac{1}{x+1} - \frac{2}{3x+2}.$$

(Check: when $x=0$, LHS $=0$ and RHS $= 1-1 = 0$.)

(b) We have

$$\frac{1}{2x(x+3)} = \frac{A}{x} + \frac{B}{x+3},$$

where A and B are constants. Using the cover-up method with $x=0$ gives

$$A = \frac{1}{2\times(0+3)} = \frac{1}{6}.$$

Using the cover-up method with $x=-3$ gives

$$B = \frac{1}{2\times(-3)} = -\frac{1}{6}.$$

So

$$\frac{1}{2x(x+3)} = \frac{\frac{1}{6}}{x} + \frac{-\frac{1}{6}}{x+3} = \frac{1}{6x} - \frac{1}{6(x+3)}.$$

(Check: when $x=1$, LHS $= \frac{1}{8}$ and RHS $= \frac{1}{6} - \frac{1}{24} = \frac{1}{8}$.)

(Notice that you cannot use $x=0$ to check this partial fraction expansion because of the linear factor x in the denominator. Instead, you should use an alternative simple value of x, such as $x=1$.)

(c) We have
$$\frac{3x-1}{(x-2)(x+3)(2x+1)} = \frac{A}{x-2} + \frac{B}{x+3} + \frac{C}{2x+1},$$
where A, B and C are constants. Using the cover-up method with $x = 2$ gives
$$A = \frac{3\times 2 - 1}{(2+3)(2\times 2+1)} = \frac{5}{5\times 5} = \frac{5}{25} = \frac{1}{5}.$$
Using the cover-up method with $x = -3$ gives
$$B = \frac{3\times(-3)-1}{(-3-2)(2\times(-3)+1)} = \frac{-10}{(-5)\times(-5)} = \frac{-10}{25} = -\frac{2}{5}.$$
Using the cover-up method with $x = -\frac{1}{2}$ gives
$$C = \frac{3\times\left(-\frac{1}{2}\right)-1}{\left(-\frac{1}{2}-2\right)\left(-\frac{1}{2}+3\right)} = \frac{-\frac{5}{2}}{\left(-\frac{5}{2}\right)\times\left(\frac{5}{2}\right)} = \frac{1}{\frac{5}{2}} = \frac{2}{5}.$$
So
$$\frac{3x-1}{(x-2)(x+3)(2x+1)} = \frac{1}{5(x-2)} - \frac{2}{5(x+3)} + \frac{2}{5(2x+1)}.$$
(Check: when $x = 0$, LHS $= \frac{-1}{-6} = \frac{1}{6}$ and RHS $= \frac{1}{-10} - \frac{2}{15} + \frac{2}{5} = \frac{1}{6}$.)

Solution to Activity 12

(a) We have
$$\frac{x+7}{(x+1)^2} = \frac{A}{x+1} + \frac{B}{(x+1)^2},$$
where A and B are constants. Using the cover-up method with $x = -1$ gives
$$B = \frac{-1+7}{1} = 6.$$
So
$$\frac{x+7}{(x+1)^2} = \frac{A}{x+1} + \frac{6}{(x+1)^2}.$$
Multiplying both sides by $(x+1)^2$ gives
$$x + 7 = A(x+1) + 6.$$
Substituting $x = 0$ gives
$$7 = A + 6, \quad \text{so} \quad A = 7 - 6 = 1.$$
Hence
$$\frac{x+7}{(x+1)^2} = \frac{1}{x+1} + \frac{6}{(x+1)^2}.$$
(Check: We can't use $x = 0$ as a check, since we've already used it to find A, so use $x = 1$. When $x = 1$, LHS $= \frac{8}{4} = 2$ and RHS $= \frac{1}{2} + \frac{6}{4} = 2$.)

(There is an alternative, quicker solution using the method demonstrated on page 31, which is easy to apply to rational expressions with simple denominators such as $(x+1)^2$. This alternative method involves rearranging the numerator, and gives the solution in one line of working:
$$\frac{x+7}{(x+1)^2} = \frac{(x+1)+6}{(x+1)^2} = \frac{1}{x+1} + \frac{6}{(x+1)^2}.)$$

(b) We have
$$\frac{x}{(3x-1)(x-1)^2} = \frac{A}{3x-1} + \frac{B}{x-1} + \frac{C}{(x-1)^2},$$
where A, B and C are constants. Using the cover-up method with $x = \frac{1}{3}$ gives
$$A = \frac{\frac{1}{3}}{\left(\frac{1}{3}-1\right)^2} = \frac{\frac{1}{3}}{\left(-\frac{2}{3}\right)^2} = \frac{\frac{1}{3}}{\frac{4}{9}} = \frac{3}{4}.$$
Using the cover-up method with $x = 1$ gives
$$C = \frac{1}{3\times 1 - 1} = \frac{1}{2}.$$
So
$$\frac{x}{(3x-1)(x-1)^2} = \frac{3}{4(3x-1)} + \frac{B}{x-1} + \frac{1}{2(x-1)^2}.$$
Multiplying both sides by $4(3x-1)(x-1)^2$ gives
$$4x = 3(x-1)^2 + 4B(3x-1)(x-1) + 2(3x-1).$$
Substituting $x = 0$ gives
$$0 = 3\times(-1)^2 + 4B\times(-1)\times(-1) + 2\times(-1)$$
$$0 = 3 + 4B - 2$$
$$-1 = 4B.$$
So $B = -\frac{1}{4}$. Hence
$$\frac{x}{(3x-1)(x-1)^2} = \frac{3}{4(3x-1)} - \frac{1}{4(x-1)} + \frac{1}{2(x-1)^2}.$$
(Check: when $x = 2$, LHS $= \frac{2}{5\times 1^2} = \frac{2}{5}$ and RHS $= \frac{3}{20} - \frac{1}{4} + \frac{1}{2} = \frac{2}{5}$.)

(c) We have

$$\frac{x^2}{(2x-1)^3} = \frac{A}{2x-1} + \frac{B}{(2x-1)^2} + \frac{C}{(2x-1)^3},$$

where A, B and C are constants. Using the cover-up method with $x = \frac{1}{2}$ gives

$$C = \frac{\left(\frac{1}{2}\right)^2}{1} = \frac{1}{4}.$$

So

$$\frac{x^2}{(2x-1)^3} = \frac{A}{2x-1} + \frac{B}{(2x-1)^2} + \frac{1}{4(2x-1)^3}.$$

Multiplying both sides by $(2x-1)^3$ gives

$$\begin{aligned} x^2 &= A(2x-1)^2 + B(2x-1) + \tfrac{1}{4} \\ &= A(4x^2 - 4x + 1) + B(2x-1) + \tfrac{1}{4} \\ &= (4Ax^2 - 4Ax + A) + (2Bx - B) + \tfrac{1}{4} \\ &= 4Ax^2 + (-4A + 2B)x + \left(A - B + \tfrac{1}{4}\right). \end{aligned}$$

Comparing coefficients of x^2 gives

$$1 = 4A, \quad \text{so} \quad A = \tfrac{1}{4}.$$

Comparing coefficients of x gives

$$-4A + 2B = 0, \quad \text{so} \quad B = 2A = \tfrac{1}{2}.$$

So

$$\frac{x^2}{(2x-1)^3} = \frac{1}{4(2x-1)} + \frac{1}{2(2x-1)^2} + \frac{1}{4(2x-1)^3}.$$

(Check: when $x = 0$, LHS $= 0$ and RHS $= -\frac{1}{4} + \frac{1}{2} - \frac{1}{4} = 0$.)

Solution to Activity 13

(a) Since

$$0^2 - 4 \times 1 \times 1 = -4 < 0,$$

the quadratic expression $x^2 + 1$ cannot be factorised. So

$$\frac{1}{(x+1)(x^2+1)} = \frac{A}{x+1} + \frac{Bx+C}{x^2+1},$$

where A, B and C are constants. Using the cover-up method with $x = -1$ gives

$$A = \frac{1}{(-1)^2 + 1} = \frac{1}{2}.$$

So

$$\frac{1}{(x+1)(x^2+1)} = \frac{1}{2(x+1)} + \frac{Bx+C}{x^2+1}.$$

Multiplying both sides by $2(x+1)(x^2+1)$ gives

$$\begin{aligned} 2 &= (x^2+1) + 2(Bx+C)(x+1) \\ &= (x^2+1) + 2(Bx^2 + Bx + Cx + C) \\ &= (x^2+1) + (2Bx^2 + 2Bx + 2Cx + 2C) \\ &= (2B+1)x^2 + (2B+2C)x + (2C+1). \end{aligned}$$

Comparing coefficients of x^2 gives

$$0 = 2B + 1, \quad \text{so} \quad 2B = -1.$$

Hence $B = -\frac{1}{2}$. Comparing constant terms gives

$$2 = 2C + 1, \quad \text{so} \quad 2C = 1.$$

Hence $C = \frac{1}{2}$. So

$$\frac{1}{(x+1)(x^2+1)} = \frac{1}{2(x+1)} + \frac{-x+1}{2(x^2+1)}.$$

(Check: when $x = 0$, LHS $= 1$ and RHS $= \frac{1}{2} + \frac{1}{2} = 1$.)

(b) Since

$$0^2 - 4 \times 2 \times 1 = -8 < 0,$$

the quadratic expression $2x^2 + 1$ cannot be factorised. So

$$\frac{x^2+1}{x(2x^2+1)} = \frac{A}{x} + \frac{Bx+C}{2x^2+1},$$

where A, B and C are constants. Using the cover-up method with $x = 0$ gives

$$A = \frac{1}{1} = 1.$$

So

$$\frac{x^2+1}{x(2x^2+1)} = \frac{1}{x} + \frac{Bx+C}{2x^2+1}.$$

Multiplying both sides by $x(2x^2+1)$ gives

$$\begin{aligned} x^2 + 1 &= (2x^2+1) + (Bx+C)x \\ &= (2x^2+1) + (Bx^2 + Cx) \\ &= (B+2)x^2 + Cx + 1. \end{aligned}$$

Comparing coefficients of x^2 gives

$$1 = B + 2, \quad \text{so} \quad B = -1.$$

Comparing coefficients of x gives $C = 0$. So

$$\frac{x^2+1}{x(2x^2+1)} = \frac{1}{x} - \frac{x}{2x^2+1}.$$

(Check: when $x = 1$, LHS $= \frac{2}{3}$ and RHS $= \frac{1}{1} - \frac{1}{3} = \frac{2}{3}$.)

(Alternatively, you could rearrange the numerator to give the following one line solution:

$$\frac{x^2+1}{x(2x^2+1)} = \frac{(2x^2+1)-x^2}{x(2x^2+1)} = \frac{1}{x} - \frac{x}{2x^2+1}.)$$

(c) Since

$$(-1)^2 - 4\times 3\times 2 = 1 - 24 = -23 < 0,$$

the quadratic expression $3x^2 - x + 2$ cannot be factorised. So

$$\frac{x-2}{(x+1)(3x^2-x+2)} = \frac{A}{x+1} + \frac{Bx+C}{3x^2-x+2},$$

where A, B and C are constants. Using the cover-up method with $x=-1$ gives

$$A = \frac{-1-2}{3\times(-1)^2-(-1)+2} = \frac{-3}{6} = -\frac{1}{2}.$$

So

$$\frac{x-2}{(x+1)(3x^2-x+2)} = -\frac{1}{2(x+1)} + \frac{Bx+C}{3x^2-x+2}.$$

Multiplying both sides by $2(x+1)(3x^2-x+2)$ gives

$$2(x-2) = -(3x^2-x+2) + 2(Bx+C)(x+1).$$

So

$$\begin{aligned}
&2x-4\\
&= -(3x^2-x+2) + 2(Bx^2+Bx+Cx+C)\\
&= (-3x^2+x-2) + (2Bx^2+2Bx+2Cx+2C)\\
&= (2B-3)x^2 + (2B+2C+1)x + (2C-2).
\end{aligned}$$

Comparing coefficients of x^2 gives

$$0 = 2B-3, \quad \text{so} \quad 2B = 3.$$

Hence $B = \frac{3}{2}$. Comparing constant terms gives

$$-4 = 2C-2, \quad \text{so} \quad 2C = -2.$$

Hence $C = -\frac{2}{2} = -1$. So

$$\begin{aligned}
\frac{x-2}{(x+1)(3x^2-x+2)} &= -\frac{1}{2(x+1)} + \frac{\frac{3}{2}x-1}{3x^2-x+2}\\
&= -\frac{1}{2(x+1)} + \frac{3x-2}{2(3x^2-x+2)}.
\end{aligned}$$

(Check: when $x=0$, LHS $= \frac{-2}{2} = -1$ and RHS $= -\frac{1}{2} + \frac{-2}{4} = -1$.)

Solution to Activity 14

(a) We have

$$\begin{aligned}
\frac{x}{(x+5)^2} &= \frac{(x+5)-5}{(x+5)^2}\\
&= \frac{x+5}{(x+5)^2} - \frac{5}{(x+5)^2}\\
&= \frac{1}{x+5} - \frac{5}{(x+5)^2}.
\end{aligned}$$

So

$$\begin{aligned}
\int \frac{x}{(x+5)^2}\,dx &= \int \left(\frac{1}{x+5} - \frac{5}{(x+5)^2}\right) dx\\
&= \int \frac{1}{x+5}\,dx - 5\int \frac{1}{(x+5)^2}\,dx\\
&= \int \frac{1}{x+5}\,dx - 5\int (x+5)^{-2}\,dx\\
&= \ln|x+5| + 5(x+5)^{-1} + c.
\end{aligned}$$

(Alternatively, you could find the partial fraction expansion of the rational expression $\frac{x}{(x+5)^2}$ by writing it in the form $\frac{A}{x+5} + \frac{B}{(x+5)^2}$, and then finding A and B using one of the standard methods that you've learned.)

(b) We have

$$\frac{1}{(x-4)(x-2)} = \frac{A}{x-4} + \frac{B}{x-2},$$

where A and B are constants. Using the cover-up method with $x=4$ gives

$$A = \frac{1}{4-2} = \frac{1}{2}.$$

Using the cover-up method with $x=2$ gives

$$B = \frac{1}{2-4} = -\frac{1}{2}.$$

So

$$\frac{1}{(x-4)(x-2)} = \frac{1}{2(x-4)} - \frac{1}{2(x-2)}.$$

(Check: when $x=0$, LHS $= \frac{1}{8}$ and RHS $= \frac{1}{-8} - \frac{1}{-4} = \frac{1}{8}$.)

So

$$\int \frac{1}{(x-4)(x-2)}\,dx$$
$$= \int \left(\frac{1}{2(x-4)} - \frac{1}{2(x-2)}\right) dx$$
$$= \tfrac{1}{2}\int \frac{1}{x-4}\,dx - \tfrac{1}{2}\int \frac{1}{x-2}\,dx$$
$$= \tfrac{1}{2}\ln|x-4| - \tfrac{1}{2}\ln|x-2| + c$$
$$= \tfrac{1}{2}\ln\left|\frac{x-4}{x-2}\right| + c.$$

(c) We have

$$\frac{1}{x(x-1)(2x-1)} = \frac{A}{x} + \frac{B}{x-1} + \frac{C}{2x-1},$$

where A, B and C are constants. Using the cover-up method with $x = 0$ gives

$$A = \frac{1}{(-1)\times(-1)} = \frac{1}{1} = 1.$$

Using the cover-up method with $x = 1$ gives

$$B = \frac{1}{1\times(2\times 1 - 1)} = \frac{1}{1} = 1.$$

Using the cover-up method with $x = \frac{1}{2}$ gives

$$C = \frac{1}{\frac{1}{2}\times\left(\frac{1}{2}-1\right)} = \frac{1}{\frac{1}{2}\times\left(-\frac{1}{2}\right)} = \frac{1}{-\frac{1}{4}} = -4.$$

So

$$\frac{1}{x(x-1)(2x-1)} = \frac{1}{x} + \frac{1}{x-1} - \frac{4}{2x-1}.$$

(Check: when $x = 2$, LHS $= \frac{1}{6}$ and RHS $= \frac{1}{2} + \frac{1}{1} - \frac{4}{3} = \frac{1}{6}$.)

So

$$\int \frac{1}{x(x-1)(2x-1)}\,dx$$
$$= \int \left(\frac{1}{x} + \frac{1}{x-1} - \frac{4}{2x-1}\right) dx$$
$$= \int \frac{1}{x}\,dx + \int \frac{1}{x-1}\,dx - 4\int \frac{1}{2x-1}\,dx$$
$$= \ln|x| + \ln|x-1| - 4\times\tfrac{1}{2}\ln|2x-1| + c$$
$$= \ln|x| + \ln|x-1| - 2\ln|2x-1| + c$$
$$= \ln|x| + \ln|x-1| - \ln(|2x-1|^2) + c$$
$$= \ln\left|\frac{x(x-1)}{(2x-1)^2}\right| + c.$$

(d) Since

$$0^2 - 4\times 3\times 1 = -12 < 0,$$

the quadratic expression $3x^2 + 1$ cannot be factorised. So

$$\frac{3x-1}{(x+1)(3x^2+1)} = \frac{A}{x+1} + \frac{Bx+C}{3x^2+1},$$

where A, B and C are constants. Using the cover-up method with $x = -1$ gives

$$A = \frac{3\times(-1)-1}{3\times(-1)^2+1} = \frac{-4}{4} = -1.$$

So

$$\frac{3x-1}{(x+1)(3x^2+1)} = -\frac{1}{x+1} + \frac{Bx+C}{3x^2+1}.$$

Multiplying both sides by $(x+1)(3x^2+1)$ gives

$$\begin{aligned}3x-1 &= -(3x^2+1) + (Bx+C)(x+1)\\ &= (-3x^2-1) + (Bx^2+Bx+Cx+C)\\ &= (B-3)x^2 + (B+C)x + (C-1).\end{aligned}$$

Comparing coefficients of x^2 gives

$$0 = B - 3, \quad \text{so} \quad B = 3.$$

Comparing constant terms gives

$$-1 = C - 1, \quad \text{so} \quad C = 0.$$

Hence

$$\frac{3x-1}{(x+1)(3x^2+1)} = -\frac{1}{x+1} + \frac{3x}{3x^2+1}.$$

(Check: when $x = 0$, LHS $= \frac{-1}{1} = -1$ and RHS $= -\frac{1}{1} + 0 = -1$.)

So

$$\int \frac{3x-1}{(x+1)(3x^2+1)}\,dx$$
$$= \int \left(-\frac{1}{x+1} + \frac{3x}{3x^2+1}\right) dx$$
$$= -\int \frac{1}{x+1}\,dx + \int \frac{3x}{3x^2+1}\,dx.$$

The first integral on the right-hand side is

$$-\int \frac{1}{x+1}\,dx = -\ln|x+1| + c.$$

For the second integral on the right-hand side, let $u = 3x^2 + 1$; then $\dfrac{du}{dx} = 6x$. So

$$\begin{aligned}\int \frac{3x}{3x^2+1}\,dx &= \tfrac{1}{2}\int \left(\frac{1}{3x^2+1}\right)(6x)\,dx\\ &= \tfrac{1}{2}\int \frac{1}{u}\,du\\ &= \tfrac{1}{2}\ln|u| + c\\ &= \tfrac{1}{2}\ln|3x^2+1| + c.\end{aligned}$$

Adding these integrals to obtain the solution, and continuing to use the symbol c for the resulting arbitrary constant, we have

$$\begin{aligned}&\int \frac{3x-1}{(x+1)(3x^2+1)}\,dx\\ &= -\ln|x+1| + \tfrac{1}{2}\ln|3x^2+1| + c\\ &= -\tfrac{1}{2}\times 2\ln|x+1| + \tfrac{1}{2}\ln|3x^2+1| + c\\ &= -\tfrac{1}{2}\ln((x+1)^2) + \tfrac{1}{2}\ln(3x^2+1) + c\\ &= \tfrac{1}{2}\ln\left(\frac{3x^2+1}{(x+1)^2}\right) + c.\end{aligned}$$

Solution to Activity 15

(a)

$$\begin{array}{r|l} & \phantom{2x+{}}2 \\ \hline x+2 & 2x+1 \\ & 2x+4 \\ \hline & -3 \end{array}$$

So the quotient is 2 and the remainder is -3.

(Check: $2(x+2) - 3 = (2x+4) - 3 = 2x+1$.)

(b)

$$\begin{array}{r|l} & \phantom{x^2+{}}x+3 \\ \hline x-3 & x^2+0x-3 \\ & x^2-3x \\ \hline & \phantom{x^2+{}}3x-3 \\ & \phantom{x^2+{}}3x-9 \\ \hline & \phantom{x^2+3x-{}}6 \end{array}$$

So the quotient is $x+3$ and the remainder is 6.

(Check:

$(x+3)(x-3) + 6 = (x^2-9) + 6 = x^2 - 3$.)

(c)

$$\begin{array}{r|l} & \phantom{x^2+x+{}}\tfrac{1}{2} \\ \hline 2x^2+x+1 & x^2+x+0 \\ & x^2+\tfrac{1}{2}x+\tfrac{1}{2} \\ \hline & \phantom{x^2+{}}\tfrac{1}{2}x-\tfrac{1}{2} \end{array}$$

So the quotient is $\tfrac{1}{2}$ and the remainder is $\tfrac{1}{2}x - \tfrac{1}{2}$.

(Check:

$$\begin{aligned}&\tfrac{1}{2}(2x^2+x+1) + \left(\tfrac{1}{2}x - \tfrac{1}{2}\right)\\ &= \left(x^2 + \tfrac{1}{2}x + \tfrac{1}{2}\right) + \left(\tfrac{1}{2}x - \tfrac{1}{2}\right)\\ &= x^2 + x.)\end{aligned}$$

(d)

$$\begin{array}{r|l} & \phantom{x^3-x^2+{}}x-1 \\ \hline x^2+0x+1 & x^3-x^2+0x+1 \\ & x^3+0x^2+x \\ \hline & -x^2-x+1 \\ & -x^2+0x-1 \\ \hline & -x+2 \end{array}$$

So the quotient is $x-1$ and the remainder is $-x+2$.

(Check:

$$\begin{aligned}&(x-1)(x^2+1) + (-x+2)\\ &= (x^3 - x^2 + x - 1) + (-x+2)\\ &= x^3 - x^2 + 1.)\end{aligned}$$

(e)

$$\begin{array}{r|l} & \phantom{x^3+{}}x^2+x+1 \\ \hline x-1 & x^3+0x^2+0x+0 \\ & x^3-x^2 \\ \hline & \phantom{x^3+{}}x^2+0x+0 \\ & \phantom{x^3+{}}x^2-x \\ \hline & \phantom{x^3+x^2+{}}x+0 \\ & \phantom{x^3+x^2+{}}x-1 \\ \hline & \phantom{x^3+x^2+x+{}}1 \end{array}$$

So the quotient is x^2+x+1 and the remainder is 1.

(Check:

$(x^2+x+1)(x-1) + 1 = (x^3-1) + 1 = x^3$.)

Solution to Activity 17

(a)

$$\begin{array}{r|l}
 & \phantom{2x^2+0x+{}}2 \\
\hline
x^2+0x-1 & 2x^2+0x+0 \\
 & 2x^2+0x-2 \\
\hline
 & \phantom{2x^2+0x+{}}2
\end{array}$$

So the quotient on dividing $2x^2$ by x^2-1 is 2 and the remainder is 2. Hence

$$\frac{2x^2}{x^2-1} = 2+\frac{2}{x^2-1} = 2+\frac{2}{(x+1)(x-1)}.$$

We have

$$\frac{2}{(x+1)(x-1)} = \frac{A}{x+1}+\frac{B}{x-1}.$$

Using the cover-up method with $x=-1$ gives

$$A = \frac{2}{(-1)-1} = \frac{2}{-2} = -1.$$

Using the cover-up method with $x=1$ gives

$$B = \frac{2}{1+1} = \frac{2}{2} = 1.$$

So

$$\frac{2}{(x+1)(x-1)} = -\frac{1}{x+1}+\frac{1}{x-1}.$$

Hence

$$\frac{2x^2}{x^2-1} = 2-\frac{1}{x+1}+\frac{1}{x-1}.$$

(Check: when $x=0$, LHS $=0$ and RHS $= 2-\frac{1}{1}+\frac{1}{-1} = 0$.)

(b)

$$\begin{array}{r|l}
 & \phantom{3x^2+0x-{}}\tfrac{3}{2} \\
\hline
2x^2+0x+1 & 3x^2+0x-1 \\
 & 3x^2+0x+\tfrac{3}{2} \\
\hline
 & -\tfrac{5}{2}
\end{array}$$

So the quotient on dividing $3x^2-1$ by $2x^2+1$ is $\frac{3}{2}$ and the remainder is $-\frac{5}{2}$.

Hence

$$\frac{3x^2-1}{2x^2+1} = \frac{3}{2}+\frac{-\frac{5}{2}}{2x^2+1} = \frac{3}{2}-\frac{5}{2(2x^2+1)}.$$

This is the required partial fraction expansion because the quadratic expression $2x^2+1$ cannot be factorised (since $0^2-4\times2\times1=-8<0$).

(Check: when $x=0$, LHS $=\frac{-1}{1}=-1$ and RHS $=\frac{3}{2}-\frac{5}{2}=-1$.)

(c)

$$\begin{array}{r|l}
 & \tfrac{1}{2}x^2+\tfrac{1}{4}x+\tfrac{1}{8} \\
\hline
2x-1 & x^3+0x^2+0x+1 \\
 & x^3-\tfrac{1}{2}x^2 \\
\hline
 & \phantom{x^3+{}}\tfrac{1}{2}x^2+0x+1 \\
 & \phantom{x^3+{}}\tfrac{1}{2}x^2-\tfrac{1}{4}x \\
\hline
 & \phantom{x^3+0x^2+{}}\tfrac{1}{4}x+1 \\
 & \phantom{x^3+0x^2+{}}\tfrac{1}{4}x-\tfrac{1}{8} \\
\hline
 & \phantom{x^3+0x^2+0x+{}}\tfrac{9}{8}
\end{array}$$

So the quotient on dividing x^3+1 by $2x-1$ is $\frac{1}{2}x^2+\frac{1}{4}x+\frac{1}{8}$ and the remainder is $\frac{9}{8}$.

Hence

$$\frac{x^3+1}{2x-1} = \frac{x^2}{2}+\frac{x}{4}+\frac{1}{8}+\frac{\frac{9}{8}}{2x-1} = \frac{x^2}{2}+\frac{x}{4}+\frac{1}{8}+\frac{9}{8(2x-1)}.$$

(Check: when $x=0$, LHS $=\frac{1}{-1}=-1$ and RHS $=0+0+\frac{1}{8}+\frac{9}{-8}=-1$.)

(d) We have

$$\frac{x^3}{(x-1)(x+3)} = \frac{x^3}{x^2+2x-3}.$$

$$\begin{array}{r|l}
 & \phantom{x^3+0x^2+{}}x-2 \\
\hline
x^2+2x-3 & x^3+0x^2+0x+0 \\
 & x^3+2x^2-3x \\
\hline
 & -2x^2+3x+0 \\
 & -2x^2-4x+6 \\
\hline
 & \phantom{x^3-2x^2+{}}7x-6
\end{array}$$

So the quotient on dividing x^3 by x^2+2x-3 is $x-2$ and the remainder is $7x-6$. Hence

$$\frac{x^3}{(x-1)(x+3)} = x-2+\frac{7x-6}{(x-1)(x+3)}.$$

We have

$$\frac{7x-6}{(x-1)(x+3)} = \frac{A}{x-1}+\frac{B}{x+3}.$$

Using the cover-up method with $x=1$ gives

$$A = \frac{7\times1-6}{1+3} = \frac{1}{4}.$$

Using the cover-up method with $x = -3$ gives

$$B = \frac{7 \times (-3) - 6}{(-3) - 1} = \frac{-27}{-4} = \frac{27}{4}.$$

So

$$\frac{7x - 6}{(x-1)(x+3)} = \frac{1}{4(x-1)} + \frac{27}{4(x+3)}.$$

Hence

$$\frac{x^3}{(x-1)(x+3)} = x - 2 + \frac{1}{4(x-1)} + \frac{27}{4(x+3)}.$$

(Check: when $x = 0$, LHS $= 0$ and RHS $= -2 + \frac{1}{-4} + \frac{27}{12} = 0$.)

Solution to Activity 18

(a) We have

$$\begin{aligned}\frac{x-1}{x+1} &= \frac{(x+1-1)-1}{x+1} \\ &= \frac{(x+1)-2}{x+1} \\ &= 1 - \frac{2}{x+1}.\end{aligned}$$

So

$$\begin{aligned}\int \frac{x-1}{x+1}\,dx &= \int \left(1 - \frac{2}{x+1}\right) dx \\ &= \int 1\,dx - 2\int \frac{1}{x+1}\,dx \\ &= x - 2\ln|x+1| + c.\end{aligned}$$

(Alternatively, you could find the partial fraction expansion of the improper rational expression

$$\frac{x-1}{x+1}$$

by using polynomial long division.)

(b)

$$\begin{array}{r|l} & \qquad\qquad \tfrac{1}{4} \\ \cline{2-2} 4x^2 + 0x + 1 & x^2 + 0x + 0 \\ & x^2 + 0x + \tfrac{1}{4} \\ \cline{2-2} & \qquad\quad\; -\tfrac{1}{4} \end{array}$$

So the quotient on dividing x^2 by $4x^2 + 1$ is $\frac{1}{4}$ and the remainder is $-\frac{1}{4}$.

Hence

$$\frac{x^2}{4x^2+1} = \frac{1}{4} + \frac{-\frac{1}{4}}{4x^2+1} = \frac{1}{4} - \frac{1}{4(4x^2+1)}.$$

This is the required partial fraction expansion, since the quadratic $4x^2 + 1$ in the denominator cannot be factorised. (Check: when $x = 0$, LHS $= 0$ and RHS $= \frac{1}{4} - \frac{1}{4} = 0$.)

So

$$\begin{aligned}\int \frac{x^2}{4x^2+1}\,dx &= \int \left(\frac{1}{4} - \frac{1}{4(4x^2+1)}\right) dx \\ &= \frac{1}{4}\int 1\,dx - \frac{1}{4}\int \frac{1}{(2x)^2+1}\,dx \\ &= \tfrac{1}{4}x - \tfrac{1}{4} \times \tfrac{1}{2}\tan^{-1}(2x) + c \\ &= \tfrac{1}{4}x - \tfrac{1}{8}\tan^{-1}(2x) + c.\end{aligned}$$

(Alternatively, you could have arrived at the partial fraction expansion by rearranging the numerator, as follows:

$$\begin{aligned}\frac{x^2}{4x^2+1} &= \frac{x^2 + \frac{1}{4} - \frac{1}{4}}{4x^2+1} \\ &= \frac{\frac{1}{4}(4x^2+1) - \frac{1}{4}}{4x^2+1} \\ &= \frac{1}{4} - \frac{1}{4(4x^2+1)}.)\end{aligned}$$

(c) We have

$$\begin{aligned}\frac{x^2}{(x+1)(x+2)} &= \frac{x^2}{x^2+3x+2} \\ &= \frac{x^2+3x+2-(3x+2)}{x^2+3x+2} \\ &= 1 - \frac{3x+2}{x^2+3x+2} \\ &= 1 - \frac{3x+2}{(x+1)(x+2)}.\end{aligned}$$

Now

$$\frac{3x+2}{(x+1)(x+2)} = \frac{A}{x+1} + \frac{B}{x+2},$$

where A and B are constants. Using the cover-up method with $x = -1$ gives

$$A = \frac{3 \times (-1) + 2}{(-1) + 2} = \frac{-1}{1} = -1.$$

Using the cover-up method with $x = -2$ gives

$$B = \frac{3 \times (-2) + 2}{(-2) + 1} = \frac{-4}{-1} = 4.$$

So

$$\frac{3x+2}{(x+1)(x+2)} = -\frac{1}{x+1} + \frac{4}{x+2}.$$

Hence

$$\frac{x^2}{(x+1)(x+2)} = 1 + \frac{1}{x+1} - \frac{4}{x+2}.$$

(Check: when $x = 0$, LHS $= 0$ and RHS $= 1 + \frac{1}{1} - \frac{4}{2} = 0$.)

So

$$\int \frac{x^2}{(x+1)(x+2)}\,dx$$
$$= \int \left(1 + \frac{1}{x+1} - \frac{4}{x+2}\right) dx$$
$$= \int 1\,dx + \int \frac{1}{x+1}\,dx - 4\int \frac{1}{x+2}\,dx$$
$$= x + \ln|x+1| - 4\ln|x+2| + c$$
$$= x + \ln|x+1| - \ln((x+2)^4) + c$$
$$= x + \ln\frac{|x+1|}{(x+2)^4} + c.$$

(Alternatively, you could have written the improper rational expression

$$\frac{x^2}{(x+1)(x+2)}$$

as the sum of a polynomial expression and a proper rational expression by using polynomial long division.)

Solution to Activity 19

(a) The denominator of $f(x)$ is 0 when $x^2 - 4 = 0$; that is, when $x^2 = 4$. So the domain consists of all numbers other than -2 and 2. Hence the domain is $(-\infty, -2) \cup (-2, 2) \cup (2, \infty)$.

(b) The denominator of $f(x)$ is never 0 (it is always positive), so the domain is $\mathbb{R}$.

(c) The denominator of $f(x)$ is 0 when $(x+1)^3 = 0$. This is only satisfied if $x = -1$, so the domain is $(-\infty, -1) \cup (-1, \infty)$.

Solution to Activity 20

(a) The y-intercept is

$$f(0) = \frac{-1}{1} = -1.$$

The x-intercepts are the solutions of $f(x) = 0$. Multiplying both sides of this equation by $2x^3 + 1$ gives

$$x^2 - 1 = 0, \quad \text{or equivalently,} \quad x^2 = 1.$$

So the x-intercepts are -1 and 1.

(b) The y-intercept is

$$f(0) = \frac{0}{1} = 0.$$

The x-intercepts are the solutions of $f(x) = 0$. Multiplying both sides of this equation by $x^2 + 1$ gives $x = 0$. So the only x-intercept is 0.

(c) The y-intercept is

$$f(0) = \frac{5}{1} = 5.$$

The x-intercepts are the solutions of $f(x) = 0$. Multiplying both sides of this equation by $x + 1$ gives

$$x^2 + 5 = 0.$$

This equation has no solutions, so there are no x-intercepts.

Solution to Activity 21

(a) By the quotient rule,

$$f'(x) = \frac{(x+1) \times (2x) - 1 \times (x^2)}{(x+1)^2}$$
$$= \frac{(2x^2 + 2x) - x^2}{(x+1)^2}$$
$$= \frac{x^2 + 2x}{(x+1)^2}$$
$$= \frac{x(x+2)}{(x+1)^2}.$$

Multiplying both sides of the equation $f'(x) = 0$ by $(x+1)^2$ gives

$$x(x+2) = 0.$$

So the stationary points of f are -2 and 0. Since

$$f(-2) = \frac{(-2)^2}{(-2)+1} = \frac{4}{-1} = -4$$

and $f(0) = 0$ the coordinates of the stationary points are $(-2, -4)$ and $(0, 0)$.

(b) For reasons of space, the following table of signs is split into two parts.

x	$(-\infty,-2)$	-2	$(-2,-1)$	-1
x	$-$	$-$	$-$	$-$
$x+2$	$-$	0	$+$	$+$
$(x+1)^2$	$+$	$+$	$+$	0
$f'(x)$	$+$	0	$-$	$*$

x	$(-1,0)$	0	$(0,\infty)$
x	$-$	0	$+$
$x+2$	$+$	$+$	$+$
$(x+1)^2$	$+$	$+$	$+$
$f'(x)$	$-$	0	$+$

Hence f is increasing on the intervals $(-\infty,-2)$ and $(0,\infty)$, and f is decreasing on the intervals $(-2,-1)$ and $(-1,0)$.

(c) Since $f'(x)$ is positive to the left and negative to the right of the stationary point -2, we deduce that -2 is a local maximum of f.

Since $f'(x)$ is negative to the left and positive to the right of the stationary point 0, we deduce that 0 is a local minimum of f.

Solution to Activity 22

(a) Since $f'(x) = -\dfrac{1}{x^2}$ we obtain the following table of signs.

x	$(-\infty,0)$	0	$(0,\infty)$
-1	$-$	$-$	$-$
x^2	$+$	0	$+$
$f'(x)$	$-$	$*$	$-$

Since $f'(x)$ is negative to the left and right of $x=0$, the graph of f looks like Figure 7(c) near $x=0$.

(b) Since $f'(x) = \dfrac{1}{x^2}$ we obtain the following table of signs.

x	$(-\infty,0)$	0	$(0,\infty)$
1	$+$	$+$	$+$
x^2	$+$	0	$+$
$f'(x)$	$+$	$*$	$+$

Since $f'(x)$ is positive to the left and right of $x=0$, the graph of f looks like Figure 7(b) near $x=0$.

(c) Since $f'(x) = -\dfrac{2}{x^3}$ we obtain the following table of signs.

x	$(-\infty,0)$	0	$(0,\infty)$
-2	$-$	$-$	$-$
x^3	$-$	0	$+$
$f'(x)$	$+$	$*$	$-$

Since $f'(x)$ is positive to the left of $x=0$ and negative to the right, the graph of f looks like Figure 7(a) near $x=0$.

(d) Since $f'(x) = \dfrac{2}{x^3}$ we obtain the following table of signs.

x	$(-\infty,0)$	0	$(0,\infty)$
2	$+$	$+$	$+$
x^3	$-$	0	$+$
$f'(x)$	$-$	$*$	$+$

Since $f'(x)$ is negative to the left of $x=0$ and positive to the right, the graph of f looks like Figure 7(d) near $x=0$.

Solution to Activity 23

(a) Since $f(x)$ is a proper rational expression, it follows that $f(x)\to 0$ as $x\to\infty$, and $f(x)\to 0$ as $x\to-\infty$, and the graph of f has a horizontal asymptote with equation $y=0$.

(b) Ignoring all terms other than the dominant terms in the numerator and denominator of $f(x)$ gives

$$g(x) = \frac{4x^2}{2x^2} = 2.$$

Since $f(x)$ has the same asymptotic behaviour as $x\to\infty$ and as $x\to-\infty$ as $g(x)$, we see that $f(x)\to 2$ as $x\to\infty$, and $f(x)\to 2$ as $x\to-\infty$, and the graph of f has a horizontal asymptote with equation $y=2$.

(c)

$$\begin{array}{r|l} & \phantom{4x^3 + 0x^2 + {}} 2x \\ \hline 2x^2+0x+1 & 4x^3 + 0x^2 + 0x - 1 \\ & 4x^3 + 0x^2 + 2x \\ \hline & \phantom{4x^3 + 0x^2 + {}} -2x - 1 \end{array}$$

(Check:

$$\begin{aligned} &2x(2x^2+1)+(-2x-1) \\ &= 4x^3+2x-2x-1 \\ &= 4x^3-1.) \end{aligned}$$

It follows that

$$f(x) = 2x - \frac{2x+1}{2x^2+1}.$$

The proper rational expression tends to 0 as $x \to \infty$ and as $x \to -\infty$. Hence $f(x) \to \infty$ as $x \to \infty$, and $f(x) \to -\infty$ as $x \to -\infty$, and the graph of f has a slant asymptote with equation $y = 2x$.

(d)

$$\begin{array}{r|l} & \phantom{4x^3 + 0x^2 + {}} -2x \\ \hline -2x^2+0x+1 & 4x^3 + 0x^2 + 0x - 1 \\ & 4x^3 + 0x^2 - 2x \\ \hline & \phantom{4x^3 + 0x^2 + {}} 2x - 1 \end{array}$$

(Check:

$$\begin{aligned} &(-2x)(-2x^2+1)+(2x-1) \\ &= 4x^3-2x+2x-1 \\ &= 4x^3-1.) \end{aligned}$$

It follows that

$$f(x) = -2x + \frac{2x-1}{2x^2+1}.$$

The proper rational expression tends to 0 as $x \to \infty$ and as $x \to -\infty$. Hence $f(x) \to -\infty$ as $x \to \infty$, and $f(x) \to \infty$ as $x \to -\infty$, and the graph of f has a slant asymptote with equation $y = -2x$.

Solution to Activity 24

(a) Since

$$f(-x) = \frac{(-x)^2}{(-x)^2+2} = \frac{x^2}{x^2+2} = f(x),$$

f is an even function.

(b) Since

$$f(-x) = \frac{-x}{(-x)^2+2} = -\frac{x}{x^2+2} = -f(x),$$

f is an odd function.

(c) Since $f(1) = 1/9$ and $f(-1) = -1$, f is neither an even function nor an odd function.

Solution to Activity 25

(a) The domain of f is $\mathbb{R}$, and there are no vertical asymptotes.

The y-intercept is $f(0) = 1$.

The equation $f(x) = 0$ is

$$\frac{1}{x^2+1} = 0,$$

which has no solutions. Hence there are no x-intercepts.

Writing $f(x) = (x^2+1)^{-1}$ and applying the chain rule gives

$$f'(x) = -(x^2+1)^{-2}(2x) = \frac{-2x}{(x^2+1)^2}.$$

Multiplying both sides of the equation $f'(x) = 0$ by $(x^2+1)^2$ gives

$$-2x = 0, \quad \text{so} \quad x = 0.$$

Hence the only stationary point of f is at $x = 0$. Since $f(0) = 1$, the coordinates of the stationary point are $(0, 1)$.

The table of signs for $f'(x)$ is as follows.

x	$(-\infty, 0)$	0	$(0, \infty)$
$-2x$	$+$	0	$-$
$(x^2+1)^2$	$+$	$+$	$+$
$f'(x)$	$+$	0	$-$

Hence f is increasing on the interval $(-\infty, 0)$ and decreasing on the interval $(0, \infty)$. The stationary point 0 is therefore a local maximum.

Since $f(x)$ is a proper rational expression, $f(x) \to 0$ as $x \to \infty$, and $f(x) \to 0$ as $x \to -\infty$, and the graph of f has a horizontal asymptote with equation $y = 0$.

Since

$$f(-x) = \frac{1}{(-x)^2+1} = \frac{1}{x^2+1} = f(x),$$

f is an even function.

The graph of f is given below.

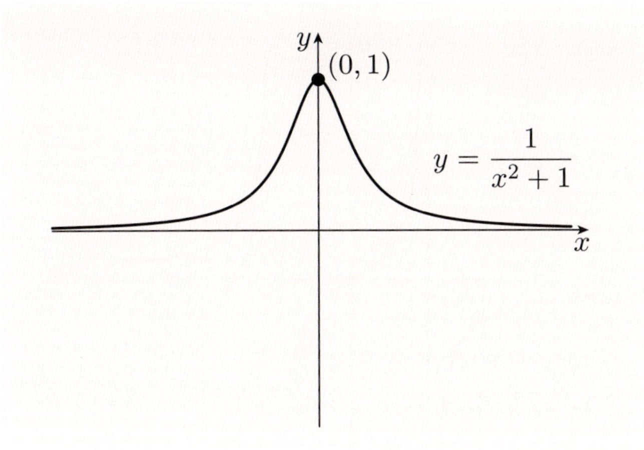

(b) The denominator $x - 2$ of $f(x)$ is 0 only when $x = 2$, so the domain of f is $(-\infty, 2) \cup (2, \infty)$. The line $x = 2$ is a vertical asymptote of the graph of f.

The y-intercept is $f(0) = \frac{5}{2}$.

Multiplying both sides of the equation $f(x) = 0$ by $x - 2$ gives

$$3x - 5 = 0, \quad \text{so} \quad x = \tfrac{5}{3}.$$

Hence the only x-intercept is $\frac{5}{3}$.

By the quotient rule,

$$\begin{aligned} f'(x) &= \frac{(x-2) \times 3 - 1 \times (3x-5)}{(x-2)^2} \\ &= \frac{(3x-6) - (3x-5)}{(x-2)^2} \\ &= \frac{-1}{(x-2)^2}. \end{aligned}$$

Thus the equation $f'(x) = 0$ has no solutions, so there are no stationary points.

The table of signs for $f'(x)$ is as follows.

x	$(-\infty, 2)$	2	$(2, \infty)$
-1	$-$	$-$	$-$
$(x-2)^2$	$+$	0	$+$
$f'(x)$	$-$	$*$	$-$

Thus f is decreasing throughout its domain, and in particular it is decreasing on both sides of the vertical asymptote $x = 2$.

Ignoring all terms other than the dominant terms in the numerator and denominator of $f(x)$ gives

$$g(x) = \frac{3x}{x} = 3.$$

Since $f(x)$ has the same asymptotic behaviour as $x \to \infty$ and as $x \to -\infty$ as $g(x)$, we see that $f(x) \to 3$ as $x \to \infty$, and $f(x) \to 3$ as $x \to -\infty$, and the graph of f has a horizontal asymptote with equation $y = 3$.

Since

$$f(1) = \frac{3 \times 1 - 5}{1 - 2} = \frac{-2}{-1} = 2$$

and

$$f(-1) = \frac{3 \times (-1) - 5}{(-1) - 2} = \frac{-8}{-3} = \frac{8}{3},$$

f is neither an even nor an odd function.

The graph of f is given below.

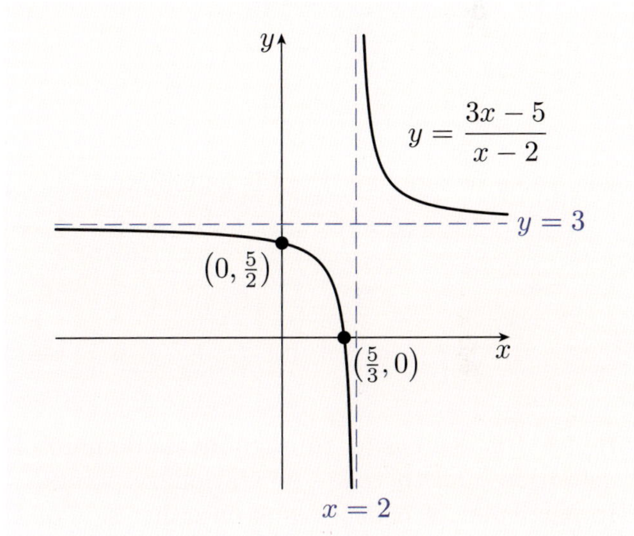

(The graph of this rational function also came up in Unit 1, Activity 5(b). The method suggested there was to write

$$\frac{3x-5}{x-2} = \frac{1}{x-2} + 3,$$

which tells you that the required graph can be obtained by translating the graph of $f(x) = 1/x$ by 2 units to the right and 3 units up. This illustrates the fact that our strategy for sketching the graphs of rational functions may not always lead to the *quickest* way of doing so.)

(c) The denominator $x^2 - 4$ of $f(x)$ is 0 when $x^2 = 4$; that is, when $x = -2$ or $x = 2$. So the domain of f is $(-\infty, -2) \cup (-2, 2) \cup (2, \infty)$, and the lines $x = -2$ and $x = 2$ are vertical asymptotes of the graph of f.

The y-intercept is $f(0) = 0$.

Multiplying both sides of the equation $f(x) = 0$ by $x^2 - 4$ gives

$$3x = 0, \quad \text{so} \quad x = 0.$$

Hence the only x-intercept is 0.

By the quotient rule,

$$\begin{aligned} f'(x) &= \frac{(x^2-4) \times 3 - (2x) \times (3x)}{(x^2-4)^2} \\ &= \frac{(3x^2 - 12) - 6x^2}{(x^2-4)^2} \\ &= \frac{-3x^2 - 12}{(x^2-4)^2} \\ &= \frac{-3(x^2+4)}{(x^2-4)^2}. \end{aligned}$$

The table of signs for $f'(x)$ is as follows.

x	$(-\infty, -2)$	-2	$(-2, 2)$	2	$(2, \infty)$
-3	$-$	$-$	$-$	$-$	$-$
$x^2 + 4$	$+$	$+$	$+$	$+$	$+$
$(x^2 - 4)^2$	$+$	0	$+$	0	$+$
$f'(x)$	$-$	$*$	$-$	$*$	$-$

Hence f is decreasing throughout its domain of definition, and there are no stationary points. In particular, f is decreasing on either side of each of the vertical asymptotes.

Since $f(x)$ is a proper rational expression, $f(x) \to 0$ as $x \to \infty$, and $f(x) \to 0$ as $x \to -\infty$, and the graph of f has a horizontal asymptote with equation $y = 0$.

Since

$$f(-x) = \frac{3(-x)}{(-x)^2 - 4} = -\frac{3x}{x^2-4} = -f(x),$$

f is an odd function.

The graph of f is given below.

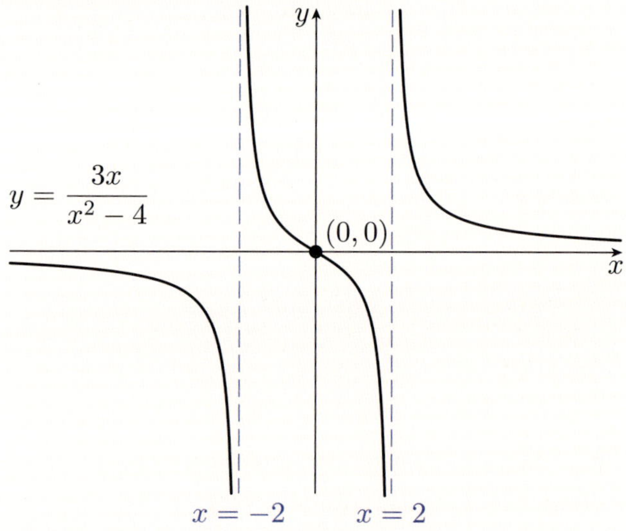

(d) The denominator $x + 1$ of $f(x)$ is 0 only when $x = -1$, so the domain of f is $(-\infty, -1) \cup (-1, \infty)$. The line $x = -1$ is a vertical asymptote of the graph of f.

The y-intercept is $f(0) = 0$.

Multiplying both sides of the equation $f(x) = 0$ by $x + 1$ gives

$$x^2 = 0, \quad \text{so} \quad x = 0.$$

Hence the only x-intercept is 0.

By the quotient rule,

$$\begin{aligned} f'(x) &= \frac{(x+1) \times (2x) - 1 \times (x^2)}{(x+1)^2} \\ &= \frac{(2x^2 + 2x) - x^2}{(x+1)^2} \\ &= \frac{x^2 + 2x}{(x+1)^2} \\ &= \frac{x(x+2)}{(x+1)^2}. \end{aligned}$$

Multiplying both sides of the equation $f'(x) = 0$ by $(x+1)^2$ gives

$$x(x+2) = 0.$$

So the stationary points of f are at $x = -2$ and $x = 0$. Since

$$f(-2) = \frac{(-2)^2}{(-2)+1} = -4$$

and $f(0) = 0$, the coordinates of the stationary points are $(-2, -4)$ and $(0, 0)$.

The table of signs for $f'(x)$, which is split into two parts for reasons of space, is as follows.

x	$(-\infty,-2)$	-2	$(-2,-1)$	-1
x	$-$	$-$	$-$	$-$
$x+2$	$-$	0	$+$	$+$
$(x+1)^2$	$+$	$+$	$+$	0
$f'(x)$	$+$	0	$-$	$*$

x	$(-1,0)$	0	$(0,\infty)$
x	$-$	0	$+$
$x+2$	$+$	$+$	$+$
$(x+1)^2$	$+$	$+$	$+$
$f'(x)$	$-$	0	$+$

Hence f is increasing on the intervals $(-\infty,-2)$ and $(0,\infty)$, and f is decreasing on the intervals $(-2,-1)$ and $(-1,0)$. In particular, f is decreasing on either side of the vertical asymptote $x=-1$.

Since $f'(x)$ is positive to the left and negative to the right of the stationary point -2, it follows that -2 is a local maximum of f.

Since $f'(x)$ is negative to the left and positive to the right of the stationary point 0, it follows that 0 is a local minimum of f.

We can divide the numerator of $f(x)$ by the denominator using polynomial long division, as follows.

$$\begin{array}{r|rr} & x & -1 \\ \hline x+1 & x^2 - 0x & +0 \\ & x^2 + x & \\ \hline & -x & +0 \\ & -x & -1 \\ \hline & & 1 \end{array}$$

(Check: $(x+1)(x-1)+1 = x^2-1+1 = x^2$.)

Hence

$$f(x) = x - 1 + \frac{1}{x+1}.$$

It follows that $f(x)\to\infty$ as $x\to\infty$, and $f(x)\to-\infty$ as $x\to-\infty$, and the graph of f has a slant asymptote with equation $y=x-1$.

Since $f(2)=\frac{4}{3}$ and $f(-2)=-4$, f is neither an even nor an odd function.

The graph of f is given below.

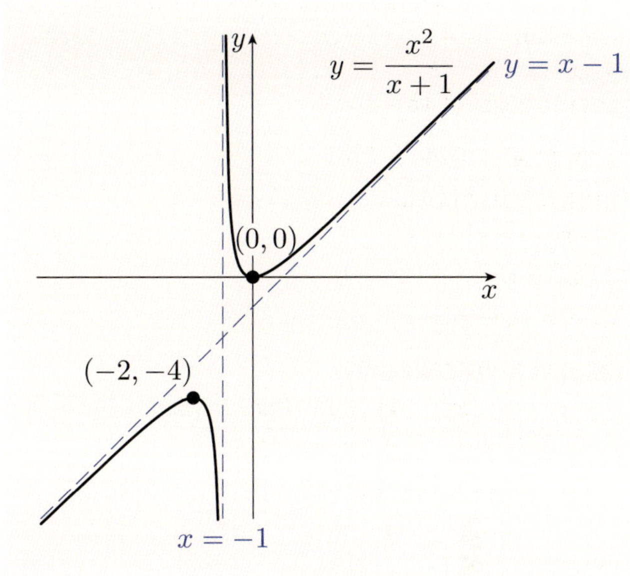

Solution to Activity 26

(a)
$$\begin{aligned}
&\int \sin(6x)\sin(4x)\,dx \\
&= \int \left(\tfrac{1}{2}\cos(6x-4x) - \tfrac{1}{2}\cos(6x+4x)\right) dx \\
&= \tfrac{1}{2}\int (\cos(2x) - \cos(10x))\,dx \\
&= \tfrac{1}{2}\left(\tfrac{1}{2}\sin(2x) - \tfrac{1}{10}\sin(10x)\right) + c \\
&= \tfrac{1}{4}\sin(2x) - \tfrac{1}{20}\sin(10x) + c.
\end{aligned}$$

(b)
$$\begin{aligned}
&\int \cos x\cos(8x)\,dx \\
&= \int \left(\tfrac{1}{2}\cos(x+8x) + \tfrac{1}{2}\cos(x-8x)\right) dx \\
&= \tfrac{1}{2}\int (\cos(9x) + \cos(-7x))\,dx \\
&= \tfrac{1}{2}\int (\cos(9x) + \cos(7x))\,dx \\
&= \tfrac{1}{2}\left(\tfrac{1}{9}\sin(9x) + \tfrac{1}{7}\sin(7x)\right) + c \\
&= \tfrac{1}{18}\sin(9x) + \tfrac{1}{14}\sin(7x) + c.
\end{aligned}$$

(c)
$$\begin{aligned}\int \sin(-3x)\cos(5x)\,\mathrm{d}x &= \int \left(\tfrac{1}{2}\sin(-3x+5x)+\tfrac{1}{2}\sin(-3x-5x)\right)\,\mathrm{d}x\\ &= \tfrac{1}{2}\int (\sin(2x)+\sin(-8x))\,\mathrm{d}x\\ &= \tfrac{1}{2}\int (\sin(2x)-\sin(8x))\,\mathrm{d}x\\ &= \tfrac{1}{2}\left(-\tfrac{1}{2}\cos(2x)-\left(-\tfrac{1}{8}\cos(8x)\right)\right)+c\\ &= -\tfrac{1}{4}\cos(2x)+\tfrac{1}{16}\cos(8x)+c.\end{aligned}$$

Solution to Activity 27

(a)
$$\begin{aligned}\int \cos^3 x\,\mathrm{d}x &= \int \cos^2 x\cos x\,\mathrm{d}x\\ &= \int (1-\sin^2 x)\cos x\,\mathrm{d}x.\end{aligned}$$

Let $u=\sin x$; then $\dfrac{\mathrm{d}u}{\mathrm{d}x}=\cos x$. The integral becomes

$$\begin{aligned}\int (1-u^2)\,\mathrm{d}u &= u-\tfrac{1}{3}u^3+c\\ &= \sin x-\tfrac{1}{3}\sin^3 x+c.\end{aligned}$$

(b)
$$\begin{aligned}\int \sin^5 x\,\mathrm{d}x &= \int (\sin^2 x)^2\sin x\,\mathrm{d}x\\ &= \int (1-\cos^2 x)^2\sin x\,\mathrm{d}x\\ &= -\int (1-\cos^2 x)^2(-\sin x)\,\mathrm{d}x.\end{aligned}$$

Let $u=\cos x$; then $\dfrac{\mathrm{d}u}{\mathrm{d}x}=-\sin x$. The integral becomes

$$\begin{aligned}&-\int (1-u^2)^2\,\mathrm{d}u\\ &= -\int (1-2u^2+u^4)\,\mathrm{d}u\\ &= \int (-1+2u^2-u^4)\,\mathrm{d}u\\ &= -u+\tfrac{2}{3}u^3-\tfrac{1}{5}u^5+c\\ &= -\cos x+\tfrac{2}{3}\cos^3 x-\tfrac{1}{5}\cos^5 x+c.\end{aligned}$$

(c)
$$\begin{aligned}\int \sin^2 x\cos^3 x\,\mathrm{d}x &= \int \sin^2 x\cos^2 x\cos x\,\mathrm{d}x\\ &= \int \sin^2 x(1-\sin^2 x)\cos x\,\mathrm{d}x.\end{aligned}$$

Let $u=\sin x$; then $\dfrac{\mathrm{d}u}{\mathrm{d}x}=\cos x$. The integral becomes

$$\begin{aligned}\int u^2(1-u^2)\,\mathrm{d}u &= \int (u^2-u^4)\,\mathrm{d}u\\ &= \tfrac{1}{3}u^3-\tfrac{1}{5}u^5+c\\ &= \tfrac{1}{3}\sin^3 x-\tfrac{1}{5}\sin^5 x+c.\end{aligned}$$

Solution to Activity 28

(a) By the half-angle identity for cosine,

$$\begin{aligned}\int \cos^2 x\,\mathrm{d}x &= \int \tfrac{1}{2}(1+\cos(2x))\,\mathrm{d}x\\ &= \tfrac{1}{2}\int (1+\cos(2x))\,\mathrm{d}x\\ &= \tfrac{1}{2}\left(x+\tfrac{1}{2}\sin(2x)\right)+c\\ &= \tfrac{1}{2}x+\tfrac{1}{4}\sin(2x)+c.\end{aligned}$$

(b) By the half-angle identity for sine,

$$\begin{aligned}\int \sin^4 x\,\mathrm{d}x &= \int (\sin^2 x)^2\,\mathrm{d}x\\ &= \int \left(\tfrac{1}{2}(1-\cos(2x))\right)^2\,\mathrm{d}x\\ &= \tfrac{1}{4}\int (1-\cos(2x))^2\,\mathrm{d}x\\ &= \tfrac{1}{4}\int (1-2\cos(2x)+\cos^2(2x))\,\mathrm{d}x.\end{aligned}$$

By the half-angle identity for cosine, the integral becomes

$$\begin{aligned}&\tfrac{1}{4}\int \left(1-2\cos(2x)+\tfrac{1}{2}(1+\cos(4x))\right)\,\mathrm{d}x\\ &= \tfrac{1}{8}\int (2-4\cos(2x)+1+\cos(4x))\,\mathrm{d}x\\ &= \tfrac{1}{8}\int (3-4\cos(2x)+\cos(4x))\,\mathrm{d}x\\ &= \tfrac{1}{8}(3x-4\times\tfrac{1}{2}\sin(2x)+\tfrac{1}{4}\sin(4x))+c\\ &= \tfrac{3}{8}x-\tfrac{1}{4}\sin(2x)+\tfrac{1}{32}\sin(4x)+c.\end{aligned}$$

(c) By the identity $\sin x \cos x = \frac{1}{2}\sin(2x)$,

$$\begin{aligned}\int \sin^2 x \cos^2 x \, dx &= \int (\sin x \cos x)^2 \, dx \\ &= \int \left(\tfrac{1}{2}\sin(2x)\right)^2 \, dx \\ &= \int \tfrac{1}{4}\sin^2(2x)\, dx \\ &= \tfrac{1}{4}\int \sin^2(2x)\, dx.\end{aligned}$$

By the half-angle identity for sine, the integral becomes

$$\begin{aligned}\tfrac{1}{4}\int \tfrac{1}{2}(1-\cos(4x))\, dx &= \tfrac{1}{8}\int (1-\cos(4x))\, dx \\ &= \tfrac{1}{8}\left(x - \tfrac{1}{4}\sin(4x)\right) + c \\ &= \tfrac{1}{8}x - \tfrac{1}{32}\sin(4x) + c.\end{aligned}$$

(Here is an alternative solution using the half-angle identities for both sine and cosine.

By the half-angle identities for sine and cosine,

$$\begin{aligned}&\int \sin^2 x \cos^2 x \, dx \\ &= \int \tfrac{1}{2}(1-\cos(2x)) \times \tfrac{1}{2}(1+\cos(2x))\, dx \\ &= \int \tfrac{1}{4}(1-\cos^2(2x))\, dx \\ &= \tfrac{1}{4}\int (1-\cos^2(2x))\, dx.\end{aligned}$$

By the half-angle identity for cosine, the integral becomes

$$\begin{aligned}&\tfrac{1}{4}\int \left(1 - \tfrac{1}{2}(1+\cos(4x))\right)\, dx \\ &= \tfrac{1}{8}\int (2-(1+\cos(4x)))\, dx \\ &= \tfrac{1}{8}\int (1-\cos(4x))\, dx \\ &= \tfrac{1}{8}\left(x - \tfrac{1}{4}\sin(4x)\right) + c \\ &= \tfrac{1}{8}x - \tfrac{1}{32}\sin(4x) + c.)\end{aligned}$$

Solution to Activity 29

The area is given by

$$\begin{aligned}&\int_{-\pi/4}^{\pi/4} \cos^2 x\, dx - \int_{-\pi/4}^{\pi/4} \sin^2 x\, dx \\ &= \int_{-\pi/4}^{\pi/4} (\cos^2 x - \sin^2 x)\, dx.\end{aligned}$$

By the identity $\cos(2x) = \cos^2 x - \sin^2 x$ from the *Handbook*, this is equal to

$$\begin{aligned}&\int_{-\pi/4}^{\pi/4} \cos(2x)\, dx \\ &= \left[\tfrac{1}{2}\sin(2x)\right]_{-\pi/4}^{\pi/4} \\ &= \tfrac{1}{2}(\sin(\pi/2) - \sin(-\pi/2)) \\ &= \tfrac{1}{2}(1-(-1)) \\ &= 1.\end{aligned}$$

(Alternatively, you could evaluate the integrals of $\cos^2 x$ and $\sin^2 x$ separately using the half-angle identities).

Solution to Activity 30

(a)
$$\begin{aligned}\int \tan x\, dx &= \int \frac{\sin x}{\cos x}\, dx \\ &= -\int \left(\frac{1}{\cos x}\right)(-\sin x)\, dx.\end{aligned}$$

Let $u = \cos x$; then $\dfrac{du}{dx} = -\sin x$. The integral becomes

$$\begin{aligned}-\int \frac{1}{u}\, du &= -\ln|u| + c \\ &= -\ln|\cos x| + c.\end{aligned}$$

(b)
$$\begin{aligned}\int \frac{\cot x}{\operatorname{cosec} x \sec x}\, dx &= \int \frac{\cos x/\sin x}{(1/\sin x)\times(1/\cos x)}\, dx \\ &= \int \cos^2 x\, dx.\end{aligned}$$

By the half-angle identity for cosine, the integral becomes

$$\begin{aligned}\int \tfrac{1}{2}(1+\cos(2x))\, dx &= \tfrac{1}{2}\int (1+\cos(2x))\, dx \\ &= \tfrac{1}{2}\left(x + \tfrac{1}{2}\sin(2x)\right) + c \\ &= \tfrac{1}{2}x + \tfrac{1}{4}\sin(2x) + c.\end{aligned}$$

(c) By the identity $\cot^2 x = \operatorname{cosec}^2 x - 1$,

$$\begin{aligned}\int \cot^2 x\, dx &= \int (\operatorname{cosec}^2 x - 1)\, dx \\ &= -\cot x - x + c.\end{aligned}$$

Solution to Activity 31

(a) Let $x = \sin u$; then $\dfrac{dx}{du} = \cos u$.

Also, $u = \sin^{-1} x$. So

$$\begin{aligned}\int \frac{x^2}{\sqrt{1-x^2}}\,dx &= \int \frac{\sin^2 u}{\sqrt{1-\sin^2 u}}(\cos u)\,du\\ &= \int \frac{\sin^2 u}{\sqrt{\cos^2 u}}(\cos u)\,du\\ &= \int \sin^2 u\,du.\end{aligned}$$

By the half-angle identity for sine, the integral becomes

$$\begin{aligned}&\int \tfrac{1}{2}(1-\cos(2u))\,du\\ &= \tfrac{1}{2}\int (1-\cos(2u))\,du\\ &= \tfrac{1}{2}\left(u - \tfrac{1}{2}\sin(2u)\right) + c\\ &= \tfrac{1}{2}u - \tfrac{1}{4}\sin(2u) + c\\ &= \tfrac{1}{2}\sin^{-1} x - \tfrac{1}{4}\sin(2\sin^{-1} x) + c.\end{aligned}$$

(b) Let $x = 4\sec u$; then $\dfrac{dx}{du} = 4\sec u \tan u$.

Also, $u = \sec^{-1}(x/4)$. So

$$\begin{aligned}&\int \frac{\sqrt{x^2-16}}{x}\,dx\\ &= \int \frac{\sqrt{(4\sec u)^2 - 16}}{4\sec u}(4\sec u\tan u)\,du\\ &= \int \sqrt{4^2\sec^2 u - 4^2}\,(\tan u)\,du\\ &= 4\int \sqrt{\sec^2 u - 1}\,(\tan u)\,du\\ &= 4\int \sqrt{\tan^2 u}\,(\tan u)\,du\\ &= 4\int \tan^2 u\,du.\end{aligned}$$

By the identity $\tan^2 u = \sec^2 u - 1$, the integral becomes

$$\begin{aligned}4\int (\sec^2 u - 1)\,du &= 4(\tan u - u) + c\\ &= 4\tan(\sec^{-1}(x/4))\\ &\quad - 4\sec^{-1}(x/4) + c.\end{aligned}$$

(c) Let $x = \tan u$; then $\dfrac{dx}{du} = \sec^2 u$.

Also, $u = \tan^{-1} x$. So

$$\begin{aligned}\int \frac{1}{(1+x^2)^2}\,dx &= \int \frac{1}{(1+\tan^2 u)^2}(\sec^2 u)\,du\\ &= \int \frac{1}{(\sec^2 u)^2}(\sec^2 u)\,du\\ &= \int \frac{1}{\sec^2 u}\,du\\ &= \int \cos^2 u\,du.\end{aligned}$$

By the half-angle identity for cosine, the integral becomes

$$\begin{aligned}\tfrac{1}{2}\int (1+\cos(2u))\,du &= \tfrac{1}{2}\left(u + \tfrac{1}{2}\sin(2u)\right) + c\\ &= \tfrac{1}{2}u + \tfrac{1}{4}\sin(2u) + c\\ &= \tfrac{1}{2}\tan^{-1} x\\ &\quad + \tfrac{1}{4}\sin(2\tan^{-1} x) + c.\end{aligned}$$

Solution to Activity 32

(a) Let $x = \sin u$; then $\dfrac{dx}{du} = \cos u$.

Also, $u = \sin^{-1} x$. So

$$\begin{aligned}\int \frac{1}{\sqrt{1-x^2}}\,dx &= \int \frac{1}{\sqrt{1-\sin^2 u}}\cos u\,du\\ &= \int \frac{1}{\sqrt{\cos^2 u}}\cos u\,du\\ &= \int 1\,du\\ &= u + c\\ &= \sin^{-1} x + c.\end{aligned}$$

(b) Let $x = \tan u$; then $\dfrac{dx}{du} = \sec^2 u$.

Also, $u = \tan^{-1} x$. So

$$\begin{aligned}\int \frac{1}{1+x^2}\,dx &= \int \frac{1}{1+\tan^2 u}\sec^2 u\,du\\ &= \int \frac{1}{\sec^2 u}\sec^2 u\,du\\ &= \int 1\,du\\ &= u + c\\ &= \tan^{-1} x + c.\end{aligned}$$

Solution to Activity 33

(a) Let $x = \frac{1}{2}\sin u$; then $\dfrac{dx}{du} = \frac{1}{2}\cos u$.

Also, $u = \sin^{-1}(2x)$. So

$$\begin{aligned}
&\int \frac{1}{x^2\sqrt{1-4x^2}}\,dx \\
&= \int \frac{1}{\left(\frac{1}{2}\sin u\right)^2\sqrt{1-4\left(\frac{1}{2}\sin u\right)^2}}\left(\tfrac{1}{2}\cos u\right)du \\
&= \frac{\frac{1}{2}}{\left(\frac{1}{2}\right)^2}\int \frac{\cos u}{(\sin^2 u)\sqrt{1-\sin^2 u}}\,du \\
&= 2\int \frac{\cos u}{(\sin^2 u)\sqrt{1-\sin^2 u}}\,du \\
&= 2\int \frac{\cos u}{(\sin^2 u)\sqrt{\cos^2 u}}\,du \\
&= 2\int \frac{1}{\sin^2 u}\,du \\
&= 2\int \operatorname{cosec}^2 u\,du \\
&= -2\cot u + c \\
&= -2\cot(\sin^{-1}(2x)) + c.
\end{aligned}$$

(b) Let $x = -1 + \sec u$, so that $x + 1 = \sec u$.

Then $\dfrac{dx}{du} = \sec u \tan u$. Also, $u = \sec^{-1}(x+1)$.

Hence

$$\begin{aligned}
&\int \frac{1}{(x+1)\sqrt{(x+1)^2-1}}\,dx \\
&= \int \frac{1}{(\sec u)\sqrt{\sec^2 u - 1}}(\sec u \tan u)\,du \\
&= \int \frac{\tan u}{\sqrt{\sec^2 u - 1}}\,du \\
&= \int \frac{\tan u}{\sqrt{\tan^2 u}}\,du \\
&= \int 1\,du \\
&= u + c \\
&= \sec^{-1}(x+1) + c.
\end{aligned}$$

(c) We have

$$10 + 6x + x^2 = 10 + (x+3)^2 - 9 = 1 + (x+3)^2.$$

Let $x = -3 + \tan u$, so that $x + 3 = \tan u$.

Then $\dfrac{dx}{du} = \sec^2 u$. Also, $u = \tan^{-1}(x+3)$. So

$$\begin{aligned}
&\int \frac{1}{10+6x+x^2}\,dx \\
&= \int \frac{1}{1+(x+3)^2}\,dx \\
&= \int \frac{1}{1+\tan^2 u}(\sec^2 u)\,du \\
&= \int \frac{\sec^2 u}{\sec^2 u}\,du \\
&= \int 1\,du \\
&= u + c \\
&= \tan^{-1}(x+3) + c.
\end{aligned}$$

(Here is an alternative solution. You've seen that the integral is equal to

$$\int \frac{1}{1+(x+3)^2}\,dx.$$

The integrand is now of the form f(linear expression), where $f(x) = 1/(1+x^2)$ and the linear expression is $x+3$. The integral of $f(x)$ is given in the standard table of indefinite integrals. By the linear expression rule for indefinite integrals you obtain

$$\int \frac{1}{1+(x+3)^2}\,dx = \tan^{-1}(x+3) + c.)$$

Solution to Activity 34

Let $x = r\sin u$; then $\dfrac{dx}{du} = r\cos u$.

Also, $u = \sin^{-1}(x/r)$.

Putting $x = 0$ into $u = \sin^{-1}(x/r)$ gives $u = 0$.

Putting $x = r$ into $u = \sin^{-1}(x/r)$ gives $u = \pi/2$.

So

$$\begin{aligned}\int_0^r \sqrt{r^2 - x^2}\,dx &= \int_0^{\pi/2} \sqrt{r^2 - (r\sin u)^2}\,(r\cos u)\,du \\ &= \int_0^{\pi/2} r^2(\cos u)\sqrt{1-\sin^2 u}\,du \\ &= r^2\int_0^{\pi/2} \cos^2 u\,du,\end{aligned}$$

and by the half-angle identity for cosine, we have

$$\begin{aligned}r^2\int_0^{\pi/2}\cos^2 u\,du &= r^2\int_0^{\pi/2}\frac{1}{2}(1+\cos(2u))\,du \\ &= \frac{1}{2}r^2\int_0^{\pi/2}(1+\cos(2u))\,du \\ &= \frac{1}{2}r^2\left[u + \frac{1}{2}\sin(2u)\right]_0^{\pi/2} \\ &= \frac{1}{2}r^2\left(\left(\frac{\pi}{2} + \frac{1}{2}\sin\pi\right) - \left(0 + \frac{1}{2}\sin 0\right)\right) \\ &= \frac{\pi r^2}{4}.\end{aligned}$$

Therefore the area of the full circle is

$$4 \times \frac{\pi r^2}{4} = \pi r^2.$$

Solution to Activity 35

(a) $\sinh 0 = \frac{1}{2}(e^0 - e^{-0}) = \frac{1}{2}(1-1) = 0$.

(b) $\cosh 0 = \frac{1}{2}(e^0 + e^{-0}) = \frac{1}{2}(1+1) = 1$.

(c) $\sinh(10) = 11\,013.232\,87$ (to 5 d.p.).

(d) $\cosh(10) = 11\,013.232\,92$ (to 5 d.p.).

(e) $\sinh(-10) = -11\,013.232\,87$ (to 5 d.p.).

(f) $\cosh(-10) = 11\,013.232\,92$ (to 5 d.p.).

Solution to Activity 36

(a) If $x > 0$, then $e^x > 1 > e^{-x}$, because e^x is an increasing function. It follows that $e^x - e^{-x} > 0$. Hence

$$\sinh x = \tfrac{1}{2}(e^x - e^{-x}) > 0.$$

Similarly, if $x < 0$, then $e^x < 1 < e^{-x}$, so $e^x - e^{-x} < 0$. Hence

$$\sinh x = \tfrac{1}{2}(e^x - e^{-x}) < 0.$$

(b) Since e^x and e^{-x} are both positive for all values of x, it follows that

$$\cosh x = \tfrac{1}{2}(e^x + e^{-x}) > 0.$$

(In fact, $\cosh x \geq 1$ for all values of x. The best way to see this is to use the identity $\cosh^2 x = 1 + \sinh^2 x$, which you'll learn later. Since $\sinh^2 x \geq 0$, this identity shows that $\cosh^2 x \geq 1$. Taking square roots then gives $\cosh x \geq 1$.)

Solution to Activity 37

(a)

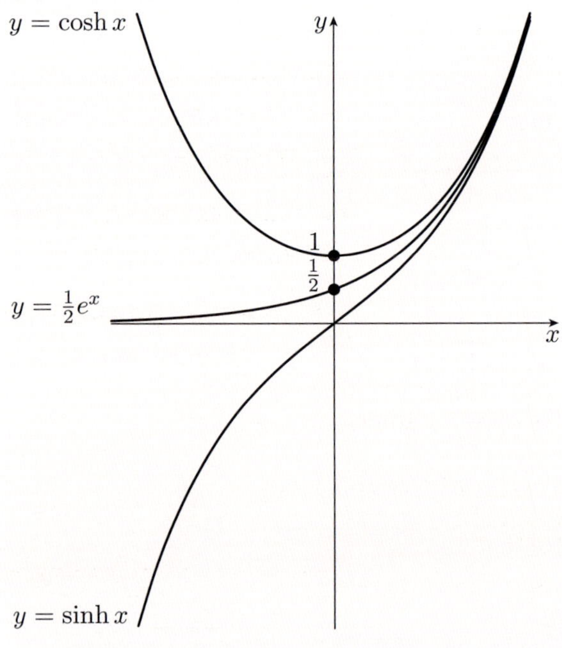

(Details of how to use the CAS to plot the graphs of $\sinh x$ and $\cosh x$ are given in the *Computer algebra guide*, in the section 'Computer methods for the CAS Activities in Books A–D'.)

(b) When x is positive and of large magnitude, the expression e^{-x} is close to 0, and e^x is positive with large magnitude. So $\sinh x$ and $\cosh x$ are both positive with large magnitude, and both close in value to $\frac{1}{2}e^x$.

(c) When x is negative and of large magnitude, the expression e^x is close to 0, and e^{-x} is positive with large magnitude. So $\sinh x$ is negative with large magnitude, and is close in value to $-\frac{1}{2}e^{-x}$, whereas $\cosh x$ is positive with large magnitude, and is close in value to $\frac{1}{2}e^{-x}$.

Solution to Activity 38

$$\begin{aligned}\tanh x &= \frac{e^x - e^{-x}}{e^x + e^{-x}} \\ &= \frac{e^x}{e^x} \times \frac{e^x - e^{-x}}{e^x + e^{-x}} \\ &= \frac{e^{2x} - 1}{e^{2x} + 1}.\end{aligned}$$

Solution to Activity 39

(a) $\tanh 0 = \dfrac{\sinh 0}{\cosh 0} = \dfrac{0}{1} = 0.$

(b) If $x > 0$, then $\sinh x$ and $\cosh x$ are both positive, so
$$\tanh x = \frac{\sinh x}{\cosh x}$$
is also positive.

If $x < 0$, then $\sinh x$ is negative, but $\cosh x$ is positive, so $\tanh x$ is negative.

(c) Since
$$\tanh(-x) = \frac{\sinh(-x)}{\cosh(-x)} = \frac{-\sinh x}{\cosh x} = -\tanh x,$$
tanh is an odd function.

Solution to Activity 40

(a) Since $\sinh 0 = 0$, $\sinh^{-1} 0 = 0$.

(b) The domain of $\cosh^{-1}$ is $[1, \infty)$, so $\cosh^{-1} 0$ is not defined.

(c) Since $\tanh 0 = 0$, $\tanh^{-1} 0 = 0$.

(d) $\sinh^{-1} 1 = 0.881\,37$ (to 5 d.p.).

(e) Since $\cosh 0 = 1$, $\cosh^{-1} 1 = 0$.

(f) The domain of $\tanh^{-1}$ is $(-1, 1)$, so $\tanh^{-1} 1$ is not defined.

Solution to Activity 41

$$\begin{aligned}&\cosh^2 x + \sinh^2 x \\ &= \left(\tfrac{1}{2}(e^x + e^{-x})\right)^2 + \left(\tfrac{1}{2}(e^x - e^{-x})\right)^2 \\ &= \tfrac{1}{4}(e^{2x} + 2e^x e^{-x} + e^{-2x}) \\ &\quad + \tfrac{1}{4}(e^{2x} - 2e^x e^{-x} + e^{-2x}) \\ &= \tfrac{1}{4}(2e^{2x} + 2e^{-2x}) \\ &= \tfrac{1}{2}(e^{2x} + e^{-2x}) \\ &= \cosh(2x).\end{aligned}$$

So $\cosh(2x) = \cosh^2 x + \sinh^2 x$.

Solution to Activity 42

Suppose that $\cosh(2x) = 3$. Then, by the half-variable identities,
$$\sinh^2 x = \tfrac{1}{2}(\cosh(2x) - 1) = \tfrac{1}{2}(3 - 1) = 1,$$
so $\sinh x = \pm 1$. Also,
$$\cosh^2 x = \tfrac{1}{2}(\cosh(2x) + 1) = \tfrac{1}{2}(3 + 1) = 2,$$
so $\cosh x = \sqrt{2}$ (because cosh only takes positive values).

Solution to Activity 43

(a) By the quotient rule,
$$\begin{aligned}\frac{d}{dx}(\tanh x) &= \frac{d}{dx}\left(\frac{\sinh x}{\cosh x}\right) \\ &= \frac{(\cosh x)(\cosh x) - (\sinh x)(\sinh x)}{(\cosh x)^2} \\ &= \frac{\cosh^2 x - \sinh^2 x}{\cosh^2 x} \\ &= \frac{1}{\cosh^2 x},\end{aligned}$$
since $\cosh^2 x - \sinh^2 x = 1$.

(Since $\dfrac{1}{\cosh x}$ is sometimes written as $\operatorname{sech} x$, you could write $\dfrac{d}{dx}(\tanh x) = \operatorname{sech}^2 x$.)

(b) Let $u = \cosh x$; then $\dfrac{du}{dx} = \sinh x$. So
$$\begin{aligned}\int \tanh x \, dx &= \int \frac{\sinh x}{\cosh x} \, dx \\ &= \int \frac{1}{u} \, du \\ &= \ln|u| + c \\ &= \ln|\cosh x| + c \\ &= \ln(\cosh x) + c,\end{aligned}$$
since $\cosh x$ is positive.

Solution to Activity 44

(a) The derivative

$$\frac{\mathrm{d}}{\mathrm{d}x}(\sinh x)$$

is positive for all values of x because it equals $\cosh x$, which is always positive.

The derivative

$$\frac{\mathrm{d}}{\mathrm{d}x}(\tanh x)$$

is positive for all values of x because it equals $1/\cosh^2 x$, which is always positive.

(b) The derivative

$$\frac{\mathrm{d}}{\mathrm{d}x}(\cosh x)$$

is equal to $\sinh x$, so it is positive if x is positive and negative if x is negative.

Solution to Activity 45

(a) By the half-variable identity for cosh,

$$\begin{aligned}\int \cosh^2 x\,\mathrm{d}x &= \int \tfrac{1}{2}(\cosh(2x)+1)\,\mathrm{d}x\\ &= \tfrac{1}{2}\int (\cosh(2x)+1)\,\mathrm{d}x\\ &= \tfrac{1}{2}\left(\tfrac{1}{2}\sinh(2x)+x\right)+c\\ &= \tfrac{1}{4}\sinh(2x)+\tfrac{1}{2}x+c.\end{aligned}$$

(b) By the linear expression rule for indefinite integrals,

$$\int \sinh(4x-7)\,\mathrm{d}x = \tfrac{1}{4}\cosh(4x-7)+c.$$

(c) Let $u=\cosh x$; then $\dfrac{\mathrm{d}u}{\mathrm{d}x}=\sinh x$. So

$$\begin{aligned}\int \sinh x\cosh^2 x\,\mathrm{d}x &= \int \cosh^2 x(\sinh x)\,\mathrm{d}x\\ &= \int u^2\,\mathrm{d}u\\ &= \tfrac{1}{3}u^3+c\\ &= \tfrac{1}{3}\cosh^3 x+c.\end{aligned}$$

Solution to Activity 46

(a) Let $x=2\sinh u$; then $\dfrac{\mathrm{d}x}{\mathrm{d}u}=2\cosh u$.
Also, $u=\sinh^{-1}(x/2)$. So

$$\begin{aligned}\int \frac{1}{\sqrt{4+x^2}}\,\mathrm{d}x &= \int \frac{1}{\sqrt{4+(2\sinh u)^2}}(2\cosh u)\,\mathrm{d}u\\ &= 2\int \frac{\cosh u}{\sqrt{2^2+2^2\sinh^2 u}}\,\mathrm{d}u\\ &= \int \frac{\cosh u}{\sqrt{1+\sinh^2 u}}\,\mathrm{d}u\\ &= \int \frac{\cosh u}{\sqrt{\cosh^2 u}}\,\mathrm{d}u\\ &= \int 1\,\mathrm{d}u\\ &= u+c\\ &= \sinh^{-1}(x/2)+c.\end{aligned}$$

(b) Let $x=\cosh u$; then $\dfrac{\mathrm{d}x}{\mathrm{d}u}=\sinh u$.
Also, $u=\cosh^{-1}x$. So

$$\begin{aligned}\int \sqrt{x^2-1}\,\mathrm{d}x &= \int \sqrt{\cosh^2 u-1}\,(\sinh u)\,\mathrm{d}u\\ &= \int \sqrt{\sinh^2 u}\,(\sinh u)\,\mathrm{d}u\\ &= \int \sinh^2 u\,\mathrm{d}u.\end{aligned}$$

Using the half-variable identity for sinh, the integral becomes

$$\begin{aligned}\int \tfrac{1}{2}(\cosh(2u)-1)\,\mathrm{d}u &= \tfrac{1}{2}\int (\cosh(2u)-1)\,\mathrm{d}u\\ &= \tfrac{1}{2}\left(\tfrac{1}{2}\sinh(2u)-u\right)+c\\ &= \tfrac{1}{4}\sinh(2u)-\tfrac{1}{2}u+c\\ &= \tfrac{1}{4}\sinh(2\cosh^{-1}x)\\ &\quad -\tfrac{1}{2}\cosh^{-1}x+c.\end{aligned}$$

(c) Let $x = \sqrt{2}\cosh u$; then $\dfrac{dx}{du} = \sqrt{2}\sinh u$.

Also, $u = \sinh^{-1}(x/\sqrt{2})$. So

$$\begin{aligned}
&\int \frac{x^2}{\sqrt{x^2-2}}\,dx \\
&= \int \frac{(\sqrt{2}\cosh u)^2}{\sqrt{(\sqrt{2}\cosh u)^2 - 2}}(\sqrt{2}\sinh u)\,du \\
&= 2\sqrt{2}\int \frac{\cosh^2 u}{\sqrt{2\cosh^2 u - 2}}(\sinh u)\,du \\
&= 2\int \frac{\cosh^2 u}{\sqrt{\cosh^2 u - 1}}(\sinh u)\,du \\
&= 2\int \frac{\cosh^2 u}{\sqrt{\sinh^2 u}}(\sinh u)\,du \\
&= 2\int \cosh^2 u\,du.
\end{aligned}$$

Using the half-variable identity for cosh, the integral becomes

$$\begin{aligned}
2\int \tfrac{1}{2}(\cosh(2u)+1)\,du &= \int (\cosh(2u)+1)\,du \\
&= \tfrac{1}{2}\sinh(2u) + u + c \\
&= \tfrac{1}{2}\sinh(2\sinh^{-1}(x/\sqrt{2})) \\
&\quad + \sinh^{-1}(x/\sqrt{2}) + c.
\end{aligned}$$

Solution to Activity 47

Each of the solutions to this activity is preceded by a comment explaining how the method of integration was chosen.

(a) You could expand the brackets, but there is no need as the integrand is a standard function of the linear expression $2x+1$.

$$\begin{aligned}
\int (2x+1)^3\,dx &= \tfrac{1}{2}\times\tfrac{1}{4}(2x+1)^4 + c \\
&= \tfrac{1}{8}(2x+1)^4 + c.
\end{aligned}$$

(b) Since the derivative of $\sin x$ is $\cos x$, the integrand is of the form

sin(something) × the derivative of the something.

You know how to integrate the sine function, so to find the integral use a substitution.

Let $u = \sin x$; then $\dfrac{du}{dx} = \cos x$. So

$$\begin{aligned}
\int \sin(\sin x)\cos x\,dx &= \int \sin u\,du \\
&= -\cos u + c \\
&= -\cos(\sin x) + c.
\end{aligned}$$

(c) Write 2^x in the form e^{kx}. The integral then becomes a standard integral modified by a linear expression.

Since $2 = e^{\ln 2}$, we see that

$$2^x = (e^{\ln 2})^x = e^{(\ln 2)x}.$$

So

$$\begin{aligned}
\int 2^x\,dx &= \int e^{(\ln 2)x}\,dx \\
&= \frac{e^{(\ln 2)x}}{\ln 2} + c \\
&= \frac{2^x}{\ln 2} + c.
\end{aligned}$$

(d) Expand the brackets to give a sum of powers of sine and cosine, which you can integrate using trigonometric identities.

$$\begin{aligned}
&\int (\sin x + \cos x)^2\,dx \\
&= \int (\sin^2 x + 2\sin x\cos x + \cos^2 x)\,dx \\
&= \int (\sin^2 x + \cos^2 x + 2\sin x\cos x)\,dx
\end{aligned}$$

Using the identity $\sin^2 x + \cos^2 x = 1$ and the double-angle identity for sine, the integral becomes

$$\int (1 + \sin(2x))\,dx = x - \tfrac{1}{2}\cos(2x) + c.$$

(e) The integrand is a rational expression, so find its partial fraction expansion.

We have $x^2 - 3x + 2 = (x-2)(x-1)$. So

$$\frac{1}{x^2-3x+2} = \frac{1}{(x-2)(x-1)} = \frac{A}{x-2} + \frac{B}{x-1},$$

where A and B are constants. Using the cover-up method with $x = 2$ gives

$$A = \frac{1}{2-1} = 1.$$

Using the cover-up method with $x = 1$ gives

$$B = \frac{1}{1-2} = -1.$$

So
$$\frac{1}{x^2-3x+2}=\frac{1}{x-2}-\frac{1}{x-1}.$$
(Check: when $x=0$, LHS $=\frac{1}{2}$ and RHS $=\frac{1}{-2}-\frac{1}{-1}=\frac{1}{2}$.)

So
$$\begin{aligned}\int\frac{1}{x^2-3x+2}\,dx &= \int\left(\frac{1}{x-2}-\frac{1}{x-1}\right)dx\\ &= \int\frac{1}{x-2}\,dx-\int\frac{1}{x-1}\,dx\\ &= \ln|x-2|-\ln|x-1|+c\\ &= \ln\left|\frac{x-2}{x-1}\right|+c.\end{aligned}$$

(f) The integrand is an odd power of $\sin(3x)$, so separate out one factor of $\sin(3x)$ and write it at the end, and express the remaining power of $\sin(3x)$ in terms of $\cos(3x)$.
$$\begin{aligned}&\int\sin^3(3x)\,dx\\ &=\int\sin^2(3x)\sin(3x)\,dx\\ &=\int(1-\cos^2(3x))\sin(3x)\,dx\\ &=-\tfrac{1}{3}\int(1-\cos^2(3x))(-3\sin(3x))\,dx.\end{aligned}$$
Let $u=\cos(3x)$; then $\frac{du}{dx}=-3\sin(3x)$. The integral becomes
$$\begin{aligned}-\tfrac{1}{3}\int(1-u^2)\,du &= -\tfrac{1}{3}\left(u-\tfrac{1}{3}u^3\right)+c\\ &= -\tfrac{1}{3}u+\tfrac{1}{9}u^3+c\\ &= -\tfrac{1}{3}\cos(3x)+\tfrac{1}{9}\cos^3(3x)+c.\end{aligned}$$

(g) The integrand involves a trigonometric function, so it's sensible to use a trigonometric identity. For powers of $\tan x$, you should use the identity $\tan^2 x=\sec^2 x-1$.

By the identity $\tan^2 x=\sec^2 x-1$,
$$\begin{aligned}\int\tan^3 x\,dx &= \int\tan x\tan^2 x\,dx\\ &= \int\tan x(\sec^2 x-1)\,dx\\ &= \int(\tan x\sec^2 x-\tan x)\,dx\\ &= \int\tan x\sec^2 x\,dx+\int(-\tan x)\,dx.\end{aligned}$$

The left-hand integral is
$$\int\sec x(\sec x\tan x)\,dx.$$
Let $u=\sec x$; then $\frac{du}{dx}=\sec x\tan x$. The integral becomes
$$\int u\,du=\tfrac{1}{2}u^2+c=\tfrac{1}{2}\sec^2 x+c.$$
The right-hand integral is
$$\int-\frac{\sin x}{\cos x}\,dx=\int\left(\frac{1}{\cos x}\right)(-\sin x)\,dx.$$
Let $v=\cos x$; then $\frac{dv}{dx}=-\sin x$. The integral becomes
$$\int\frac{1}{v}\,dv=\ln|v|+c=\ln|\cos x|+c,$$
where c is a constant which, in general, will differ from the constant in the left-hand integral. Adding the two integrals, and continuing to use the letter c for the new arbitrary constant, we have
$$\int\tan^3 x\,dx=\tfrac{1}{2}\sec^2 x+\ln|\cos x|+c.$$

(Alternatively, you can find the integral
$$\int\tan x\sec^2 x\,dx$$
by writing the integrand in terms of sine and cosine. You obtain
$$\int\frac{\sin x}{\cos^3 x}\,dx,$$
which you can integrate by making the substitution $u=\cos x$.)

(h) The integrand is an improper rational expression, so find its partial fraction expansion.

We have
$$\begin{aligned}\left(\frac{x}{x+3}\right)^2 &= \left(\frac{x+3-3}{x+3}\right)^2\\ &= \left(1-\frac{3}{x+3}\right)^2\\ &= 1-2\times\left(\frac{3}{x+3}\right)+\left(\frac{3}{x+3}\right)^2\\ &= 1-\frac{6}{x+3}+\frac{9}{(x+3)^2}.\end{aligned}$$

So

$$\int \left(\frac{x}{x+3}\right)^2 \mathrm{d}x$$
$$= \int \left(1 - \frac{6}{x+3} + \frac{9}{(x+3)^2}\right) \mathrm{d}x$$
$$= \int 1 \, \mathrm{d}x - 6 \int \frac{1}{x+3} \, \mathrm{d}x + 9 \int \frac{1}{(x+3)^2} \, \mathrm{d}x$$
$$= \int 1 \, \mathrm{d}x - 6 \int \frac{1}{x+3} \, \mathrm{d}x + 9 \int (x+3)^{-2} \, \mathrm{d}x$$
$$= x - 6 \ln|x+3| - 9(x+3)^{-1} + c.$$

(Alternatively, you could have found the partial fraction expansion of the expression $\left(\frac{x}{x+3}\right)^2$ by using polynomial long division, and then following the usual strategy for finding partial fraction expansions of improper rational expressions.)

(i) The integrand involves the square root of the expression $4 - x^2$, so try a trigonometric substitution.

Let $x = 2\sin u$; then $\dfrac{\mathrm{d}x}{\mathrm{d}u} = 2\cos u$.
Also, $u = \sin^{-1}(x/2)$. So

$$\int x\sqrt{4 - x^2} \, \mathrm{d}x$$
$$= \int (2\sin u)\sqrt{4 - (2\sin u)^2}(2\cos u) \, \mathrm{d}u$$
$$= \int 4\sin u \cos u \sqrt{4 - 4\sin^2 u} \, \mathrm{d}u$$
$$= \int 8\sin u \cos u \sqrt{1 - \sin^2 u} \, \mathrm{d}u$$
$$= 8\int \sin u \cos u \sqrt{\cos^2 u} \, \mathrm{d}u$$
$$= 8\int \sin u \cos^2 u \, \mathrm{d}u$$
$$= -8\int \cos^2 u(-\sin u) \, \mathrm{d}u.$$

Let $v = \cos u$; then $\dfrac{\mathrm{d}v}{\mathrm{d}u} = -\sin u$. The integral becomes

$$-8\int v^2 \, \mathrm{d}v = -8 \times \tfrac{1}{3}v^3 + c$$
$$= -\tfrac{8}{3}v^3 + c$$
$$= -\tfrac{8}{3}\cos^3 u + c$$
$$= -\tfrac{8}{3}\cos^3(\sin^{-1}(x/2)) + c.$$

(j) When written in the form $(\tan^{-1} x) \times 1$, the integrand is suitable for integration by parts.

Integrating by parts gives

$$\int \tan^{-1} x \, \mathrm{d}x$$
$$= \int (\tan^{-1} x) \times 1 \, \mathrm{d}x$$
$$= (\tan^{-1} x) \times x - \int \left(\frac{1}{1+x^2}\right) \times x \, \mathrm{d}x$$
$$= x\tan^{-1} x - \int \frac{x}{1+x^2} \, \mathrm{d}x$$
$$= x\tan^{-1} x - \tfrac{1}{2}\int \left(\frac{1}{1+x^2}\right)(2x) \, \mathrm{d}x.$$

Let $u = 1 + x^2$; then $\dfrac{\mathrm{d}u}{\mathrm{d}x} = 2x$. So

$$\tfrac{1}{2}\int \left(\frac{1}{1+x^2}\right)(2x) \, \mathrm{d}x = \tfrac{1}{2}\int \frac{1}{u} \, \mathrm{d}u$$
$$= \tfrac{1}{2}\ln|u| + c$$
$$= \tfrac{1}{2}\ln|1 + x^2| + c.$$

Hence, continuing to use c for the arbitrary constant in the final integral,

$$\int \tan^{-1} x \, \mathrm{d}x = x\tan^{-1} x - \tfrac{1}{2}\ln|1 + x^2| + c$$
$$= x\tan^{-1} x - \tfrac{1}{2}\ln(1 + x^2) + c,$$

since the expression $1 + x^2$ is always positive.

(k) The integrand is an improper rational expression, so find its partial fraction expansion.

$$\begin{array}{r|l} & x+1 \\ \hline x^2-x & x^3+0x^2+0x+1 \\ & x^3-x^2 \\ \hline & \quad x^2+0x+1 \\ & \quad x^2-x \\ \hline & \qquad x+1 \end{array}$$

So the quotient on dividing x^3+1 by x^2-x is $x+1$ and the remainder is $x+1$. Hence

$$\begin{aligned}\frac{x^3+1}{x^2-x} &= x+1+\frac{x+1}{x^2-x}\\ &= x+1+\frac{x+1}{x(x-1)}.\end{aligned}$$

We have

$$\frac{x+1}{x(x-1)} = \frac{A}{x}+\frac{B}{x-1}.$$

Using the cover-up method with $x=0$ gives

$$A = \frac{1}{-1} = -1.$$

Using the cover-up method with $x=1$ gives

$$B = \frac{1+1}{1} = 2.$$

So

$$\frac{x+1}{x(x-1)} = -\frac{1}{x}+\frac{2}{x-1}.$$

Hence

$$\frac{x^3+1}{x^2-x} = x+1-\frac{1}{x}+\frac{2}{x-1}.$$

(Check: when $x=-1$, LHS $=0$ and RHS $=(-1)+1-\frac{1}{-1}+\frac{2}{-2}=0$.)

So

$$\begin{aligned}&\int \frac{x^3+1}{x^2-x}\,\mathrm{d}x\\ &= \int\left(x+1-\frac{1}{x}+\frac{2}{x-1}\right)\mathrm{d}x\\ &= \int x\,\mathrm{d}x+\int 1\,\mathrm{d}x-\int\frac{1}{x}\,\mathrm{d}x+2\int\frac{1}{x-1}\,\mathrm{d}x\\ &= \tfrac{1}{2}x^2+x-\ln|x|+2\ln|x-1|+c\\ &= \tfrac{1}{2}x^2+x-\ln|x|+\ln((x-1)^2)+c\\ &= \tfrac{1}{2}x^2+x+\ln\frac{(x-1)^2}{|x|}+c.\end{aligned}$$

(l) The integrand involves the square root of the expression $1+x^2$, so try either a trigonometric or hyperbolic substitution. It turns out that a hyperbolic substitution is more effective in this case.

Let $x=\sinh u$; then $\dfrac{\mathrm{d}x}{\mathrm{d}u}=\cosh u$.

Also, $u=\sinh^{-1}x$. So

$$\begin{aligned}\int\frac{x^2}{\sqrt{1+x^2}}\,\mathrm{d}x &= \int\frac{\sinh^2 u}{\sqrt{1+\sinh^2 u}}(\cosh u)\,\mathrm{d}u\\ &= \int\frac{\sinh^2 u}{\sqrt{\cosh^2 u}}(\cosh u)\,\mathrm{d}u\\ &= \int\sinh^2 u\,\mathrm{d}u.\end{aligned}$$

Using the identity $\sinh^2 u=\frac{1}{2}(\cosh(2u)-1)$, the integral becomes

$$\begin{aligned}&\int\tfrac{1}{2}(\cosh(2u)-1)\,\mathrm{d}u\\ &= \tfrac{1}{2}\int(\cosh(2u)-1)\,\mathrm{d}u\\ &= \tfrac{1}{2}\left(\tfrac{1}{2}\sinh(2u)-u\right)+c\\ &= \tfrac{1}{4}\sinh(2u)-\tfrac{1}{2}u+c\\ &= \tfrac{1}{4}\sinh(2\sinh^{-1}x)-\tfrac{1}{2}\sinh^{-1}x+c.\end{aligned}$$

(m) First use integration by parts, and then integrate the resulting improper rational expression in the usual way.

Integrating by parts gives

$$\begin{aligned}&\int x\ln(x+1)\,\mathrm{d}x\\ &= \tfrac{1}{2}x^2\ln(x+1)-\int\tfrac{1}{2}x^2\times\left(\frac{1}{x+1}\right)\mathrm{d}x\\ &= \tfrac{1}{2}x^2\ln(x+1)-\tfrac{1}{2}\int\frac{x^2}{x+1}\,\mathrm{d}x.\end{aligned}$$

To find the partial fraction expansion of the integrand on the right, you could use polynomial long division, but in this case there's an easier way.

Since $x^2-1=(x+1)(x-1)$, we have

$$\frac{x^2}{x+1}=\frac{(x+1)(x-1)+1}{x+1}=x-1+\frac{1}{x+1}.$$

Hence

$$\begin{aligned}
&\tfrac{1}{2}\int \frac{x^2}{x+1}\,\mathrm{d}x \\
&\quad= \tfrac{1}{2}\int \left(x-1+\frac{1}{x+1}\right)\mathrm{d}x \\
&\quad= \tfrac{1}{2}\int x\,\mathrm{d}x - \tfrac{1}{2}\int 1\,\mathrm{d}x + \tfrac{1}{2}\int \frac{1}{x+1}\,\mathrm{d}x \\
&\quad= \tfrac{1}{4}x^2 - \tfrac{1}{2}x + \ln|x+1| + c.
\end{aligned}$$

Now $x+1$ must be positive, for otherwise the original integrand $x\ln(x+1)$ would not be defined. Hence, continuing to use c for the arbitrary constant, we obtain

$$\begin{aligned}
&\int x\ln(x+1)\,\mathrm{d}x \\
&\quad= \tfrac{1}{2}x^2\ln(x+1) - \tfrac{1}{2}\int \frac{x^2}{x+1}\,\mathrm{d}x \\
&\quad= \tfrac{1}{2}x^2\ln(x+1) - \tfrac{1}{4}x^2 + \tfrac{1}{2}x - \ln(x+1) + c \\
&\quad= \tfrac{1}{2}(x^2-1)\ln(x+1) - \tfrac{1}{4}x^2 + \tfrac{1}{2}x + c.
\end{aligned}$$

Acknowledgements

Grateful acknowledgement is made to the following sources:

Page 101: Figure 20. Kamel 15 /
http://en.wikipedia.org/wiki/File:Kette_Kettenkurve_Catenary_2008_PD.JPG.
This file is licensed under the Creative Commons Attribution-Share Alike Licence http://creativecommons.org/licenses/by-sa/3.0/

Page 113: Courtesy of Mathematical Gazette & The Mathematical Association

Every effort has been made to contact copyright holders. If any have been inadvertently overlooked the publishers will be pleased to make the necessary arrangements at the first opportunity.

Index